SIGMUND FREUD'S WRITINGS

A Comprehensive Bibliography

SIGMUND FREUD'S WRITINGS

A Comprehensive Bibliography

ALEXANDER GRINSTEIN, M.D.

INTERNATIONAL UNIVERSITIES PRESS, INC.
New York

Library of Congress Cataloging in Publication Data

Grinstein, Alexander.
  Sigmund Freud's writings.

  1. Freud, Sigmund, 1856-1939—Bibliography.
2. Psychoanalysis—Bibliography. I. Title.
[DNLM: 1. Psychoanalysis—History. WZ100 F889GD]
Z8315.5.G75   [BF173]   016.150'19'52   76-46812
ISBN 0-8236-6076-1

Manufactured in the United States of America

CONTENTS

INTRODUCTION

When the first volume of the *Index of Psychoanalytic Writings* was published in 1956, the centenary of Sigmund Freud's birth, *The Standard Edition of the Complete Psychological Works of Sigmund Freud* had not been completed. References in Volume I of the *Index* showing the location of Freud's papers in the various volumes of the *Standard Edition* were provided through the graciousness of James Strachey. Subsequently, in Volumes V, VI and X of the *Index* additions and corrections to the Freud bibliography from the *Standard Edition* and from other sources were included. Dispersion of the important Freud reference material into four volumes of the *Index* created obvious difficulties for the reader. *Sigmund Freud's Writings: A Comprehensive Bibliography* was conceived to remedy this awkward arrangement and became a *separatum* to the *Index*.

The present work, originally initiated to update and correct the bibliographic citations in the *Index*, soon came to have somewhat more ambitious goals. We decided to include references to new published material including Freud's previously unpublished letters and to list new translations of his works in diverse languages.

The basic principles governing our orientation have been rather arbitrary and pragmatic. All Freud's writings are listed alphabetically according to the title of the original publication followed by reference to the bibliographic citation of the original publication. This catalog of Freud's writings includes abstracts, articles, books, introductions, letters, postscripts, prefaces, publications honoring his friends and colleagues, obituaries, reviews, and translations. We have attempted to provide information as to where and when papers were originally presented and to arrange in chronological sequence of publication, the various editions first in the original language and then in translation.

The original citation is usually followed by detailed information about English translations. This sequence was chosen because in recent years the predominant language of psychoanalysis has become English. Also, the most complete translation of Freud's work has been into English by James Strachey and his collaborators in the *Standard Edition*.

Citations of English translations are followed by citations in other languages in which the translated work was published. All available bibliographical information about the published translations is given as well as the names of the translators when known.

The bibliographical material has been derived from several sources and wherever possible the original sources of the publication were consulted. In addition, we have relied on the material provided in all of the collections of Freud's works (*Gesammelte Schriften, Gesammelte Werke, Standard Edition, Obras Completas*, etc.). Libraries both here and abroad have been consulted for information about collections and translations of Freud's writings in different languages. We have corresponded with publishers seeking knowledge of new publications or hitherto little-known publications and translations of Freud's writings. Apart from the sources we were able to call upon for our work in connection with the *Index,* we had the particular advantage of the cooperation of Dr. K. R. Eissler and the Sigmund Freud Archives. Moreover, Ernst Freud and the Freud Copyrights Ltd. were especially helpful in supplying us with data about the "out of the way" translations of Freud's writings. After his death, his widow Lucie Freud and Mark Paterson kindly turned over to us their entire file of correspondence and information about these translations.

There is a veritable jungle of whole or partial translations and editions some of which were authorized while others were pirated. Translations of Freud's works and letters vary in completeness as well as in quality. As we had done in the *Index,* we followed the bibliographic principle of nonevaluatory listing of translations, without considering whether or not permission had been obtained from Sigmund Freud Copyrights. Nor did we attempt to verify the completeness of translations. Often there were serious impediments to obtaining and checking some of the "out of the way" published translations, and verification of each with the original was beyond the scope of this project. Language was not only a barrier, but the matter of transliteration of titles into English made for inconsistencies of rendering. Although our research disclosed that many of Freud's papers, or portions of them, especially the shorter ones, appeared in popular magazines and newspapers throughout the world, listing all of them would have been economically unfeasible and of questionable value. We reasoned that even if we could provide such a listing, it would not really serve the needs of the scholar or the student of psychoanalysis.

GENERAL FORMAT AND ORGANIZATION

Sigmund Freud's Writings: A Comprehensive Bibliography is divided into eight sections: Freud's early, primarily nonpsychological writings; his psychological writings; Freud's introductions and prefaces to his own works and to those of others; his abstracts and reviews; Freud's translations of the works of others; his published letters; a chronological listing of Freud's writings; and an alphabetical listing of Freud's works in English under familiar words or titles.

All citations are numbered sequentially, centered at the top of the entire body of the citation. Below this number, on the left side, is the Tyson-Strachey number where one has been assigned. This number refers to the year of publication and corresponds to the identifying number in the *Standard Edition.* Another number in parentheses may appear below this in those instances where the year of writing of a particular work is known to be different from the year of publication. The original number used in the *Index* appears in the left margin, in italics. No attempt has been made to include all pertinent numbers used in subsequent volumes of the *Index.*

All citations are listed in alphabetical order according to the language of the original publication. Most of Freud's writings were in German; however, a few were first published in other languages (French, English, Spanish). Sometimes they were written by Freud in another language; at other times they were written in German, but translated for publication. The name of the translator is given when known. Some of the original German texts were subsequently published, others are not extant.

The first letter of the first *main* word in the title was used as the basis for alphabetization. Articles and prepositions were not considered in the alphabetization.

Available information about where, when, and by whom the paper was originally presented follows the title. A chronological listing of the various publications in the particular language is given next. Although Freud's own abstracts of a number of his early papers such as those in the *Inhaltsangabe der wissenschaftlichen Arbeiten* are included, abstracts or reviews of Freud's works by others are not.

The English translations in chronological order are listed next, followed by the names or abbreviations for the editors and translators. Other languages in which translations appeared are given in alphabetical sequence after the English translations. Among the languages represented are Arabic, Chinese, Czechoslovakian, Danish, Dutch, Finnish, French, Greek, Hebrew, Hindu, Hungarian, Italian, Japanese, Jugoslavian, Korean, Norwegian, Persian, Portuguese, Russian, Spanish, Swedish and Yiddish. Whenever possible titles are transliterated into English.

For purposes of this work, a number of changes from the organization of Freud material in the *Index* have been made. The inclusion under the general heading of "Psychological Writings" of Freud's introductions, prefaces, and letters did not seem strictly accurate. Listing such publications in alphabetical order, as they are in the *Index*, under "introduction," "foreword," "Geleitwort," "preface," "Vorrede," and "Vorwort" was not only confusing, but did not always follow the actual wording of the original title. This was also true for "Briefe" and "letters," especially since some of them were published as prefaces to books.

To circumvent this confusion, we have listed in Section III all of Freud's introductions, forewords, and prefaces alphabetically under the author for whom Freud wrote them. When the word "preface," "Geleitwort," "Vorrede," "Vorwort" was specifically designated in the original title, it is given here preceding the actual title. If no specific designation is indicated, it is to be understood that Freud's published remarks served the purpose of a preface. As the various German terms were used interchangeably, any attempt to use them for alphabetization or other categorization would have been artificial.

Section III also contains those letters Freud wrote to be used as prefaces. In certain instances Freud's letter was published in facsimile and used as a preface (e.g., to Richard Sterba and to *Das Psychoanalytische Volksbuch*). We have included them under PREFACES, but have indicated in brackets, before the original title, that the letters were published in facsimile [Facsimile], even though Strachey, in the *Standard Edition*, entitled them "prefaces."

The names of the recipients of these letters used as prefaces are also listed in Section IV (LETTERS), but are unnumbered there. The reader is referred to the entry number in Section III where the complete bibliographic information is given.

The remainder of Freud's letters and correspondence is listed in Section VI, chronologically, under the name of the recipient. If there are one to three letters the dates, if known, of these letters are given at the beginning of the citation. When there are four or more letters, the dates of the first and last letters of the series are indicated. Only those letters that have special significance (e.g., the Freud letters to Fliess in *The Origins of Psychoanalysis*) and those that were initially "open letters" (e.g., the letters to Professor Einstein or to Romain Rolland) are included in Section II.

Letters listed in Ernest Jones' *The Life and Work of Sigmund Freud* refer to the

English-language editions only. For translations of the letters into other languages, it is suggested that readers consult editions of Jones' book in other languages.

The full bibliographical reference for *Briefe 1873-1939* (German) or the collected *Letters of Sigmund Freud* (English) showing all known translations of this collection of Freud letters is given only once, at the beginning of Section VI (p. 129). Thereafter, this work in *all* its translations, is referred to as *Briefe; Letters*. The reader should be aware that the abbreviated reference *Briefe; Letters* implicitly includes the existence of French, Italian, Norwegian, and Spanish translations.

Pagination is not provided for letters listed in Jones' book or in *Briefe; Letters* because it varies in the diverse editions of these works.

Although we have relied heavily on the material in the *Index*, we have not found it necessary to include in this present work the various collections of Freud's writings. For this material, the reader is referred to Volumes I, VI and X of the *Index*.

This bibliography of Freud's work, while comprehensive, must be regarded as incomplete. The growth of interest in psychoanalysis will bring about new translations of his writings. Only a portion of Freud's correspondence with men such as Fliess, Abraham, and Jung has been published. In due time, we hope the entire correspondence will be released for publication. As new material and new translations appear, they will certainly be included in subsequent editions of this work.*

Despite the fine assistance we received, our efforts to achieve scrupulous accuracy in compiling as thorough and complete a bibliography as possible, errors and omissions are inevitable. We urge the readers of this work to call our attention to such errors and omissions so that they may be corrected in future editions.

ACKNOWLEDGMENTS

Many individuals and organizations were helpful in the preparation of this work, which goes back to the labors involved in the preparation of the first volume of the *Index of Psychoanalytic Writings*, over twenty-five years ago. I wish to express sincere gratitude and appreciation:

To the late Ernst Freud for his kind help, to Mrs. Lucie Freud, and to Mark Paterson and his assistant Mrs. Virginia J. Thomas of the Sigmund Freud Copyrights Ltd. Their work put us in touch with Dr. Rosie M. Klaar who provided them and us with many of the "out of the way" translations.

To K. R. Eissler, M.D. and the Sigmund Freud Archives, Inc. for providing us with many references over the years. Dr. Eissler's secretary, Mona M. Karff, has been instrumental in keeping us informed of these developments.

To the late James Strachey and his assistants, the late Alix Strachey, Alan Tyson, and Angela Richards. In the course of our correspondence throughout many years, Mr. Strachey provided us with his discoveries of new translations.

* After the galley proofs of this work were received, we learned of the recent publication of the following book: *Sigmund Freud: Sein Leben in Bildern und Texten*. (Eds: Freud, E. L.; Freud, L.; & Grubrich-Simitis, I.) (Intro: Grubrich-Simitis, I.; Biographical sketch: Eissler, K. R.) Frankfurt: Suhrkamp Verlag 1976, 352 p. This work contains a number of previously unpublished letters.

To Alan W. Fraser, M.D. for his work on the translations of Freud into Japanese and his careful transliteration of the Japanese titles. His scholarship in this difficult and complicated area was exceedingly conscientious and meticulous. When in doubt, we deferred to his judgment and research.

To Roger A. Dufresne, M.D. for his work on the French translations, for his helpful additions to and corrections of our material. We relied heavily on his publication, *Bibliographie des Écrits de Freud.*

To Joseph Placek of the Slavic Division of the University of Michigan Library for his careful transliteration of Russian titles and his verification of the Russian translations.

To Phyllis Rubinton of the Abraham A. Brill Library of The New York Psychoanalytic Institute.

To Glenn Miller, Librarian, The McLean Library of The Institute for Psychoanalysis, Chicago, Illinois.

To Hans W. Bentz and his work as editor of *Sigmund Freud in Über-setzungen.*

To various professional organizations, their facilities, and their librarians, archivists or officers who provided us with help in researching. Among these are the:

Chicago Institute for Psychoanalysis
Columbia University in the City of New York, Kenneth A. Lohf
Detroit Psychiatric Institute, Merry Miller
Detroit Public Library
Harvard University
Israel Psychoanalytical Society, S. Nagler
Japan Psycho-Analytical Society, Michio Yamamura
Jewish Nation and University Library (Jerusalem), Dr. C. Wormann
Library of Congress
Library of the Jewish Theological Seminary of America, Ora Hamels-dorf
Menninger Foundation Museum, Verne B. Horne
Michigan Psychoanalytic Institute and Society, Marlene Handler
National Palace (Taipei, Taiwan)
New York Psychoanalytic Institute, Abraham A. Brill Library, Ms. Wolpe, Jeanette Taylor
New York Public Library
Otto Rank Association, Anita J. Faetz
Psychoanalytisch Instituut van de Nederlansche Vereeniging voor Psychoanalyse Library, Dr. P. Hirschler
Shiffman Medical Library, Wayne State University (Detroit, Michigan)
Società Psicoanalitica Italiana, Francesco Corrao
Svenska Psykoanalytiska Förenigen, Olof Billingberg
University of Michigan Library (Ann Arbor, Michigan)
Wilson Library, University of Minnesota (Minneapolis, Minnesota)
Wayne State University, Department of Psychiatry

To all the publishers who provided us with listings of their Freud publications. Among them are:

Bokförlaget Forum Publishers (Stockholm), Lisbet Ekberg
Albert Bonniers Förlag (Stockholm), Wolfgang Hirsch
Arnoldo Mondatori Editore, Armaroh

Dall 'Oglio, Editore (Milan)
Gyldendal Norsk Förlag (Oslo), Barbra C. Ugland
Iwanami Shoten Publishers (Tokyo), Kazuo Otsuka
Natur och Kultur Kunskapsförlaget (Stockholm), Barbro Johansson
Paolo Boringheiri Editore (Torino)
Ruiz-Castillo Y, Editorial Biblioteca Nueva (Madrid), Jose Ruiz-Castillo
Ugo Mursia Editore, Dr. Flavio Fagnani
To the many people who provided assistance in supplying information,
tracking down, correcting, translating, and verifying references. Among them
are:
Ruth Betlheim
Mrs. Smiley Blanton
Professor A. Bourguignon
Dr. Aldo Carotennto
Dr. N. N. Dracoulides
Dr. Theodore Dusužkov
Prof. Dr. G. Fichtner
Martin Grotjahn, M.D.
Dr. Imre Hermann
Sandor Lorand, M.D.
Marvin Margolis, M.D.
Prof. Dott. Emilio Servadio
Deena Silverman
Editha Sterba, Ph.D.
Richard F. Sterba, M.D.
Mayer Subrin, M.D.
To Edith C. Polk who did a good deal of the preliminary work by sifting
through and resolving many of the intricate and tangled problems of the
Freud translations. Associated with the original work in the first volume of the
Index, she followed the manifold changes and additions throughout the
complete series. Her experience and knowledge of the material and her
dedication over the years proved invaluable in the execution of this project.

To Jacqueline Olivanti who was responsible for the completion of the
manuscript, its final organization, and the ultimate resolution of the innumer-
able problems inherent in this work. Her dedication and conscientious
devotion to the labors involved were without parallel.

To my wife, Adele, for her continuing help, support and encouragement in
these bibliographic endeavors.

ALEXANDER GRINSTEIN, M.D.

ABBREVIATIONS

ABBREVIATIONS OF NAMES OF
PERIODICALS AND COLLECTED WORKS

Abbreviations of periodicals in the Bibliography, other than those listed below, were taken from the *World List of Scientific Periodicals, 1900-1950*, 3rd Edition, New York: Academic Press; London: Butterworth Publications, Ltd., 1952.

Almanach	Almanach der Psychoanalyse. Earlier title: Almanach für das Jahr ... Vienna, Int Psa Verlag 1926-1938.
Briefe	Freud, E. L. (ed) *Briefe 1873-1939*. Frankfurt: S. Fischer 1960. Freud, E. L. & Freud, L. (eds) 2nd ed, 1968.
Bull Am Psa Ass	Bulletin of the American Psychoanalytic Association
Bull Phila Ass Psa	Bulletin of the Philadelphia Association for Psychoanalysis
Bull Soc fr Philos	Bulletin de la Société Française de Philosophie
BWSF	Brill, A. A. (ed) *The Basic Writings of Sigmund Freud*. NY: Random House 1938.
C	Zentralblatt für Psychoanalyse. Wiesbaden.
CP	Freud, Sigmund *Collected Papers*. London: Hogarth; NY: Basic Books 1924-1950, 5 Volumes.
CW-Ars	[Collected Works of Sigmund Freud.] Tokyo: Ars 1929-1941.
Dichtung und Kunst	Freud, Sigmund *Psychoanalytische Studien an Werken der Dichtung und Kunst*. Leipzig/Vienna/Zurich: Int Psa Verlag 1924.
Erf Beisp Psa Prx	Freud, Sigmund *Erfahrungen und Beispiel aus der analytischen Praxis*. Z 1913, 1:377-382.
FCW-S	[Collected Works of Sigmund Freud.] Tokyo: Shunyodo 1929-1934.
GS	Freud, Sigmund *Gesammelte Schriften*. Leipzig/Vienna/Zurich: Int Psa Verlag 1924-1934.
GW	Freud, Sigmund *Gesammelte Werke*. London: IPC 1940-1952.
HPI	The Hogarth Press and Institute of Psycho-Analysis.
Inhalts wiss Arb	Freud, Sigmund *Inhaltsangabe der wissenschaftlichen Arbeiten*. Vienna: Deuticke 1897.
Int Psa Pr	International Psychoanalytic Press
Int Psa Verlag	Internationaler psychoanalytischer Verlag
IPC	Imago Publishing Company
IUP	International Universities Press
J	International Journal of Psycho-Analysis
J Am Psa Ass	Journal of the American Psychoanalytic Association
JMS	Journal of Mental Science

JNMD	Journal of Nervous and Mental Diseases
Jones	Jones, Ernest *The Life and Work of Sigmund Freud*. NY: Basic Books. London: Hogarth Pr 1953-1957, 3 Volumes.
Kitvei	*Kitvei Sigmund Freud*. Tel-Aviv: Dvir 1966-1969, 5 Volumes.
Letters	Freud, E. L. (ed) *Letters of Sigmund Freud*. NY: Basic Books 1960.
Major Works	*Major Works*. Chicago: Encyclopaedia Britannica 1952, 1955. Great Books of the Western World, Vol. 54.
Neurosen-lehre und Technik	Freud, Sigmund *Schriften zur Neurosenlehre und zur psychoanalytischen Technik* (1913-1926). Vienna: Int Psa Verlag 1931.
NMDP	Nervous and Mental Diseases Publishing Company
Obr Comp 1948	*Sigmund Freud. Obras Completas*. Madrid: Editorial Biblioteca Nueva 1948, 2 Volumes.
Obr Comp 1967/1968	
Obr Comp-BA	*Sigmund Freud. Obras Completas*. Buenos Aires: Santiago Rueda 1952-1956, 22 Volumes.
Obr Comp-Madrid	*Obras Completas del Professor S. Freud*. Madrid: Biblioteca Nueva 1922-1934, 17 Volumes.
Obr Comp-P	*Obras Completas de Sigmund Freud*. Rio de Janeiro, S. Paulo, etc.: Editora Delta S.A., 18 Volumes.
Opere	Musatti, C. L. (ed) *Opere di Sigmund Freud*. Torino: Boringhieri 1967-1972, 5 Volumes, [1972-, Volumes 6-11]
Psa B	Psychoanalytische Bewegung
Psa Clin Inter	Paul, L. (ed) *Psychoanalytic Clinical Interpretation*. NY: The Free Pr of Glencoe 1963.
Psa Forum	The Psychoanalytic Forum
Psa P	Zeitschrift für psychoanalytische Pädagogik
Psikholog i psikhoanal	*Psikhologicheskaia i psikhoanaliticheskaia Biblioteka*, Moskva/Petrograd: Gos. Izd-vo 1923.
Psychiat-neurol Wsch	Psychiatrisch-neurologische Wochenschrift
Psychoan-alyse der Neurosen	Freud, Sigmund *Studien zur Psychoanalyse der Neurosen aus den Jahren 1913-1925*. Leipzig/Vienna/Zurich: Int Psa Verlag 1926.
Psychoanaly-sis, J Nat Psychol Ass Psycho-analysis	Psychoanalysis, Journal of the National Psychological Association for Psychoanalysis
PUF	Presse Universitaire de France
Q	Psychoanalytic Quarterly
Rev Psico-anál	Revista de Psicoanálisis
RFPsa	Revue Française de Psychanalyse
Riv Psa	Rivista di Psicoanalise
SE	Strachey, James (ed) *Standard Edition of the Complete Psychological Works of Sigmund Freud*. London: HPI, 1953-1974.

SelFr-JinSh   [Selections from the writings of Sigmund Freud.] Kyoto: Jinbun
              Shoin Pr 1968-1971, 6 Volumes.
SelFr-K   [Selections from the Writings of Sigmund Freud.] Tokyo:
              Kyobunsha 1952-1960; revised 1969-1970, 17 Volumes.
Sexualtheorie Freud, Sigmund *Kleine Schriften zur Sexualtheorie und zur
und Traum-   Traumlehre.* Vienna: Int Psa Verlag 1931.
lehre
SKSN   Freud, Sigmund *Sammlung kleiner Schriften zur Neurosenlehre.*
              Leipzig/Vienna: Deuticke 1906-1913; Heller 1918; Int Psa
              Verlag 1922.
SPH   Freud, Sigmund *Selected Papers on Hysteria.* NY: NMDP 1909,
              1912.
Technik und   Freud, Sigmund *Zur Technik der Psychoanalyse und zur Meta-
Metapsy-   psychologie.* Leipzig/Vienna/Zurich: Int Psa Verlag 1924.
chologie
Theoretische Freud, Sigmund *Theoretische Schriften.* Vienna: Int Psa Verlag
Schriften   1931.
Traumlehre   Freud, Sigmund *Kleine Beiträge zur Traumlehre.* Leipzig/
              Vienna/Zurich: Int Psa Verlag 1925.
Vier Kran-   Freud, Sigmund *Vier psychoanalytische Krankengeschichten.*
kengeschich- Vienna: Int Psa Verlag 1932.
ten
Wien med   Wiener medizinische Wochenschaft
Wschr
Y   Jahrbuch für psychoanalytische und psychopathologische For-
              schungen; Jahrbuch der Psychoanalyse.
YBPsa   Lorand, Sándor (ed) *The Yearbook of Psychoanalysis.* NY: IUP
              1945-1952.
Z   Internationale Zeitschrift für ärztliche Psychoanalyse; Inter-
              nationale Zeitschrift für Psychoanalyse.

ABBREVIATIONS USED
FOR NAMES OF TRANSLATORS

AAB	Abraham A. Brill
AB	Anne Berman
ASt	Alix Strachey
CJMH	C. J. M. Hubback
CLM	Cesare Luigi Musatti
CMB	Cecil M. Baines
CMdeF	C. Magalhães de Freitas
DB	Douglas Bryan
EBH	Ethilde B. M. Herford
ECM	E. Colburn Mayne
ED	Elias Davidovich
EG	Edward George Glover
EJ	Ernest Jones
GP	Gladstone Parente
IFGD	I. F. Grant Duff
IsIz	Isaac Izecksohn
JLa	Jean Laplanche
JPP	José Pires Porto-Carrero
JR	John Rickman
JRiv	Joan Riviere
JS	James Strachey
KA	Karl Abraham
KO	Kenji Ohtsuki
LLBT	Luis López-Ballesteros Y de Torres
LR	Ludovico Rosenthal
MB	Marie Bonaparte
MG	Moyses Gikovate
MLB	Marco Levi Bianchini
MV	Moshe V. Vul'f
OG	Odilon Gallotti
RCM	R. C. McWatters
RL	Rudolph Maurice Loëwenstein
SFe	Sándor Ferenczi
YT	Yoshitaka Takahashi

NAMES OF TRANSLATORS

A. [unidentified]
Abd El Moneim Al Meleigy
Abraham, Hilda C.
Adami, Francesco
Agō, Shinji
Agō, Yukihiro
Albinski, Marian
Allers, Rudolph
Al-Nafseah, Nafsy Wa Amrad
Andersson, Ola
Anzieu, Didier
Aoki, Hiroyuki
Asker, Assar
Athanassopoulos, G.

Baba, Ken-ichi
Baer, Aryeh
Baines, Cecil M.
Balint, Michael
Ballardini, Arrigo
Barbaro, Umberto
Bazlin, Roberto
Becker, Hortense Koller
Bekić, Tomislav
Bekonyi, S.
Benedicty, Gustavo de
Berachyahu, Mordekhay
Berger, Denise
Berman, Anne
Bernays, J.
Beucler, A.
Bissery, J.
Bjelousov (Belousov, V. A.)
Bjerre, Poul Carl
Bogičević, Djordje
Boisen, Mogens
Bonaparte, Marie
Bratt, Signe
Briand, J. B.
Brill, Abraham A.
Briod, Blaise
Brøgger, Waldemar
Brüel, Oluf
Bruno, P.
Brunswick, David

Bryan, Clement A. Douglas
Buchet, E.
Buda, Bela
Budinský, J.
Bullitt, William Christian
Bunker, Henry Alden
Bychowski, G.
Byck, Robert

Cabo, Matilde Rodríquez
Cabral, Alvaro
Cambon, F.
Campione, Adele
Candreva, Sandro
Chase, Harry W.
Chino, Shōjyō
Choisy, Maryse
Cinato, Ada
Clark, L. P.
Cohen, Avraam
Cohen, Israel
Cohen, R.
Corrêa, J. Barbosa

Daniele, Silvano
David, Sante
Davidovich, Elias
Demet, M. F.
Deri, Frances
Devereux, George
Dimakou, E.
Dogana, Marilisa Tonin
Dogana, Fernando
Doi, Masanori
Donoghue, A. K.
Dosužkov, B.
Douglas Scotti, G. L.
Downey, Helen M.
Dudnick, I.
Duff, I. F. Grant
Dukesz, Geza
Duquenne, P.
Dvossis, I.

Ebon, Martin
Eder, Montague David
Edminster, Steven A.
Eissler, Kurt R.
Eissler, Ruth S.

Emden, J. E. G. van
Engel, Fred
Erikson, Erik H.
Ermakov, I. D.
E. S. G. [unidentified]

Fachinelli, Elvio
Fel'tsman, O.
Ferenczi, Sándor
Ferentinos, S.
Ferrarotti, Franco
Flatterer, Richard
Fleck, Stephen
Flescher, Joachim
Fodor, Nandor
Fonseca, Ramiro da
Foxe, Arthur N.
Fraenkel, Ernest
Franghias, A.
Freisinger, Leona A.
Freitas, C. Magalhães de
Freud, Anna
Freud, Ernst L.
Freud, Martin
Friedmann, Ota
Friedman, Paul
Fu, Kao Chio
Furrer, Albert

Gabler, Rosalie
Gallotti, Odilon
Gelsted, Otto
Gergely, Erzsébet
Gikovate, Moysés
Gilbert, Stuart
Giordano, Alberto
Glaser, K.
Glaser, Mrs.
Glover, Edward George
Golan, S.
Gounili, Abolhasen H.
Green, A.
Groddek, E.
Grossein, Jean-Pierre
Grotjahn, Etelka
Grotjahn, Martin
Guérineau, D.
Guterman, Norbert
Gyorgyey, Ferenc

Hagerup, A.
Hagerup, I.
Hall, G. Stanley
Hamakawa, Sakae
Hamano, Osamu
Hasegawa, Masaya
Hasegawa, Seiya
Havelková, M.
Hawelka, E. R.
Hawelka, P.
Hayashi, Takashi
Hejazi, Mohammad
Heller, Judith Bernays
Herbert
Herford, Ethilde B. M.
Hermann, Imre
Hesnard, Angelo Louis Marie
Hilav, Selâhattin
Hill, R. F. C.
Hillman, James
Hoesli, Henry
Hollós, István
Holstijn, A. J. Westerman
Horn, M. W.
Hosoki, Akitoshi
Houwaard, C.
Hubback, C. J. M.

Ignotus
Iida, Makato
Ikeda, Kazuyoshi
Ikemi, Torijiro
Ikonen, Pentti
Ikumatsu, Keizō
Imura, Tsunero
Ishinaka, Shōji
Itō, Toyoo
Ivanka, Helena
Izecksohn, Isaac

Jackson, Edith B.
Jankélévitch, S.
Javaher-Kalam, Farid
Jekels, Ludwig
Jelliffe, Smith Ely
Jensen, Brynjulf
Jeretić, Vladeta
Jones, Ernest
Jones, Katherine

Jumel, Lily
Jury, Paul

Kahr, Madlyn
Kahr, Sidney
Kaila, Eino
Kakeda, Katsumi
Kao, Chio-Fu
Katō, Masaaki
Kikuchi, Eiichi
Kikumori, Hideo
Kimura, Kinji
Kimura, Masashi
Kirin, Vladimir
Klajn, Hugo
Klempnerówna, S.
Kogan, IA. M.
Konuma, Masuho
Konuma, Tosuo
Kopřiva, K.
Kosawa, Heisaku
Koteliansky, S. S.
Kotik, M.
Kovács, Vilma
Kraak-de Looze, E. M. A.
Kratochvíl, Ladislav
Kris, Ernst
Kubo, Yoshiihide
Kučera, O.
Kumada, Masaharu
Kuttner, Alfred Booth
Kyprianos, C.

Lacan, Jacques
Landquist, John
Landquist, Solveig
Laplanche, Jean
Larsen, Petter
Lauzun, Gérard
Legros, Hélène
LeLay, Yves
Lengyel, József
Lerman, Sarah
Levi Bianchini, Marco
Lewinter, R.
Lillis, M.
Loewenstein, Rudolph Maurice
Löfgren, Ingeborg
Lorenc, Borislav

Low, Barbara
Lucentini, Mauro
Lukács, Katalin
Lūqā, Nazmī
Luriia, Alexander R.
Luserna, Enzo

Mackenzie, W. L.
Maerker-Branden, A. P.
Mahmud 'Ali, Sāmī
Manheim, Ralph
Marcondes, Durval
Marsh, Bernard
Martet, P.
Marty, Mme. Edouard
Marui, Kiyoyasu
Masaki, Fujokyu
Matić, Vojin
Mayne, E. Colburn
Mazer, Milton
McWatters, R. C.
Medem, V.
Meranaios, C.
Meranaios, K. C.
Merino Pérez, Joaquin
Meron, J.
Meyer, Monroe
Meyerson, Ignace
Milekić, Pavle
Milillis
Molinari, Egon
Montinari, Mazzino
Moriyama, Kimio
Mosbacher, Eric
Münz, T.
Musatti, Cesare Luigi

Naitō, Kōbun
Najātī, Muḥammad 'uthmān
Nathan, Marcel
Navrátil, F.
Neergaard, Jørgen
Niizeki, Ryōzō
Noda, Taku
Nousiainen, Pulma
Nousiainen, Tapio
Novoda, C.

Odier, Charles
Odier, Mme. Charles

O'Donovan, J. F.
Ohtsuki, Kenji
Okonogi, Keigo
Oliveira, Osório de
Oppenot, F.
Osipov, N. E.
Othman, Nagāti M.
Ozorai, Gizella

Pachta, Jan
Palmen, Rolf
Panaitescu, Emilio Alessandro
Pangalos, A.
Parente, Gladstone
Pártos, Zoltán
Paul, Cedar
Paul, Eden
Payne, Charles R.
Petrillo, Raffaele
Petrović, Gruja
Pherentinou, Stathe
Piazza, Carlo Fredrico
Pichon, Edouard
Poliakov, I. E.
Polianskiĭ, V. F.
Pollak, S.
Pontalis, Jean-Bertrand
Porto-Carrero, José Pires
Potash, Robert S.
Prica, Srda
Proctor-Gregg, Nancy
Puranen, Erkki
Pur-Bager, Iraj
Putnam, James Jackson

Querido, Arie

Ramzi, Ishaq
Ranchetti, Michele
Rank, Beata
Rapaport, David
Raun, Conrad
Razi, Hashem
Redlich, Frederick C.
Reik, Theodor
Renterghem, A. W. van
Reverchon, Blanche
Richards, A. M. O.
Richards, Angela
Rickman, John

Rieff, Philip
Riviere, Joan
Robbins, F.
Robert, M.
Robson-Scott, Elaine
Robson-Scott, William D.
Rocheblave, Anne-Marie
Rodker, John
Romero, H.
Rosenthal, Ludovico
Rousseau, P.
Russin, Lester A.

Sachs, B.
Sachs, Hanns
Safouan, Moustafa
Sagittario, Ermanno
Saheboz-Zamani, M. H. N.
Santala, Marjatta
Sauvage Nolting, W. J. J.
Schedin, Göran
Schiff, A.
Schjelderup, Kristian
Schönberger, István
Schrier, Ilse
Schur, Max
Schütz, Harry
Schwarz, Laura
Searl, M. Nina
Seki, Eikichi
Servadio, Emilio
Shimura, Hirotsugu
Shinoda, Hideo
S. J. S.
Soavi, Giulio Cesare
Sohar, Zwi
Sorani, Rosanna
Sprott, W. J. H.
Srdce, Václav
Stärcke, August
Stärcke, Johan
Staude, Angela
Stern, James
Stern, Tania
Stierlin, Helm
Straat, E.
Strachey, Alix
Strachey, James
Suchtelen, Nicholaas Johannes van
Sulzberger, Carl Fulton

Syrros, P.
Szilágyi, Géza

Tadié, Marie
Taft, Jessie
Tait, D. F.
Takács, Maria
Takahashi, Yoshitaka
Takala, Martti
Tanaka, Machiko
Teslaar, James S. van
Thompson, Clara
Törngren, Pehr Henrik
Torres, Luis López-Ballesteros Y de
Tort, Michel
Toyokawa, Noboru
Tsushima, Kanji
Tyson, Alan

Varsamis, N.
Vedalanker, Devendrakumar
Veen, Joseph van
Veltri, Pietro
Viakhirev, A. V.
Vilhar, Albin
Vojslavsky, Zevi
Volf, Nikola
Vul'f, M. V.
Vygotskiĭ, L. S.

Weibel, L.
Weinrich, Wilna
Weiss, Edoardo
Winston, Clara
Winston, Richard
Wiškowský, E.
Witenberg, Earl G.
Woolf, Virginia
Wortis, Joseph
Wulff, Moshe
Wygotski, L.
Wyrubow, N. A. von

Yabe, Yaekichi
Yamamoto, Iwao
Yamamoto, Yoshiko
Yasuda, Ichiro
Yasuda, Tokutaro
Yi, Yong-ho

Yoshida, Masami
Yoshioka, Nakayoshi

Zalszupin, H.
Zaniewicki, W.
Zewar, Moustafa
Zographou, Mina
Zohn, Harry
Zuring, J.

SECTION I

EARLY, PRIMARILY NONPSYCHOLOGICAL WRITINGS

In addition to his nonpsychological writings, this section includes three of Freud's early papers: "Beobachtung einer hochgradigen Hemianästhesie bei einem hysterischen Manne" [8]; "Hypnose" [22]; "Zerstreute Gedanken" [40].

1

1885b   Über die Allgemeinwirkung des Cocaïns. (Lecture before the Psychiatr
10351   Verein, 5 Mar 1885) Med-chirug Centralbl 1885, (20:7 Aug):374-376.

On the general effect of cocaine. (Tr: Edminster, S.A.) in Donoghue, A. K. & Hillman, J. (eds) *The cocaine papers*. Vienna/Zurich: Dunquin Pr 1963, 45-49. In "Drug Dependence" 1970, 1(5:Oct):15-17. In Byck, R. (ed) *Cocaine papers by Sigmund Freud*. NY: Stonehill 1974, 113-118.

2

1891b   Zur Auffassung der Aphasien. Eine kritische Studie. Leipzig/Vienna:
10352   Deuticke 1891, 107 p.
         Abs Inhalts wiss Arb 19.

On aphasia, a critical study. (Tr: Stengel, E.) NY: IUP; London: IPC 1953, xv + 105 p.

On the interpretation of the aphasias, a critical study.
         Abs (Tr:JS) SE 3:240-241.

3

1886a   Akute multiple Neuritis der spinalen und Hirnnerven. Wien med Wschr
10350   1886 (Feb 6), 36(6), cols 168-172.
         Abs Inhalts wiss Arb 13.

Acute multiple neuritis of the spinal and cranial nerves.
         Abs (Tr:JS) SE 3:236.

4

         (Unsigned) The bacillus of syphilis. Medical News, Phila 1884, 45
73569   (14 Dec):673-674. In Grinstein, A. "Freud's first publications in
         America," J Am Psa Ass 1971, 19:257-258.

5

1882a   Über den Bau der Nervenfasern und Nervenzellen beim Flusskrebs.
10353   (Presented at Academy of Science session, 15 Dec 1881) S B Akad Wiss
         Wien (Math-Naturwiss Kl), III Abt, 85:9-46.
         Abs Inhalts wiss Arb 5.

On the structure of the nerve fibres and nerve cells of the river crayfish.
Abs (Tr:JS) SE 3:230.

6

1887d Beiträge über die Anwendung des Cocaïn. Zweite Serie. I. Bemerkungen
10355 über Cocaïnsucht und Cocaïnfurcht mit Beziehung auf einem Vortrag
W. A. Hammond's. Wien med Wschr 1887, 37(28):cols 929-932.
Abs Inhalts wiss Arb 17.

Contributions about the applications of cocaine. Second series. I. Remarks on craving for and fear of cocaine with reference to a lecture by
W. A. Hammond. (Tr: Freisinger, L. A.) In Donoghue, A. K. &
Hillman, J. (eds) *The cocaine papers*. Vienna/Zurich: Dunquin Pr 1963,
57-62. In Byck, R. (ed) *Cocaine papers by Sigmund Freud*. NY: Stonehill
1974, 171-176.
Abs (Tr:JS) SE 3:239.

7

1885a Beitrag zur Kenntnis der Cocawirkung. Wien med Wschr 1885, 35
10354 (5:31 Jan):cols 129-133.
Abs Inhalts wiss Arb 10.

Contribution to the knowledge of the effect of cocaine. (Tr: Potash,
R. S.) In Donoghue, A. K. & Hillman, J. (eds) *The cocaine papers*.
Vienna/Zurich: Dunquin Pr 1963, 35-41. In Byck, R. (ed) *Cocaine
papers by Sigmund Freud*. NY: Stonehill 1974, 97-104.
Abs (Tr:JS) SE 3:234.

8

1886d Beobachtung einer hochgradigen Hemianästhesie bei einem hysterischen
10356 Manne. (Beiträge zur Kasuistik der Hysterie I.) (Paper read before K.K.
Ges der Ärzte in Vienna, 26 Nov 1886). Wien med Wschr 1886, 36:(49,
50):cols 1633-1638, 1674-1676.
Abs Inhalts wiss Arb 16.

Observations of a severe case of hemi-anaesthesia in a hysterical male.
(Contributions to the clinical study of hysteria, I.) (Tr:JS) SE 1:25-31.
Abs (Tr:JS) SE 3:238.

It: Osservazione di un caso grave di emianestesia in un paziente isterico.
(Tr: Schwarz, L.) Opere 1, 25-34.

9

1877b Beobachtungen über Gestaltung und feineren Bau der als Hoden be-
10357 schriebenen Lappenorgane des Aals. (Presented at Academy of Science
session, 15 Mar 1877 by Prof Claus) S B Akad Wiss Wien (Math-
Naturwiss Kl), I Abt, 75 (4):419.
Abs Inhalts wiss Arb 1.

Observations on the configuration and finer structure of the lobed organs

in eels described as testes.
Abs (Tr:JS) SE 3:227.

10

1895e   Über die Bernhardt'sche Sensibilitätsstörungen am Oberschenkel. Neurol
10358   Zbl 1895, 14(11):491-492.
Abs Inhalts wiss Arb 34.

On Bernhardt's disturbance of sensibility in the thigh.
Abs (Tr:JS) SE 3:253.

11

1886b   (& Darkschewitsch, L.) Über die Beziehung des Strickkörpers zum
10359   Hinterstrang und Hinterstrangskern nebst Bemerkungen über zwei
Felder der Oblongata. Neurol Zbl 1886, 5(6):121-129.
Abs Inhalts wiss Arb 14.

On the relation of the restiform body to the posterior column and its
nucleus with some remarks on two fields of the medulla oblongata.
Abs (Tr:JS) SE 3:237.

12

1898c   Cerebrale Kinderlähmung. In Mendel, E. (ed) *Jahresbericht über die*
1899b   *Leistungen und Fortschritte auf dem Gebiete der Neurologie und Psy-*
1900b   *chiatrie* [Annual report on the achievements and progress in the fields of
10360   neurology and psychiatry] 30 reviews and abstracts for 1897. Berlin:
Karger 1898, 1:613-632. 29 reviews and abstracts for 1898. Berlin:
Karger 1899, 2:632-642. 22 reviews and abstracts for 1899. Berlin:
Karger 1900, 3:611-618.

Infantile cerebral paralysis. (Tr: Russin, L. A.) Coral Gables, Florida:
Univ Miami Pr 1968.

13

1891a   (& Rie, Oscar) Cerebrale Kinderlähmung und Poliomyelitis infantilis.
10361   [Infantile cerebral paralysis and infantile poliomyelitis.] Wien med
Wschr 1891, 41(5, 6, 7):cols 193-196, 244-246, 292-294. In *Klinische
Studie über die halbseitige Cerebrallähmung der Kinder.*

14

1884e   Ueber Coca. Zbl ges Therap 1884, 2(7):289-314.
10362   Abs Inhalts wiss Arb 9.

Coca. (Abbrev tr: Pollak, S.) St. Louis Med Surg J 1884, 47(6):502-505.

On Coca. (Tr: Edminster, S. A.) In Donoghue, A. K. & Hillman, J. (eds)
The cocaine papers. Vienna/Zurich: Dunquin Pr 1963, 1-26. (Tr:
Edminster, S. A.; additions: Redlich, F. C.) In Byck, R. (ed) *Cocaine
papers by Sigmund Freud.* NY: Stonehill 1974, 49-74.
Abs (Tr:JS) SE 3:233.

15

(Unsigned) Cocaine. Medical News, Phila 1884, 45 (1 Nov):502. In
73570 Grinstein, A. "Freud's first publications in America." J Am Psa Ass 1971,
19:255-256.

16

1893e Les diplégies cérébrales infantiles. Rev Neurol Paris 1893, 1:177-183.
10366 Abs Inhalts wiss Arb 27.

Cerebral diplegias in childhood.
Abs (Tr:JS) SE 3:247.

17

1884a Ein Fall von Hirnblutung mit indirekten basalen Herdsymptomen bei
10367 Skorbut. Wien med Wschr 1884, 34(9, 10):cols 244-246, 276-279.
Abs Inhalts wiss Arb 8.

A case of cerebral hemorrhage with indirect basal focal symptoms in
scurvy.
Abs (Tr:JS) SE 3:232.

18

1885c Ein Fall von Muskelatrophie mit ausgebreiteten Sensibilitätsstörungen
10368 (Syringomyelie). Wien med Wschr 1885, 35(13, 14):cols 389-392,
425-429.
Abs Inhalts wiss Arb 12.

A case of muscular atrophy with extensive disturbances of sensitivity
(syrongomyelia).
Abs (Tr:JS) SE 3:235.

19

1893d Über familiäre Formen von cerebralen Diplegien. Neurol Zbl 1893, 12
10369 (15, 16):512-515, 542-547.
Abs Inhalts wiss Arb 26.

On familiar forms of cerebral diplegias.
Abs (Tr:JS) SE 3:247.

20

1885e [Gutachten über das Parke Cocaïn.] In Gutt[macher, H.], "Neue Arznei-
10370 mittel und Heilmethoden. Über die verschiedenen Cocäin-Präparate und
deren Wirkung." Wien med Presse 1885, 26(32:9 Aug):1036.

Opinion on Parke's cocaine. (Tr: Freisinger, L. A.) In Donoghue, A. K.
& Hillman, J. (eds) *The cocaine papers.* Vienna/Zurich: Dunquin Pr
1963, 53. (Tr: Fleck, S.; Gyorgyey, F.; & Byck, R.) in Byck, R.
(ed) *Cocaine papers by Sigmund Freud.* NY: Stonehill 1974, 122-
123.

21

1888a   Über Hemianopsie im frühesten Kindesalter. Wien med Wschr 1888, 38
10371   (32, 33):cols 1081-1086, 1116-1121.
        Abs Inhalts wiss Arb 18.

        On hemianopsia in early childhood.
        Abs (Tr:JS) SE 3:239.

22

1891d   Hypnose. In Bum, A. *Therapeutisches Lexikon*, Vienna: Urban &
73580   Schwarzenberg 1891, 724-734. 2nd ed 1893, 896-904. 3rd ed 1900,
        1:1110-1119.

        Hypnosis. (Tr:JS) SE 1:105-114.

23

1897a   Die infantile Cerebrallähmung. In Nothnagel *Specielle Pathologie und*
10372   *Therapie*. Vienna: Hölder 1897, vi+327 p, IX Bd, II Teil, II Abt.
        Abs Inhalts wiss Arb 38.

        Infantile cerebral paralysis.
        Abs (Tr:JS) SE 3:256.

24

1897b   Inhaltsangaben der wissenschaftlichen Arbeiten des Privatdocenten Dr.
10373   Sigm. Freud (1877-1897). Vienna: Deuticke 1897, 24 p. Contains ab-
        stracts of [9], [37], [34], [31], [5], [35], [30], [17], [14], [7], [26], [18], [3],
        [11], [38], [8], [6], [21], [2], [27], [97], [69], [36], [185], [25], [19], [16],
        [200], [42], [173], [214], [59], [138], [10], [250], [50], [118], [23].

        Bibliographie und Inhaltsangaben der Arbeiten Freuds bis zu den
        Anfängen der Psychoanalyse. Z 1940, 25(1):69-93. GW 1952, 1:461-488.

        Abstracts of the scientific writings of Dr. Sigm. Freud 1877-1897.
        (Tr:JS) SE 3:227-257.

    It: Somnari dei lavori scientifici del libero docente dottor Sigmund Freud,
        1877-1897. (Tr: Campione, A.) Opere 2, 365-394.

    Sp: Sinopsis de los trabajos cientificos del Docente Privado Dr. Sigmund
        Freud 1877-1897. (Tr:LR) Obr Comp-BA 22:457-476.

25

1893b   Zur Kenntnis der cerebralen Diplegien des Kindesalters (im Anschluss an
10374   die Little'sche Krankheit). In Kassowitz *Beiträge zur Kinderheilkunde*,
        Neue Folge, No. 3, Leipzig/Vienna: Deuticke 1893, iii+168 p.
        Abs Inhalts wiss Arb 25.

        Contribution to the knowledge of cerebral diplegias in childhood, in
        connection with Little's disease.
        Abs (Tr:JS) SE 3:245-247.

26

1885d   Zur Kenntnis der Olivenzwischenschicht. Neurol Zbl 1885, 4(12):
10375   268-270.
        Abs Inhalts wiss Arb 11.

        Concerning the knowledge of the intermediary layer of the olive.
        Abs (Tr:JS) SE 3:234.

27

1891a   (& Rie, Oscar) Klinische Studie über die halbseitige Cerebrallähmung
10376   der Kinder. In Kassowitz *Beiträge zur Kinderheilkunde*. No. 3. Vienna:
        Perles 1891, 221.
        Abs Inhalts wiss Arb 20.

        Clinical study of hemilateral cerebral paralysis in children.
        Abs (Tr:JS) SE 3:241-242.

28

1885f   Nachträge über [Ueber] Coca. In revised, enlarged, separate reprint
        "Über Coca." Zbl ges Therap, Vienna: Von Moritz Perles, 11:1-26.
        Abs Inhalts wiss Arb 10.

        Addenda to "On Coca." (Tr: Edminster, S. A.) In Donoghue, A. K. &
        Hillman, J. (eds) *The cocaine papers*. Vienna/Zurich: Dunquin Pr 1963,
        27-29. (Tr: Edminster, S. A.; additions: Redlich, F. C.) In Byck, R. (ed)
        Cocaine papers by Sigmund Freud. NY: Stonehill 1974, 107-110.
        Abs (Tr:JS) SE 3:233.

29

1887f   Das Nervensystem. [The nervous system.] Abschnitt V of Buchheim (ed)
10378   *Ärztliche Versicherungsdiagnostik* 1887.

30

1884b   Eine neue Methode zum Studium des Faserverlaufeṣ im Centralnerven-
10379   system. Zbl med Wiss 1884, 22(11):161-163.

1884c   A new histological method for the study of nerve-tracts in the brain and
10381   spinal cord. (Tr: Freud, S. & Sachs, B.) Brain 1884, 7:86-88.

1884d   Eine neue Methode zum Studium des Faserverlaufes im Centralnerven-
10380   system. (Expanded version of [1884b].) Archiv Anat Physiol Anatomische
        Abt. 1884, Heft 5-6:453-460.
        Abs Inhalts wiss Arb 7.

        A new method for the study of the course of nerve fibers in the central
        nervous system.
        Abs (Tr:JS) SE 3:231.

31

1879a   Notiz über eine Methode zur anatomischen Präparation des Nerven-

10382 systems. Zbl med Wiss 1879, 17(26):468-469.
Abs Inhalts wiss Arb 4.

Note on a method for anatomical preparation of the nervous system.
Abs (Tr:JS) SE 3:229.

32

[Contribution to] Rosenberg, Ludwig *Casuistische Beiträge zur Kenntnis*
10363 *der cerebralen Kinderlähmungen und der Epilepsie.* In Kassowitz, M.
Beiträge zur Kinderheilkunde. Vienna: Deuticke 1893, 4:92-111.

33

[Contribution to] Rosenthal, Emil (ed) *Contribution à l'étude des*
10364 *diplégies cérébrales de l'enfance.* [In French] Thèse de Lyon 1892, 152 p.
Les diplégies cérébrales de l'enfance. Paris: J. B. Ballière 1893, 160 p.

34

1878a Über Spinalganglien und Rückenmark des Petromyzon. (Presented at
10383 Academy of Science session, 18 July, 1878 by Prof Brücke) S B Akad Wiss
Wien (Math-Naturwiss Kl), III Abt, 78(2):81-167.
Abs Inhalts wiss Arb 3.

On the spinal ganglia and spinal cord of the petromyzon.
Abs (Tr:JS) SE 3:228-229.

35

1884f Die Struktur der Elemente des Nervensystems. Vortrag im psych-
10384 iatrischen Verein. [1882 according to Freud but no reference in 1882
minutes of the Society.] Jahrb Psychiat 1884, 5(3):221-229.
Abs Inhalts wiss Arb 6.

The structure of the elements of the nervous system. Lecture at the
psychiatric society 1882.
Abs (Tr:JS) SE 3:230.

36

1893g Über ein Symptom, das häufig die Enuresis nocturna der Kinder
10385 begleitet. Neurol Zbl 1893, 12(21):735-737.
Abs Inhalts wiss Arb 23.

On a symptom frequently accompanying nocturnal enuresis in children.
Abs (Tr:JS) SE 3:243.

37

1877a Über den Ursprung der hinteren Nervenwurzeln im Rückenmarke von
10386 Ammocoetes. (Petromyzon Planeri). (Presented at Academy of Science
session, 4 Jan 1877 by Prof Brücke). S B Akad Wiss Wien (Math-
Naturwiss Kl), III Abt, 75(1):15-27.
Abs Inhalts wiss Arb 2.

On the origin of the posterior nerve-roots in the spinal cord of the
ammocoetes.
Abs (Tr: JS) SE 3:228.

38

1886c   Über den Ursprung der Nervus acusticus. Monatschr Ohrenheilk 1886,
10387   Neue Folge 20(8,9):245-251, 277-282.
        Abs Inhalts wiss Arb 15.

On the origin of the acoustical nerve.
Abs (Tr: JS) SE 3:238.

39

1888b   [Contributions to] Villaret, Albert (ed) *Handwörterbuch der gesamten*
10365   *Medizin*. Unter Mitwirkung von Baginsky, A.; Baginsky, B.; u.s.
        Stuttgart: Enke 1888-1891, 2 vol.
            Aphasis, 1:88-90.
            Gehirn, 1:684-697.
            Hysterie, 1:886-892. Psyche 1953, 7:486-500.
            Hysteria. (Tr: JS) SE 1:41-57.
   It: Isteria. (Tr: Schwarz, L.) Opere 1, 43-64.

            Hysteroepilepsie. 1:892.
            Hystero-epilepsy. (Tr: JS) SE 1:58-59.
   It: Isteroepilessia. (Tr: Schwarz, L.) Opere 1, appendix.

            Kinderlähmung, spinale, 2:91-93.
            Lähmung, 2:169-171.

40

Zerstreute Gedanken. ["Scattered thoughts" written in 1871 for student
paper "Musarion," published by Grades V, VI, Leopoldstaedter Gym-
nasium.] In Eissler, K. R. "Psychoanalytische Einfälle zu Freuds
'Zerstreute(n) Gedanken.'" *Jahrbuch der Psychoanalyse* Bern: Hans
Huber 1974, 101.

SECTION II
PSYCHOLOGICAL WRITINGS

This section does not include Introductions and Prefaces, Abstracts and Reviews, Translations, or Letters. Separate sections are provided elsewhere for these listings. A few letters of special significance (e.g., the letters to Fliess in *The origins of psychoanalysis*) and those which were initially "open letters" (e.g., the letters to Romain Rolland) are included in this section.

41

1940a Abriss der Psychoanalyse. Z 1940, 25(1):7-67. GW 1941, 17:63-138.
(1938) Frankfurt/M: Fischer 1953.
10388

  An outline of psycho-analysis. (Tr:JS) J 1940, 21(1):27-82. (Revised tr: JS) London:HPI 1949, ix+84 p. NY: Norton 1949, 127 p. (Revised tr:JS) SE 23:144-207.

Arab: Ma'ālim al-tahlīl al-nafsānī. (Tr: Najatī, M.) Cairo: Maktabit al-Mahdah al-Misriyyah 1958.

  Al-mujaz fī al tahlīl al-nafsi. (Tr: Mahmud 'Ali, S.) Cairo: Dar al-Mā'arif 1962.

Fr: Abrégé de psychanalyse. (Tr:AB) Paris: PUF 1950, 1953, 1955, 1964, 1967, 87 p.

It: Sommario di psicoanalisi. (Tr: David, S.) (Pref: Servadio, E.) Florence: Ed. Universitaria 1951, 103 p; 1957, 104 p; 1967, 87 p.

  Compendio di psicoanalisi. (Tr: Lucentini, M.) In *Casi clinici*, Turin: Boringhieri 1952, 1962. Opere 11. (Tr: Fachinelli, E.; Staude, A.; & Montinari, M.) In *Psicoanalisi. Esposizione divulgative*, Turin: Boringhieri 1963, 1965.

Jap: (Tr: Kosawa, H.) SelFr-K 1958, 15. Rev ed (Tr: Okonogi, K.) SelFr-K 1969, 15:103 p.

Nor: Slik den var-op slik den ble. (Tr: Brøgger, W.) In Psykoanalysen, Cappelens realbøker 1965, 135 p.

Pers: Nokāte omdehe ravānshenāsiye tahlili. (Tr: Gounili, A. H.) Tehran: Tehran Univ Pr 1962, 66+5 p.

Sp: Compendio del psicoanálisis. (Tr:LR) Obr Comp-BA 21:67-126. Obr Comp 1967/1968, 3:392-440.

  Esquema del psicoanálisis. (Tr:LR) Buenos Aires: Nova 1953. Obr Comp 1967/1968, 3:1009-1061.

Prólogo de la edición alemena Esquema del Psicoanálisis. (Tr:LR)
Obr Comp-BA 21:13-16. Obr Comp 1967/1968, 3:361-362.

42

1894a   Die Abwehr-Neuropsychosen. Versuch einer psychologischen Theorie der
10389   akquirierten Hysterie, vieler Phobien und Zwangsvorstellungen und
        gewisser hallucinatorischer Psychosen. Neurol Zbl 1894, 13(10:15 May):
        362-364; (11:1 June):402-409. SKSN 1906, 1:45-59. 2nd ed, 1911.
        3rd ed, 1920. 4th ed, 1922. GS 1925, 1:290-305. GW 1952, 1:59-74.
        Abs Inhalts wiss Arb 29.

        The defense neuro-psychoses. An endeavor to provide a psychological
        theory of acquired hysteria, many phobias and obsessions, and certain
        hallucinatory psychoses. (Tr:AAB) SPH 1909, 121-132. 2nd ed, 1912.
        3rd ed, 1920.

        The defence neuro-psychoses. A tentative psychological theory of
        acquired hysteria, many phobias and obsessions, and certain halluci-
        natory psychoses. (Tr:AAB) In *Major Works* 81-87.

        The defence neuro-psychoses. (Tr:JR) CP 1924, 1:59-75.

        The neuro-psychoses of defence (an attempt at a psychological theory of
        acquired hysteria, of many phobias and obsessions and of certain halluci-
        natory psychoses). (Tr:JR) SE 3:45-61.
        Abs (Tr:JS) SE 3:249.

  Fr: Les psychonévroses de défense. (Tr:JLa) In *Névrose, psychose et
        perversion.* Paris: PUF 1973, 1-14.

  It: Le neuropsicosi da difesa: abbozzo di una teoria psicologica dell'isteria
        acquisita, di molte fobie e ossessioni e di certe psicosi allucinatorie. (Tr:
        Campione, A.) Opere 2:121-136.

  Jap: (Tr: Imura, T.) SelFr-JinSh 1970, 6:11 p.

  Por: As neuropsicoses de defesa. Ensaio de uma teoria psicológica da histeria
        adquirida, de muitas fobias e representações obsessivas e de certas
        psicoses alucinatórias. (Tr:CMdeF) Obr Comp-P 2:119-138.

  Sp: Las neuropsicosis de defensa: ensayo de una teoría psicológica de la
        histeria adquirida, de muchas fobias y representaciones obsesivas y de
        ciertas psicosis alucinatorias. (Tr:LLBT) Obr Comp-Madrid 11:115-132.
        Obr Comp-BA 11:85-98. Obr Comp 1948, 1:175-197. Obr Comp 1967/
        1968, 1:173-179.

43

1909a   Allgemeines über den hysterischen Anfall. Z Psychother med Psychol
(1908)   1909, 1(1 Jan):10-14. SKSN 1909, 2:146-150. 2nd ed, 1912. 3rd ed, 1921.
10390   GS 1924, 5:255-260. GW 1941, 7:235-240.

         General remarks on hysterical attacks. (Tr:DB) CP 1924, 2:100-104.

         Some general remarks on hysterical attacks. (Revised tr:JS) SE 9:
         229-234.

Fr: Considérations générales sur l'attaque hystériqùe. (Tr: Guérineau, D.) In *Névrose, psychose et perversion.* Paris: PUF 1973, 161-165.

It: Osservazioni generali sull'attacco isterico. (Tr: Dogana, M. T.) Opere 5: 441-448.

Jap: Hisuteri hossa no ippanteki chōsō. (Tr: KO) In *Bunseki renai ron,* FCW-S 1932, 9:113-121.

Por: Generalidades sôbre o ataque histérico. (Tr: OG & MG) Obr Comp-P 5: 155-160.

Sp: Generalidades sobre el ataque histérico. (Tr: LLBT) Obr Comp-Madrid, 13:142-147. Obr Comp-BA 13:115-119. Obr Comp 1948, 1:971-973. Obr Comp 1967/1968, 1:960-962.

44

1912d   Über die allgemeinste Erniedrigung des Liebeslebens. (Beiträge zur
10391   Psychologie des Liebeslebens II). Y 1912, 4(1):40-50. SKSN 1918, 4: 213-218, 2nd ed, 1922. GS 1924, 5:198-211. In *Beiträge zur Psychologie des Liebeslebens,* Leipzig/Vienna/Zurich: Int Psa Verlag 1924, 15-28. Sexualtheorie und Traumlehre 1931, 80-95. GW 1943, 8:78-91.

The most prevalent form of degradation in erotic life. (Contributions to the psychology of love II). (Tr: JRiv) CP 1925, 4:203-216.

On the universal tendency to debasement in the sphere of love. (Contributions to the psychology of love II). (Tr: Tyson, A.) SE 11:179-190.

Fr: Contribution à la psychologie de la via amoureuse. II: Considérations sur le plus commun des ravalements de la vie amoureuse. (Tr: MB & AB) RFPsa 1936, 9(1):10-21. (Tr: JLa) In *La vie sexuelle,* Paris: PUF 1969, 55-65.

Heb: Al hahashpala haklalit beyoter shel chaye haahava. Kitvei 2, chap. 10.

It: Le degradazione della vita erotica. In Zolla, E. *La psicoanalisi,* Milan: Grazanti 1960, 210-223.

Sulla più comune degradazione della vita amorosa. (Tr: Campione, A.; Candreva, S.; Montinari, M.; CLM; & Sagittario, E.) In *La vita sessuale,* Turin: Boringhieri 1970. Opere 6.

Jap: Renai seikatsu no ippanteki iyashime ni tsuite. Renai no seikatsu no shinri—dai ni rombun. In *Bunseki renai ron,* FCW-S 1932, 9:17-35.

Por: Sôbre uma degradação geral da vida erótica. (Tr: OG & MG) Obr Comp-P 5:171-183.

Sp: Sobre una degradación general de la vida erótica. (Tr: LLBT) Obr Comp-Madrid 13. Obr Comp-BA 13:70-80. Obr Comp 1948, 1:978-984. Obr Comp 1967/1968, 1:967-972.

45

1909b   Analyse der Phobie eines fünfjährigen Knaben. Y 1909, 1(1):1-109.
10392   SKSN 1913, 3:1-122. GS 1924, 8:129-263. *Vier Krankengeschichten*

1932, 142-281. GW 1941, 7:243-377. *See also* Nachschrift zur Analyse des kleinen Hans [161].

Analysis of a phobia in a five-year-old boy. (Tr:ASt & JS) CP 1925, 3:149-287. SE 10:5-147.

Cz: Analyse fobie petileteho hosika. (Tr: Friedmann, O.) In *Psychoanalytické chorobopisy*, Prague: Julius Albert 1937.

Fr: Analyse d'une phobie d'un petit garçon de cinq ans (le petit Hans). (Tr:MB) RFPsa 1928, 2:411-538. (Tr:MB & RL) In *Cinq psychanalyses*, Paris: Denoël & Steele 1935, 111-228; Paris: PUF 1954, 1966, 1967, 1970, 93-198.

It: Analisi della fobia di un bambino di cinque anni (caso clinico del piccolo Hans). (Tr: Lucentini, M.) In *Casi clinici*, Turin: Editore Boringhieri 1952, 1962. Opere 5:481-590. (Tr:CLM; Panaitescu, E. A.; & Lucentini, M.) In *Psicanalisi infantile*, Turin: Boringhieri 1969, 1970.

Jap: (Tr:YT & Noda, T.) Tokyo: Ars 1930. SelFr-JinSh 1969, 5:103 p.

Por: Análise da fobia de um minino de cinco anos. (Tr:OG) Obr Comp-P 15: 127-264.

Rus: Psikhoanaliz dietskago strakha. Analiz fobii 5-lietnego mal'chika. (Tr: Fel'tsman, O. ?) In *Psikhoterapevticheskaia biblioteka*, vyp. IX, Moskva: Nauka 1913, 150 p.

Sp: Análisis de la fobia de un niño de cinco años. (Tr:LLBT) Obr Comp-Madrid 15. Obr Comp-BA 15:115-225. Obr Comp 1948, 2:566-623. Obr Comp 1967/1968, 2:658-714.

Sw: Lille Hans. Analys av fobi hos en femårig pojke. (Tr: Löfgren, I.) Stockholm: Aldus/Bonniers 1970, 137 p.

46

1950a   Aus den Anfängen der Psychoanalyse; Briefe an Wilhelm Fliess.
10393   Abhandlungen und Notizen aus den Jahren 1887-1902. London: IPC 1950, viii+477 p. *See also* Wilhelm Fliess [382].

The origins of psychoanalysis. Letters to Wilhelm Fliess, drafts and notes: 1887-1902. (Ed: Bonaparte, M.; Freud, A.; Kris, E.) (Tr: Mosbacher, E. & JS) (Intro: Kris, E.) NY: Basic Books; London: IPC 1954, xi+486 p. NY: Doubleday 1957, Anchor Books, Vol. A 112.

Extracts from the Fliess Papers. Includes: Draft A, B, D-N; Letters 14, 18, 21, 22, 46, 50, 52, 55-57, 59-61, 64, 66, 67, 69-73, 75, 79, 84, 97, 101, 102, 105, 125. (Tr:JS) SE 1:177-280.

Fr: La naissance de la psychanalyse, Lettres à Wilhelm Fliess, notes et plans (1887-1902). (Ed: Bonaparte, M.; Freud, A.; Kris, E.) (Tr:AB) Paris: PUF 1956, 1969, 424 p.

It: Le origini della psicoanalisi. Lettere a Wilhelm Fliess (1887-1902). (Tr: Soavi, G.) (Pref: Servadio, E.) (Intro: Kris, E.) *Epistolari di Sigmund Freud*, Vol. 2. Turin: Boringhieri 1961, 2nd ed (revised), 1968, 298 p.

Minute teoriche per Wilhelm Fliess [le minute sono dincate con le lettere da A a N]. Opere 2:7-68.

Sp: Los orígenes del psicoanálisis. Cartas a Wilhelm Fliess, manuscritos y notas de los años 1887 a 1902. (Tr:LR) Obr Comp-BA 22:77-372. Obr Comp 1967/1968, 3:585-882.

In part: Cuatros cartas a Wilhelm Fliess. [Letters 69-72]. (Tr:LR) Rev Psicoanál 1955, 13:404-414.

47

1941e Ansprache an die Mitglieder des Vereins B'nai B'rith. [Read on
(1926) Freud's 70th birthday, 6 May 1926.] GW 1941, 17:51-53. *Briefe.*
10394
Address to the society of B'nai B'rith. (Tr:JS) SE 20:273-274. *Letters.*

It: Discorso ai membri della Associazone B'nai-B'rith. Opere 10.

Sp: Discurso a los miembros de la sociedad B'nai B'rith. (Tr:LR) Obr Comp-BA 21:55-58. Obr Comp 1967/1968, 3:387-388.

48

1930e Ansprache im Frankfurter Goethe-Haus. [Read by Anna Freud on
10395 28 Aug 1930] Psa B 1930, 2(5:Sept-Oct):421-426. GS 1934, 12:408-411. GW 1948, 14:547-550. *See also* Alfons Paquet [455].

Address delivered in the Goethe House at Frankfurt. (Tr: Richards, A.) SE 21:208-212.

Sp: Discurso en la casa de Goethe en Frankfurt. (Tr:LR) Obr Comp-BA 20:234-238.

49

1938c Anti-semitism in England. [To the editor of *Time and Tide.*] Time
73574 and Tide, London 1938, 26 Nov:1649. SE 23:301. *Briefe; Letters.*

It: Antisemitismo in Inghilterra. Opere 11.

Sp: Antisemitismo en Inglaterra. Obr Comp 1967/1968, 3:341-342.

50

1896c Zur Ätiologie der Hysterie. (Read at Verein für Psychiatrie und
10397 Neurologie, 21 Apr 1896) Wien klin Rdsch 1896, 10(22, 31 May): 379-381; (23, 7 June):395-397; (24, 14 June): 413-415; (25, 21 June):432-433; (26, 28 June):450-452. SKSN 1906, 1:149-180. GS 1925, 1:404-438. GW 1952, 1:425-459.
Abs Inhalts wiss Arb 36.

The aetiology of hysteria. (Tr:CMB) CP 1924, 1:183-219. (Revised tr:JS) SE 3:191-221.
Abs (Tr:JS) SE 3:254.

Fr: L'étiologie de l'hystérie. (Tr: Bissery, J. & JLa) In *Névrose, psychose et perversion.* Paris: PUF 1973, 83-112.

It: Etiologia dell'isteria. (Tr: Campione, A.) Opere 2:333-362.

Jap: Hisuteri byōin ron. (Tr: Kakeda, K. & Yoshida, M.) In *Hisuteri kenkyū,* SelFr-K 1955, 9.

Por: A etiologia da histeria. (Tr:CMdeF) Obr Comp-P 2:7-46.

Sp: La etiología de la histeria. (Tr:LLBT) Obr Comp-Madrid 12. Obr Comp-BA 12:157-184. Obr Comp 1948, 1:131-145. Obr Comp 1967/ 1968, 1:131-145.

51

1913h   Auftreten der Krankheitssymptome im Traume. Erf Beisp Psa Prx [89]
10398   no. 22. Z 1913, 1:377-382. GS 1928, 11:301-303. Neurosenlehre und Technik 1931, 303-308. GW 1946, 10:40-42.

Appearance in the dream of the symptoms of the illness. (Tr:JS) SE 13:198.

52

1901c   Autobiographical note. In Pagel, J. L. *Biographisches Lexicon hervor-*
(1899)   *ragender Ärzte des neunzehnten Jahrhunderts* [Biographical Lexicon of
10399   Eminent Doctors of the Nineteenth Century]. Berlin/Vienna 1901, col 545.

Autobiographical note. (Tr:JS) SE 3:325.

It: Nota autobiografica. Opere 2:459-462.

53

1911d   Die Bedeutung der Vokalfolge. C 1911, 2:105. GS 1928, 11:301.
10400   Neurosenlehre und Technik 1931, 306. GW 1943, 8:348.

The significance of sequences of vowels. (Tr:JS) SE 12:341.

It: Il significato della successione delle vocali. Opere 6. In *Saggi sull'arte, la letteratura e il linguaggio,* Turin: Boringhieri 1969, vol. 1.

Sp: El significado de la aliteración de las vocales. (Tr:LR) Obr Comp-BA 19: 260. Obr Comp 1967/1968, 3:177.

54

1910j   Beispiele des Verrats pathogener Phantasien bei Neurotikern. C 1910,
10401   1:43-44. GS 1928, 11:300-301. Neurosenlehre und Technik 1931, 305-306. GW 1943, 8:228.

Two instances of pathogenic phantasies revealed by the patients themselves. (Tr:JS) SE 11:236-237.

It: Esempi del modo come si tradiscono le fantasie patogene dei nevrotici. Opere 6.

Sp: Ejemplos de cómo los neuróticos revelan sus fantasías patógenas. (Tr: LR) Obr Comp-BA 19:259. Obr Comp 1967/1968, 3:176.

55

1911i Ein Beitrag zum Vergessen von Eigennamen. C 1911, 1:407-408.
10402 Example 11, chapter 3 in *Zur Psychopathologie des Alltagslebens*, 4th ed, 1912, 31-32 and later editions.

A contribution to the forgetting of proper names. (Tr:JS) SE 6:30-32.

FOR OTHER LANGUAGES, see under *Zur Psychopathologie des Alltagslebens* [197].

56

1910h, Beiträge zur Psychologie des Liebeslebens. SKSN 1918, 4:200-251.
1912d, GS 1924, 5:186-231. Leipzig/Vienna/Zurich: Int Psa Verlag 1924, 49 p.
1918a Sexualtheorie und Traumlehre 1931, 69-115. GW 1943, 8:66-91; III
(1917) 1947, 12:161-180. [Includes 44, 60, 215]
10403 Contributions to the psychology of love. (Tr:JRiv) CP 1925, 4:192-235.
I, II (Tr: Tyson, A.) SE 11:165-175; 179-190. III (Tr: Richards, A.)
SE 11:193-208.

Dan: Bidrag til kaerlighedslivets psykologi. (Tr: Boisen, M.) In *Nye forelaesninger om psykoanalysen*, Copenhagen: Hans Reitzel 1959.

Fr: Contributions à la psychologie de la vie amoureuse. (Tr:MB & AB) RFPsa 1936, 9:2-21. (Tr:JLa & Berger, D.) In *La vie sexuelle*, Paris: PUF 1969, 47-80.

It: Contributi alla psicologia della vita amorosa: 1. Su un tipo particulare di scelta oggettuale nell'uomo. 2. Sulla più comune degradazione della vita amorosa. 3. Il tabù della verginità. (Tr: Campione, A.; Candreva, S.; Montinari, M.; CLM; & Sagittario, E.) In *La vie sessuale*, Turin: Boringhieri 1970. Opere 6.

Jap: (Tr:KO) Tokyo: Ars 1932, 1939. (Tr: Kimura, K.) CW-Ars, 5. Bunseki renai ron. (Tr:KO) Tokyo: Shunyodo 1939.

Aijō seikatsu no shinrigaku. (Tr: Yasuda, T. & Yasuda, I.) In *Sei to aijō no shinri*, Tokyo: Kadokawa Shoten 1955. (Tr: Imura, T. & YT) In *Sei no seishin bunseki*, Tokyo: Kawade Shobō Shinsha 1957.

Aijō seikatsu no shinrigaku eno sho kiyo. (Tr:YT) In *Aijō no shinrigaku*, SelFr-K 1960, 14:62p.

Por: Contribuições à psicologia da vida erótica. (Tr:OG & MG) Obr Comp-P 5:161-202.

Rus: Moscow: Staatsverlag 1925.

Sp: Aportaciones a la psicología de la vida erótica. (Tr:LLBT) Obr Comp-Madrid, 13:72-118. Obr Comp-BA 13:61-96. Obr Comp 1948, 1:974-992. Obr Comp 1967/1968, 1:963-981.

57

1909d   Bemerkungen über einen Fall von Zwangsneurose. Y 1909, 1(2):357-421.
10405   SKSN 1913, 3:123-197, 2nd ed, 1921. GS 1924, 8:269-351. *Vier Krankengeschichten* 1932, 284-376. GW 1941, 7:381-463. *L'homme aux rats. Journal d'une analyse.* Paris: PUF 1974, 287 p. [Complete German text, including the first sessions.] *See also* Original record of the case of obsessional neurosis [177].

Notes upon a case of obsessional neurosis. (Tr:ASt & JS) CP 1925, 3:293-383. (Revised tr:ASt & JS) SE 10:155-318. [Does not include first sessions.]

Cz: Poznamky k pripadu nutkave neurosy. (Tr: Friedmann, O.) In *Psycho-analytické chorobopisy*, Prague: Julius Albert 1937.

Fr: Remarques sur un cas de névrose obsessionnelle (L'homme aux rats). (Tr:MB & RL) RFPsa 1932, 5(3):322-390. In *Cinq psychanalyses*, Paris: Denoël & Steele 1935, 229-299; PUF 1954, 1966, 1967, 1970, 199-261.

L'homme aux rats. Journal d'une analyse. (Tr: Hawelka, E. R. & Hawelka, P.) [Contains the complete German text] Paris: PUF 1974, 287 p.

It: Osservazioni su un caso di nevrosi ossessive (caso clinico dell'uomo dei topi). (Tr: Lucentini, M.) In *Casi clinici*, Turin: Boringhieri 1952, 1962. Opere 6.

Jap: Kyōhaku shinkeishō no ichirei. (Tr: Tsushima, K.) FCW-S 1930, 4:105-254.

Kyōhaku shinkeishō no ichirei ni kansuru kōsatsu. (Tr: Kumada, M. & Okonogi, K.) In *Shōrei no kenkyū*, SelFr-K 1959, 16:106 p.

Por: Um caso de neurose obsessiva. (Tr:ED & OG) Obr Comp-P 16:5-94.

Sp: Análisis de un caso de neurosis obsesiva. (Tr:LLBT) Obr Comp-Madrid 16:7-85. Obr Comp-BA 16:13-80. Obr Comp 1948, 2:624-660. Obr Comp 1967/1968, 2:715-751.

58

1923c   Bemerkungen zur Theorie und Praxis der Traumdeutung. Z 1923, 9(1):
10406   1-11. GS 1925, 3:305-318. Traumlehre 1925, 49-62. Sexualtheorie und Traumlehre 1931, 354-368. GW 1940, 13:301-314.

Remarks upon the theory and practice of dream-interpretation. (Tr:JS) J 1943, 24:66-71. YBPsa 1945, 1:13-30. (Revised tr) CP 1950, 5:136-149.

Remarks on the theory and practice of dream-interpretation. (Revised tr) SE 19:109-121.

It: Osservazioni sulla teoria e pratica dell'interpretazione dei sogni. Opere 9.

Sp: Observaciones sobre la teoría y la práctica de la interpretación onírica. (Tr:LR) Obr Comp-BA 19:165-178. Obr Comp 1967/1968, 3:116-125.

59

1895b Über die Berechtigung, von der Neurasthenie einen bestimmten Symp-
(1894) tomenkomplex als "Angstneurose" abzutrennen. Neurol Zbl 1895,
10407 14(2, 15 Jan):50-66. SKSN 1906, 1:60-85. 2nd ed, 1911. 3rd ed, 1920.
4th ed, 1922. GS 1925, 1:306-333. GW 1952, 1:315-342.
Abs Inhalts wiss Arb 32.

On the right to separate from neurasthenia a definite symptom-complex
as "anxiety neurosis." (Tr:AAB) SPH 1909, 133-154. 2nd ed, 1912.
3rd ed, 1920. In *Major Works* 87-97.

The justification for detaching from neurasthenia a particular syndrome:
the anxiety neurosis. (Tr:JR) CP 1924, 1:76-106.

On the grounds for detaching a particular syndrome from neurasthenia
under the description "anxiety neurosis." (Tr:JR) SE 3:90-115.
Abs (Tr:JS) SE 3:251.

Fr: Qu'il est justifié de séparer de la neurasthénie un certain complexe
symptomatique sous le nom "névrose d'angoisse." (Tr:JLa) In *Névrose,
psychose et perversion*. Paris: PUF 1973, 15-38.

It: Legittimità di separare dall nevrastenia un preciso complesso di sintomi
come "nevrosi d'angoscia." (Tr: Campione, A.) Opere 2:153-176.

Jap: "Fuan shinkeishō" to yu tokutei shōjōgun o shinkei. (Tr: Imura, T. &
Katō, M.) In *Fuan no mondai*, SelFr-K 1955. Rev ed (Tr: Katō, M.)
SelFr-K 1969, 10:30 p.

Por: A neurastenia e a "neurose de angústia." Sôbre a justificação de separar
da neurastenia certo complexo de sintomas sob o título de "neurose de
angústia." (Tr:CMdeF) Obr Comp-P 2:139-172.

Sp: La neurastenia y la "neurosis de angustia": sobre la justificación de
separar de la neurastenia un cierto complejo de síntomas a título de
"neurosis de angustia." (Tr:LLBT) Obr Comp-Madrid 11:133-164.
Obr Comp-BA 11:99-122. Obr Comp 1948, 1:180-192. Obr Comp 1967/
1968, 1:180-191.

60

1910h Über einen besonderen Typus der Objektwahl beim Manne. (Beiträge
10409 zur Psychologie des Liebeslebens I) Y 1910, 2(2):389-397. SKSN 1918,
4:200-212. GS 1924, 5:186-197. In *Beiträge zur Psychologie des Liebeslebens*, Leipzig/Vienna/Zurich: Int Psa Verlag 1924, 3-14. Sexualtheorie
und Traumlehre 1931, 69-80. GW 1943, 8:66-77. [The gist of this paper
presented to Vienna Psa Soc., 19 May 1909.]

A special type of choice of object made by men (contributions to the
psychology of love I). (Tr:JRiv) CP 1925, 4:192-202. (Tr: Tyson, A.)
SE 11:165-175.

Fr: D'un type particulier de choix objectal chez l'homme. Contribution à la
psychologie de la vie amoureuse. I. (Tr:MB & AB) RFPsa 1936, 9(1):
2-10. (Tr:JLa) In *La vie sexuelle*, Paris: PUF 1969, 47-55.

It: Su un tipo particolare di scelta oggettuale nell'uomo. (Tr: Campione, A.; Candreva, S.; Montinari, M.; CLM; & Sagittario, E.) In *La vita sessuale*, Turin: Boringhieri 1970. Opere 6.

Jap: Otoko no ko taishō sentaku ni okeru tokushu no kei. Renai no seikatsu no shinri-dai ichi rombun. (Tr:KO) In *Bunseki renai ron*, FCW-S 1932, 9:2-16.

Por: Sôbre um tipo especial de escolha de objeto. (Tr:OG & MG) Obr Comp-P 5:161-170.

Sp: Sobre un tipo especial de la elección de objeto en el hombre. (Tr:LLBT) Obr Comp 1948, 1:974-977. Obr Comp-BA, 13:61-69. Obr Comp 1967/ 1968, 1:963-966.

61

1916c   Eine Beziehung zwischen einem Symbol und einem Symptom. Z 1916,
10410   4(2):111-112. SKSN 1918, 4:198-199, 2nd ed, 1922. GS 1924, 5:310-
          311. Psychoanalyse der Neurosen 1926, 38-39. Neurosenlehre und
          Technik 1931, 21-23. GW 1946, 10:394-395.

A connection between a symbol and a symptom. (Tr:DB) CP 1924, 2:162-163. SE 14:339-340.

Fr: Rapport entre un symbole et un symptôme. (Tr: Jury, P.) RFPsa 1935, 8(3):447-448.

It: Una relazione fra un simbolo e un sintomo. Opere 8.

Jap: (Tr:KO) FCW-S 1933, 9.

Por: Uma relação entre um símbolo e um sintoma. (Tr:OG & MG) Obr Comp-P 5:253-254.

Sp: Una relación entre un símbolo y un síntoma. (Tr:LLBT) Obr Comp-Madrid, 13:197-198. Obr Comp-BA 13:158-159. Obr Comp 1948, 1:1015-1016. Obr Comp 1967/1968, 1:1003-1004.

62

1931e   Brief an den Bürgermeister der Stadt Příbor. [25 Oct 1931. Read by Anna
10411   Freud at ceremony in Příbor.] Psa B 1931, 3(6):566. GS 1934, 12:414.
          GW 1948, 14:561. *Briefe*.

Letter to the Burgomaster of Příbor. (Tr:JS) SE 21:259. *Letters*.

It: Lettera al borgomastro di Pribor. Opere 11.

Sp: Carta al burgomaestre de la ciudad de Pribor. (Tr:LR) Obr Comp-BA 20:239-240. Obr Comp 1967/1968, 3:351.

63

1925b   Brief an den Herausgeber der *Jüdische Presszentrale Zürich*. *Jüdische*
10412   *Presszentrale* 1925, 26 Feb. GS 1928, 11:298. GW 1948, 14:556.

Letter to the Editor of the *Jewish Press Centre in Zurich*. (Tr:JS) SE 19:291.

It: Lettera al direttore del periodico "Jüdische Presszentrale Zürich." Opere 10.

Sp: Carta sobre la posición frente al judaísmo. (Tr:LR) Obr Comp-BA 19:257. Obr Comp 1967/1968, 3:175. (Tr: Romero, H.) In *Autobiografía*, Santiago: Edicion Pax, n.d.

64

1910f Brief an Dr. Friedrich S. Krauss über die *Anthropophyteia* (26 June
10414 1910). Anthropophyteia 1910, 7:472-473. Sexualprobleme 1911, 7:
73-75. GS 1928, 11:242-243. Sexualtheorie und Traumlehre 1931,
240-242. GW 1943, 8:224-225.

Letter to Dr. Friedrich S. Krauss on *Anthropophyteia*. (Tr:JS) SE 11:
233-235.

It: Lettera al dottor F. S. Krauss a proposito della rivista "Anthropophyteia." Opere 6.

Sp: Carta al doctor Friedrich S. Krauss sobre la "Anthropophyteia." (Tr:LR)
Obr Comp-BA 20:139-141. Obr Comp 1967/1968, 3:288-289.

65

1941d Brief an Josef Breuer, 29 June 1892. GW 1941, 17:5-6. *See also* Josef
(1892) Breuer [362].
10417
Letter to Josef Breuer. (Tr:JS) CP 1950, 5:25-26. (Revised tr:JS) SE 1:
147-148.

Sp: Obr Comp 1967/1968, 3:363.

66

1936a Brief an Romain Rolland (Eine Erinnerungsstörung auf der Akropolis).
10420 Almanach 1937, 1936:9-21. GW 1950, 16:250-257. *See also* Romain
Rolland [464].

A disturbance of memory on the Acropolis. An open letter to Romain
Rolland on the occasion of his seventieth birthday. (Tr:JS) J 1941,
22:93-101. CP 1950, 5:302-312. (Corrected tr:JS) SE 22:239-248.

Fr: Un trouble de mémoire sur l'Acropole (Lettre à Romain Rolland). (Tr:
Robert, M.) In L'Ephémère, Éditions de la Fondation Maeght, Paris
1967, (2:Apr):3-13.

It: Un disturbo della memoria sull'Acropolis. Riv Psa 1966, 12:61-67.

Un errore di memoria sull'Acropoli: lettera aperta a Romain Rolland.
Opere 11.

Sp: Un trastorno de la memoria en la Acrópolis. Carta abierta a Romain
Rolland, en ocasión de su septuagésima aniversario. (Tr:LR) Obr
Comp-BA 20:241-250. Obr Comp 1967/1968, 3:352-360.

67

1905e Bruchstück einer Hysterie-Analyse. Mschr Psychiat Neurol 1905,
(1901) 18(4, Oct):285-310; (5, Nov):408-467. SKSN 1909, 2:1-110. 2nd ed,
10421 1912. 3rd ed, 1921. GS 1924, 8:3-126. In *Vier Krankengeschichten* 1932,
5-141. GW 1942, 5:163-286.

Fragment of an analysis of a case of hysteria. (Tr:JS & ASt) CP 1925,
3:13-146. In *The case of Dora*, NY: Norton 1952. (Revised) SE 7:7-122.

Cz: Uryvek z analusy hysterie. (Tr: Friedmann, O.) In *Psychoanalytické
chorobopisy*, Prague: Julius Albert 1937.

Fr: Fragment d'une analyse d'hystérie (Dora). (Tr:MB & RL) RFPsa 1928,
2(1):1-112. (Revised tr:AB) In *Cinq Psychanalyses*, Paris: Denoël &
Steele 1935, 7-109; PUF 1954, 1966, 1967, 1970, 1-91.

It: Frammento di un'analisis d'isteria (Caso clinico di Dora). (Tr: Lucentini,
M.) In *Casi clinici*, Turin: Boringhieri 1952, 1962. (Tr: Lucentini, M. &
Ranchetti, M.) Opere 4:305-404.

Jap: (Tr: Hosoki, A. & Iida, M.) SelFr-JinSh 1969, 5:91 p.

Por: Análise fragmentária de uma histeria. (Tr:OG) Obr Comp-P 15:15-115.

Sp: Análisis fragmentario de una histeria. (Tr:LLBT) Obr Comp-Madrid 15.
Obr Comp-BA 15:17-114. Obr Comp 1948, 2:513-565. Obr Comp 1967/
1968, 2:605-657.

68

1908b Charakter und Analerotik. Psychiat-neurol Wsch 1908. 9(52, Mar):
10422 465-467. SKSN 1909, 2:132-137. GS 1924, 5:261-267. Sexualtheorie
und Traumlehre 1931, 62-68. GW 1941, 7:203-209.

Character and anal erotism. (Tr:RCM) CP 1924, 2:45-50. In Thompson,
C.; Mazer, M.; Witenberg, E. (eds) *The outline of psychoanalysis*.
NY: Random House 1955, 277-282. (Revised tr:JS) SE 9:169-175.

Fr: Caractère et érotisme anal. (Tr: Berger, D.; Bruno, P.; Guérineau, D.;
Oppenot, F.) In *Névrose, psychose et perversion*. Paris: PUF 1973,
143-148.

It: Carattere ed erotismo anale. (Tr:CLM) In *Freud con antologia
freudiana*, Turin: Boringhieri 1959, 1970. Opere 5:401-408.

Jap: Seikaku to komon seiyoku. (Tr: Konuma, M.) In *Ijō seiyoku no bunseki*,
CW-Ars 1933, 15:180-189.

Seikaku to komon seikan. (Tr:KO) In *Bunseki byōhō ron*, FCW-S 1932,
8:337-345.

(Tr: Kakeda, K.) SelFr-K 1953, 5:12 p. (Tr: Kakeda, K. & Shimura, H.)
SelFr-JinSh 1969, 5:6 p.

Por: O caráter e o erotismo anal. (Tr:OG & MG) Obr Comp-P 5:149-154.

Rus: (Tr: Belousov, V. A.) In *Psikhoanaliz i uchenie o kharakterakh. Psikholog i psikhoanal*, vyp. V, 192 p.

Sp: El carácter y el erotismo anal. (Tr:LLBT) Obr Comp-Madrid 13: 148-153. Obr Comp-BA 13:120-124. Obr Comp 1948, 1:969-970. Obr Comp 1967/1968, 1:958-959.

69

1893f   Charcot (obituary). Wien Med Wschr 1893, 43(37):cols 1513-1520.
10423   SKSN 1906, 1:1-13. 2nd ed, 1911. 3rd ed, 1920. 4th ed, 1922. GS 1925, 1:243-257. GW 1952, 1:21-35.
Abs Inhalts wiss Arb 22.

Charcot. (Tr: Bernays, J.) CP 1924, 1:9-23. SE 3:11-23.
Abs (Tr:JS) SE 3:243.

It: Charcot. (Tr: Campione, A.) Opere 2:105-118.

Por: Charcot. (Tr:CMdeF) Obr Comp-P 1:1-16.

Sp: Charcot. (Tr:LLBT) Obr Comp-Madrid 10:279-294. Obr Comp-BA 10:195-206. Obr Comp 1948, 1:17-24. Obr Comp 1967/1968, 1:17-24.

70

1914e   Darstellung der "grossen Leistung" im Traume. Z 1914, 2:384-385.
10424   In part: in Die Traumdeutung, GS 1925, 3:130. GW 1942, 2-3:416-417.

A "great achievement" in a dream. (Complete) (Tr:JS) SE 5:412-413.

Fr: La représentation d'un "grand exploit" dans un rêve. (Tr: Meyerson, I.; rev. Berger, D.) In L'interprétation des rêves, Paris: PUF 1967, 352-353.

Sp: Representación de la "gran hazaña" en el sueño. (Tr:LR) Obr Comp-BA 19:135-136. Obr Comp 1967/1968, 3:94.

FOR OTHER LANGUAGES, see under Die Traumdeutung, Chapter 6, Section F, example 13.

71

1913h   Darstellung von Lebenszeiten im Traume. Erf Beisp Psa Prx [89] no. 3.
10425   Z 1913, 1:377-382. GS 1925, 3:127. GW 1942, 2-3:413-414.

Representation in dreams of times of life. (Tr:AAB) In The interpretation of dreams, 3rd ed 1932, 383-384. (Tr:JS) SE 5:409-410.

Representation of ages in dreams. (Tr:JS) SE 13:195.

FOR OTHER LANGUAGES, see under Die Traumdeutung, Chapter 6, Section F.

72

1899a   Über Deckerinnerungen. Mschr Psychiat Neurol 1899, 6(3, Sept):
10426   215-230. GS 1925, 1:465-488. GW 1952, 1:531-554.

Screen memories. (Tr:JS) CP 1950, 5:47-69. SE 3:303-322.

Fr: Les souvenirs-écrans. (Tr: Anzieu, D. & AB) In Anzieu, D. L'auto-analyse, Paris: PUF 1959, 277-286.

Sur les souvenirs-écrans. (Tr: Berger, D.; Bruno, P.; Guérineau, D.; & Oppenot, F.) In *Névrose, psychose et perversion.* Paris: PUF 1973, 113-132.

Heb: Al sichronot mechapim. Kitvei 4, chap. 11.

It: Ricordi di copertura. (Tr: Campione, A.) Opere 2:435-456.

Jap: (Tr: Okonogi, K.) SelFr-JinSh 1970, 6:18 p.

Por: As recordações encobridoras. (Tr: CMdeF) Obr Comp-P 2:75-100.

Sp: Los recuerdos encubridores. (Tr: LLBT) Obr Comp-Madrid 12. Obr Comp-BA 12:205-222. Obr Comp 1948, 1:157-166. Obr Comp 1967/ 1968, 1:157-166.

73

1908e   Der Dichter und das Phantasieren. (Lecture, 6 Dec 1907) Neue Revue
10427   1908, 1(10, Mar):716-724. SKSN 1909, 2:197-206. GS 1924, 10:229-239. *Dichtung und Kunst* 1924, 3-14. GW 1941, 7:213-223.

The relation of the poet to day-dreaming. (Tr: IFGD) CP 1925, 4: 172-183; Boston: Beacon Pr 1956. In Vivas, E. & Krieger, M. *The problems of aesthetics,* NY: Holt, Rinehart & Winston 1960, 153-160. In Dulany, D. E., Jr. et al: *Contributions to modern psychology,* NY: Oxford Univ Pr 1964, 196-204.

Creative writers and day-dreaming. (Revised tr: JS) SE 9:143-153.

Fr: La création littéraire et le rêve éveillé. (Tr: Marty, Mme. E. & MB) In *Essais de psychanalyse appliquée,* Paris: Gallimard 1933, 1971, 69-81.

Heb: Hameshorer vehahasaya. Kitvei 2, chap 1.

It: Il poeta e la fantasia. (Tr: CLM) In *Freud con antologia freudiana,* Turin: Boringhieri 1959, 1970. Opere 5:375-386.

Jap: Shijin to kūsō. (Tr: KO) In *Bunseki geijutsu ron,* FCW-S 1932, 1937, 6:144-158.

Kūsō suru koto shijin. (Tr: YT) In *Geijutsu ron,* SelFr-K 1953, 7:18 p. Rev ed (Tr: YT & Ikeda, K.) SelFr-K 1970, 7:20 p. (Tr: YT) Tokyo: Shinchô-sha 1957. SelFr-JinSh 1969, 3:9 p.

Por: O poeta e a fantasia. (Tr: ED) Obr Comp-P 11:117-128.

Rus: Poèt i fantazii. In *Psikhologicheskie ètiudy. Biblioteka "Psikhoterapiia,"* no. 1. Izd. 2-e. Moskva: Red. zhurnala "Psikhoterapiia" 1912, 55 p.

Sp: La creación poética y la fantasía. (Tr: LR) Obr Comp-BA 18:47-58. Obr Comp 1948, 2:965-969. Obr 1967/1968, 2:1057-1061.

74

1913i   Die Disposition zur Zwangsneurose. Ein Beitrag zum Problem der
10428   Neurosenwahl. (Read at 4th Int Psa Cong, Munich, Sept 1913) Z 1913, 1(6):525-532. SKSN 1918, 4:113-124. GS 1924, 5:277-278. Psychoan-

analyse der Neurosen 1926, 3-15. Neurosenlehre und Technik 1931, 5-16. GW 1943, 8:442-452.

The predisposition to obsessional neurosis: a contribution to the problem of the option of neurosis. (Tr:EG & ECM) CP 1924, 2:122-132.

The disposition to obsessional neurosis. A contribution to the problem of choice of neurosis. (Tr:JS) SE 12:317-326.

Fr: La prédisposition à la névrose obsessionnelle. (Tr: Pichon, E. & Hoesli, H.) RFPsa 1929, 3(3):437-447.

La disposition à la névrose obsessionnelle. Une contribution au problème du choix de la névrose. (Tr: Berger, D.; Bruno, P.; Guérineau, D.; & Oppenot, F.) In *Névrose, psychose et perversion*. Paris: PUF 1973, 189-197.

It: La disposizione alla nevrosi ossessiva. Opere 7.

Jap: Kyōhaku shinkei-shō no soin. (Tr: Imura, T. & Katō, M.) In *Fuan no mondai*, SelFr-K 1955, 10. Rev ed (Tr: Katō, M.) SelFr-K 1969, 10:16 p.

Por: A predisposição à neurose obsessiva. (Tr:OG & MG) Obr Comp-P 5: 221-232.

Sp: La disposición a la neurosis obsesiva. Una aportacion al problema de la eleccion de neurosis. (Tr:LLBT) Obr Comp-Madrid 13:163-174. Obr Comp-BA 13:132-140. Obr Comp 1948, 1:1001-1005. Obr Comp 1967/1968, 1:989-993.

75

1920c [Possibly written with Otto Rank] Dr. Anton v. Freund. (obituary)
10429 Z 1920, 6:95-96 [with signature "Redaktion und Herausgeber der Internationalen Zeitschrift für Psychoanalyse"]. GS 1928, 11:280-281. GW 1940, 13:435-436.

Dr. Anton von Freund. (Tr:JS) SE 18:267-268.

It: Il dottor Anton von Freund. Opere 9.

Sp: En memoria de Antón Von Freund. (Tr:LR) Obr Comp-BA 20:204-205. Obr Comp 1967/1968, 3:326-327.

76

1923i Dr. Ferenczi Sándor (zum 50. Geburtstag). [Signed "Herausgeber und
10430 Redaktion"] Z 1923, 9(3):257-259. GS 1928, 11:273-275. GW 1940, 13:443-445.

Dr. Sándor Ferenczi (on his 50th birthday). (Tr:JS) SE 19:267-269.

It: Il dottor Sándor Ferenczi (per il cinquantesimo compleanno). Opere 9.

Sp: A Sándor Ferenczi. (Tr:LR) Obr Comp-BA 20:206-208. Obr Comp 1967/1968, 3:328-329.

77

1926   Dr. Reik und Kurpfuschereifrage. A letter to the *Neue Freie Presse.*
73577   Neue Freie Presse 1926, (18 July):12.

   Dr. Reik and the problem of quackery. A letter to the *Neue Freie Presse.*
   Bull Am Psa Ass 1948, 4:56. (Tr:JS) SE 21:247-248.

 It: Il dottor Reik e il problema dei medici empirici. Opere 10.

78

1928b   Dostojewski und die Vatertötung. In Fülop-Müller & Eckstein, F. *Die*
10431   *Urgestalt der Brüder Karamasoff,* Munich: Piper 1928, xi-xxxvi.
   Almanach 1930, 1929:9-31. GS 1934, 12:7-26. GW 1948, 14:399-418.

   Dostoevski and parricide. (Tr: Tait, D. F.) The Realist 1929, 1(4):18-23.

   Dostoevsky and parricide. (Tr:JS) J 1945, 26(1/2):1-8. Partisan Review,
   1945, 12(4):530-544. (Tr: Woolf, V. & Koteliansky, S. S.) In Dostoevsky, F. M. *Stavrogin's confession,* NY: Lear Publications 1947, 87-114.
   CP 1950, 5:222-242. SE 21:177-194. In Phillips, W. *Art and psycho-*
   analysis, NY: Criterion Pr 1957, 3-20. In Ruitenbeek, H. M. *The literary*
   imagination, NY: Quadrangle Books 1965, 329-348.

 Fr: Dostoiewski et le parricide. (Tr: Beucler, A.) In Dostoiewska, A. G.
   Dostoiewski, Paris: Gallimard 1930, 15-33.

 Heb: Dostojewski verezach av. Kitvei 2, chap. 8.

 It: Dostoevskij e il parricidio. Opere 10. In *Saggi sull'arte, la letteratura e*
   il linguaggio, Turin: Boringhieri 1969, vol. 1.

 Jap: Dosutoiefusuki to chichi goroshi. (Tr:KO) In *Bunseki geijutsu ron,*
   FCW-S 1937, 6. (Tr:YT) In *Geijutsu ron,* SelFr-K 1953, 7:36 p. Rev ed
   (Tr:YT & Ikeda, K.) SelFr-K 1970, 7:36 p. (Tr:YT) SelFr-JinSh 1969,
   3:19 p. (Tr: Kikumori, H.) Tokyo: Kawade Shobō Shinsha Pr 1972,
   38 p.

 Jug: Dostojevski i oceubistvo. (Tr: Matić, V.; Jeretić, V.; & Bogičević, D.)
   In *Iz kulture i umetnosti,* [Collected Works, Vol. 3] Novi Sad: Matica
   Srpska 1969.

 Por: Dosteoievsky e o parricídio. (Tr:ED) Obr Comp-P 11:299.

 Sp: Dostoievsky y el parricidio. (Tr:LLBT) Obr Comp 1948, 2:1044.
   Obr Comp 1967/1968, 2:1136. (Tr:LR) Obr Comp-BA 21:253-272.

79

1905d   Drei Abhandlungen zur Sexualtheorie. Leipzig/Vienna: Deuticke 1905,
10432   ii+83 p. 2nd ed (with preface and additions), 1910, iii+87 p. 3rd ed (with
   new preface and additions), 1915, vi+101 p. 4th ed (with different
   preface and additions), 1920, xiii+104 p. 5th ed, 1922 (with additions),
   GS 1924, 5:3-119. 6th ed, Leipzig/Vienna: Deuticke 1925, 120 p.
   GW 1942, 5:29-145. *See also* Vorwort zur vierten Auflage der *Drei*
   Abhandlungen zur Sexualtheorie [265].

Three contributions to the sexual theory. (Tr: AAB) (Intro: Putnam, J. J.) NY: NMDP 1910, x+91 p.

Three contributions to the theory of sex. (Tr: AAB) (Intro: Putnam, J. J.) NY: NMDP 2nd ed (with additions), 1916, xi+117 p. 3rd ed, 1918, xii+117 p. 4th ed (revised intro: AAB & Putnam, J. J.), 1930, xiv+104 p. BWSF 1938, 553-629.

Three essays on the theory of sexuality. (Tr: JS) London: IPC 1949, 133 p. (corrected, expanded, & with all prefaces) SE 7:130-243. NY: Basic Books 1962, 130 p.

Arab: Thalāth rasā'il fi nazariyyat al-jins. (Tr: Najātī, M.) Cairo: Dār al Qalam 1960.

Thalāth maqālat fī nazarīyat al-jinsiyah. (Tr: Mahmud 'Ali, S.) Cairo: Dār al-Ma-Ārif 1963.

Cz: Tři úvahy o sexuální teorii. (Tr: Srdce, V.) Prague: Alois Srdce 1926, 136 p.

Dan: Tre afhandlinger om Seksualteori. (Tr: Neergaard, J.) Copenhagen: Store Nordiske Videnskabsboghandel 1934, 120 p. (Tr: Boisen, M.) In *Nye forelaesninger om psykoanalysen,* Copenhagen: Hans Reitzel 1959. (Tr: Boisen, M.) Copenhagen: Hans Reitzel 1961, 1963, 96 p. (Tr: Löfgren, I.) 1965, 136 p.

Fr: Trois essais sur la théorie de la sexualité. (Tr: Reverchon, B.) Paris: Gallimard 1923. (Tr: JLa & Pontalis, J. B.) Paris: Gallimard 1962, 1968, 190 p.

Gr: Tris Meletes ghia tin Sexoualiki zoi. (Tr: Milillis) Athens: Maris 1949. (Tr: Syrros, P.) Athens: Panekdotiki 1964.

Heb: Shalosh massot al hateoria haminit. (Tr: Ebon, M.) Merchavia: Sifriyat Hapoalim 1954.

Hun: Három értekezés a szexualitás elméletéről. (Tr: SFe) Budapest: Manó Dick 1915, 91 p; 1919, 93 p.

It: Tre contributi alla teoria sessuale. (Tr: MLB) Zurich/Naples/Vienna: Nocera Inferiore, Libreria Psicoanalitica Internationale 1921, 112 p.

Enciclopedia sessuale. (Tr: Adami, F.) Rome: Elios 1947, 384 p.

Tre saggi sulla teoria della sessualità. (Tr: Douglas Scotti, G. L.) Milan: Mondadori 1960, 198 p.

Tre saggi sulla teoria sessuale. (Tr: Montinari, M.) Opere 4:447-546. (Tr: Campione, A.; Candreva, S.; Montinari, M.; CLM; & Sagittario, E.) In *La vita sessuale,* Turin: Boringhieri 1970.

Jap: Seizei ni kansuru mitsu rombun. (Tr: Yabe, Y.) In *Seiyoku ron, kinsei ron,* FCW-S 1931, 5:1-174.

Furoido seiyoku ron, sei riron ni kansuru san ronbun. (Tr: KO) Tokyo: Seishin Bunsekigaku kenkyūjo Shuppanbu 1952, 161 p.

Seiyoku ron. (Tr: Kakeda, K.) SelFr-K 1953, 5:170 p.

Sei no riron ni kansuru mittsu no ronbun. (Tr: Yasuda, T. & Yasuda, I.)
In *Sei to aijō shinri*, Tokyo: Kadokawa Shoten 1952. (Tr: Imura, T. &
YT) In *Sei no seishin bunseki*, Tokyo: Kawade Shobō Shinsha 1957.
(Tr: Kakeda, K. & Shimura, H.) SelFr-JinSh 1969, 5:88 p.

Jug: Prilozi teoriji seksualnosti. Tri rasprave. (Tr: Petrović, G. & Prica, S.)
Zagreb: Universum 1934, 120 p.

O seksualnoj teoriji. (Tr: Milekić, P.) [Collected Works, Vol. 4] Novi
Sad: Matika Srpska 1969.

Nor: Seksualteorien. (Tr: Jensen, B.) Oslo: Cappelen 1966, 111 p.

Pers: Se resāle darbāreye teoriye meyle jensi. (Tr: Razi, H.) Tehran: Asia
Publ 1964, 256 p.

Pol: Trzy Rosprawy z Teorji Seksualnej. (Tr: Jekels, L. & Albinski, M.)
Polska Bibljoteka Psychoanalityczna, vol. 2, Międzynarodowe Wydawnictwo Psychoanalityczne 1924, 216 p.

Por: Sexualidade. (Tr: Oliveira, O. de) Colecção Scientiae Vitae. Lisbon:
Editorial Atica 1932, 161 p.

Psicologia da vida erótica. (Tr: Gikovate, M.) Rio de Janeiro: Editora
Guanabara 1934.

Três ensaios sobre a teoria da sexualidade. (Tr: Fonseca, R. da) Lisbon:
Livros do Brasil 1966, 1967, 142 p.

Uma teoria sexual. (Tr:CMdeF) Obr Comp-P 8:5-126.

Rus: Tri stat'i o teorii polovogo vlecheniia. (Tr: Viakhirev, A. V. & Poliakov,
E.) In *Psikhoterapevticheskaia biblioteka*, vyp. 3, Moskva: Nauka 1911,
116 p.; 1912, 166 p.

Ocherki po psikhologii seksual'nosti. (Tr:MV) In *Psikholog i psikhoanal*,
vyp. VIII, 188 p.

Sp: Una teoria sexual. (Tr:LLBT) Obr Comp-Madrid, 2:5-144. Obr Comp-
BA 2:7-100. Obr Comp 1948, 1:779-832. Obr Comp 1967/1968,
1:771-824.

Sw: Sexualteori. Tre studier i sexualteoretiska frågor. (Tr: Löfgren, I.)
Stockholm: Aldus/Bonniers 1965, 136 p.

80

1912b   Zur Dynamik der Übertragung. C 1912, 2(4):167-173. SKSN 1918,
10433   4:388-398. Technik und Metapsychol 1924, 53-63. GS 1925, 6:53-63.
Neurosenlehre und Technik 1931, 328-340. GW 1943, 8:364-374.

The dynamics of transference. (Tr:JRiv) CP 1924, 2:312-322. (Tr:JS)
SE 12:99-108.

Fr: La dynamique du transfert. (Tr:AB) RFPsa 1952, 16(1-2):170-177.
In *La technique psychanalytique*, Paris: PUF 1953, 1967, 1970, 50-60.

It: Dinamica della traslazione. Opere 6.

Jap: (Tr:KO) FCW-S 1933, 8:16 p. Kanjō teni no rikidōsei ni tsuite. (Tr: Kosawa, H.) SelFr-K 1958, 15:74-90. Rev ed (Tr: Okonogi, K.) 1969, 15:17 p.

Por: A dinâmica da transferência. (Tr:JPP, OG & GP) Obr Comp-P 10: 223-234.

Rus: (Tr:MV) Moscow 1913. In [Method and technique of psychoanalysis], Moscow/Leningrad: Psychological and psychoanalytical library 1923, vol. 4, 136 p.

Sp: La dinámica de la transferencia. (Tr:LLBT) Obr Comp-Madrid, 14. Obr Comp-BA 14:95-143. Obr Comp 1948, 2:321-325. Obr Comp 1967/1968, 2:413-417.

81

1914c Zur Einführung des Narzissmus. Y 1914, 6:1-24. SKSN 1918, 4:78-112,
10434 2nd ed 1922. Leipzig/Vienna/Zurich: Int Psa Verlag 1924, 35 p. GS 1925, 6:155-187. Theoretische Schriften 1931, 25-57. GW 1946, 10:138-170.

On narcissism: an introduction. (Tr:CMB) CP 1925, 4:30-59. (Revised) SE 14:73-102. In *Major Works* 399-411.

Extracts. In Rickman, J. (ed) *A general selection from the works of Sigmund Freud*, London: HPI 1937, 118-141.

Fr: Pour introduire le narcissisme. (Tr:JLa) In *La vie sexuelle*, Paris: PUF 1969, 81-105.

It: Il narcisismo. In Zolla, E. *La psicanalisi*, Milan: Garzanti 1960, 141-159.

Introduzione al narcisismo. Riv Psa 1962, 8:155-175. Opere 7.

Jap: Jiko aishō joron. (Tr: Hayashi, T.) In *Ijō seiyoku no bunseki*, CW-Ars 1933, 15:4-53.

Naruchisumusu gairon. (Tr:KO) In *Bunseki renai ron*, FCW-S 1932, 9:230-274.

(Tr: Kakeda, K.) SelFr-K 1953, 5:44 p. (Tr: Kakeda, K. & Shimura, H.) SelFr-JinSh 1969, 5:24 p.

Por: Introdução ao narcisismo. (Tr:CMdeF) Obr Comp-P 7:247-276.

Rus: (Tr:MV) In *Psikholog i psikhoanal*, vyp. VIII, 188 p.

Sp: Introducción al narcisismo. (Tr:LLBT) Obr Comp-Madrid, 14:215-246. Obr Comp-BA 14:171-196. Obr Comp 1948, 1:1097-1110. Obr Comp 1967/1968, 1:1083-1096.

82

1916d Einige Charaktertypen aus der psychoanalytischen Arbeit. Imago 1916,
10435 4(6):317-336. SKSN 1918, 4:521-552, 2nd ed, 1922. GS 1924, 10: 287-314. *Dichtung und Kunst* 1924, 59-86. Section I: Almanach 1926, 1925:21-26. Section III: Psa P 1935, 9:193-194. GW 1946, 10:364-391.

Some character-types met with in psycho-analytic work. (Tr:ECM)
CP 1925, 4:318-344. (Revised) SE 14:311-333. Extracts in Rickman, J.
(ed) A general selection from the works of Sigmund Freud, London:
HPI 1937, 111-117.

Fr: Quelques types de charactères dégagés par la psychanalyse. (Tr: Marty,
Mme. E. & MB) In Essais de psychanalyse appliquée, Paris: Gallimard
1933, 1971, 105-136.

Heb: Tipusei ofi achadim min hamechkar hapsichoanaliti. Kitvei 2, chap. 9.

It: Alcuni tipi di carattere tratti dal lavoro psicoanalitico. Opere 8. In Saggi
sull'arte, la letteratura e il linguaggio, Turin: Boringhieri 1969, vol. 1.
(Tr:CLM) Excerpts in Freud con antologia freudiana, Turin: Boringhieri 1959, 1970.

Jap: Seishin bunseki kara mita seikaku-gata no nisan. (Tr: Shinoda, H. &
Hamano, O.) In Geijutsu no bunseki, Tokyo: Ars 1933.

Seishin bunseki teki kenkyū kara mita jakkan no seikaku tenkei. (Tr:YT)
SelFr-K 1953, 7:42 p. In Sei no seishin bunseki, Tokyo: Kawade Shobō
Shinsha 1957. Rev ed (Tr:YT & Ikeda, K.) SelFr-K 1970, 7:44 p.
(Tr: Kikumori, H.) Tokyo: Kawade Shobō Shinsha Pr 1972, 25 p.

Por: Vários tipos de caráter descobertos no trabalho psicanalítico. (Tr:ED)
Obr Comp-P 11:177-204.

Rus: (Tr: Belousov, V. A.) In Psikhoanaliz i uchenie o kharakterakh. Psikholog
i psikhoanal, vyp. V, 192 p.

Sp: Algunos tipos caractéricos revelados por el psicoanálisis. (Tr:LR)
Obr Comp-BA 18:111-134.

Varios tipos de carácter descubiertos en la labor psicoanalítica. Obr
Comp 1948, 2:990-1001. Obr Comp 1967/1968, 2:1082-1093.

83

1925i Einige Nachträge zum Ganzen der Traumdeutung. (1) Die Grenzen
10436 der Deutbarkeit. (2) Die sittliche Verantwortung für den Inhalt der
Träume. (3) Die okkulte Bedeutung des Traumes. GS 1925, 3:172-184.
Traumlehre 1925, 63-76. GW 1952, 1:559-573. Parts I, II only: Sexualtheorie und Traumlehre 1931, 369-381. Part III only: Imago 1925,
11(3):234-238. Almanach 1926, 1925:27-31.

Some additional notes upon dream-interpretation as a whole. (1) The
possible limits of dream interpretation. (2) Moral responsibility for the
content of dreams. (3) The occult significance of dreams. (Tr:JS) J 1943,
24:71-75. (Revised tr) CP 1950, 5:150-162. (Revised tr) SE 19:127-138.
Part III: in Devereux, G. Psychoanalysis and the occult, NY: IUP 1953,
87-90.

It: Alcune aggiunte d'insieme alla "Interpretazione dei sogni." Opere 10.

Sp: Los límites de la interpretabilidad de los sueños. La responsibilidad moral
por el contenido de los sueños. La significación ocultista del sueño.
(Tr:LR) Obr Comp-BA 19:185-202. Obr Comp 1967/1968, 3:128-136.

84

1922b Über einige neurotische Mechanismen bei Eifersucht, Paranoia und
10437 Homosexualität. Z 1922, 8(3):249-258. GS 1924, 5:387-399. Psychoanalyse der Neurosen 1924, 125-139. Neurosenlehre und Technik, 1931,
173-186. GW 1940, 13:195-207.

Certain neurotic mechanisms in jealousy, paranoia and homosexuality.
(Tr:JRiv) J 1923, 4:1-10. CP 1924, 2:232-243. Complex 1950(1):3-13.

Some neurotic mechanisms in jealousy, paranoia and homosexuality.
(Revised tr:JS) SE 18:223-232.

Fr: De quelques mécanismes névrotiques dans la jalousie, la paranoïa et
l'homosexualité. (Tr: Lacan, J.) RFPsa 1932, 5(3):391-401. (Tr:
Guérineau, D.) In *Névrose, psychose et perversion*. Paris: PUF 1973,
271-281.

It: Alcuni meccanismi nevrotici nella gelosia, paranoia e omosessualità.
Opere 9.

Jap: Shito, henshū, dōseiai ni okeru ni, san no shinkeishōteki kikō ni tsuite.
(Tr: Konuma, M.) In *Ijō seiyoku bunseki*, CW-Ars 1933, 15:156-176.

Shito, bōsō, dōseiai ni okeru ni, san shinkeishōteki kisei ni tsuite.
(Tr:KO) In *Bunseki renai ron*, FCW-S 1932, 9:178-195.

Shito, paranoia, dōseiai ni okeru ni-san no shineishō mekanizumu ni
tsuite. (Tr: Imura, T. & Katō, M.) In *Fuan no mondai*, SelFr-K 1955,
10. Rev ed (Tr: Katō, M.) SelFr-K 1969, 10:18 p. (Tr: Imura, T.)
SelFr-JinSh 1970, 6:8 p.

Por: Sôbre alguns mecanismos neuróticos nos ciumes, na paranóia e na
homossexualidade. (Tr:OG & MG) Obr Comp-P 5:285-296.

Sp: Sobre algunos mecanismos neuróticos en los celos, la paranoia y la
homosexualidad. (Tr:LLBT) Obr Comp-Madrid 13:277-290. Obr
Comp-BA 13:219-229. Obr Comp 1948, 1:1030-1035. Obr Comp 1967/
1968, 1:1018-1022.

85

1925j Einige psychische Folgen des anatomischen Geschlechtsunterschieds.
10438 [Read by Anna Freud, 3 Sept 1925, 9th Int Psa Congress, Hamburg]
Z 1925, 11(4):401-410. Psychoanalyse der Neurosen 1926, 205-219.
GS 1928, 11:8-19. Sexualtheorie und Traumlehre 1931, 207-220. GW
1948, 14:19-30.

Some psychological consequences of the anatomical distinction between
the sexes. (Tr:JS) J 1927, 8(2):133-142. (Revised tr:JS) CP 1950, 5:
186-197.

Some psychical consequences of the anatomical distinction between the
sexes. (Corrected tr:JS) SE 19:248-258.

Fr: Quelques conséquences psychologiques de la différence anatomique entre
les sexes. (Tr: Berger, D.) In *La vie sexuelle*, Paris: PUF 1969, 123-132.

It: Alcune conseguenze psichiche della differenza anatomica tra i sessi.
(Tr: Campione, A.; Candreva, S.; Montinari, M.; CLM; & Sagittario,
E.) In *La vita sessuale*, Turin: Boringhieri 1970. Opere 10.

Jap: (Tr: Kakeda, K.) SelFr-K 1953, 5:20 p. (Tr: Kakeda, K. & Shimura, H.)
SelFr-JinSh 1969, 5:10 p.

Sp: Algunas consecuencias psíquicas de la diferencia sexual anatómica.
(Tr: LR) Obr Comp-BA 21:203-216. Obr Comp 1967/1968, 3:482-491.

86

1910g   Zur Einleitung der Selbstmord-Diskussion. Schlusswort der Selbstmord-
10597   Diskussion. In "Über den Selbstmord, insbesondere den Schülerselbst-
mord," *Diskussionen des Wiener psychoanalytischen Vereins*, Wiesbaden: Bergmann 1910, 1:19, 59-60. GS 1925, 3:321-323. Neurosenlehre und Technik 1931, 309-310. GW 1943, 8:62-64.

Contributions to a discussion on suicide. (Tr: JS) SE 11:231-232. In
Friedman, P. (ed) *On suicide*, NY: IUP 1967.

It: Contributi a una discussione sul suicidio. Opere 6.

Sp: Contribuciones al simposio sobre el suicidio. (Tr: LR) Obr Comp-BA,
21:169-172. Obr Comp 1967/1968, 3:469.

87

1937c   Die endliche und unendliche Analyse. Z 1937, 23(2):209-240. In part
10440   Almanach 1938, 1937:44-50. GW 1950, 16:59-99.

Analysis terminable and interminable. (Tr: JRiv) J 1937, 18(4):373-405.
CP 1950, 5:316-357. (Tr: JS) SE 23:216-253.

Fr: Analyse terminée et analyse interminable. (Tr: AB) RFPsa 1939, 11(1):
3-38.

It: Analisi terminabile e interminabile. Opere 11.

Jap: Owariaru bunseki to owarinaki bunseki. (Tr: Kosawa, H.) In *Seishin
bunseki ryoho*, SelFr-K 1958, 15:237-299. Rev ed (Tr: Okonogi, K.)
SelFr-K 1969, 15:63 p. (Tr: Baba, K.) SelFr-JinSh 1970, 6:37 p.

Sp: Análisis terminable e interminable. (Tr: LR) Rev Psicoanál B. Aires 1946,
4:224-257. Obr Comp-BA 315-352. Obr Comp 1967/1968, 3:540-572.

88

1950a   [Entwurf einer Psychologie.] In *Aus den Anfängen der Psychoanalyse*,
(1895)   London: IPC 1950, 371-466.
73578
Project for a scientific psychology. (Tr: JS) In *The origins of psycho-
analysis*, London: IPC; NY: Basic Books 1954, 347-445. (Revised tr: JS)
SE 1:295-397.

Fr: Esquisse d'une psychologie scientifique. (Tr: AB) In *La naissance de la
psychanalyse*. Paris: PUF 1956, 307-396.

It: Progetto di una psicologia. Opere 2:201-286.

Sp: Proyecto de un psicologia para Neurologos. Obr Comp-BA 22:373-456. Obr Comp 1967/1968, 3:883-968.

89

1913h Erfahrungen und Beispiele aus der analytischen Praxis. Z 1913, 1(4):
10442 377-382. (Nos. 1, 2, 3, 4, 9, 10, 13, 15, 19, 20, 21, 22). Introduction & Nos. 13, 15, 19, 22 in GS 1928, 11:301-303; Neurosenlehre und Technik 1931, 306-308. GW 1946, 10:40-42. Nos. 1, 2, 3, 9, 10, 19, 20 included in *Die Traumdeutung* from 4th ed (1914) onwards. *See also* [225], [216], [71], [179], [264], [145], [241], [210], [207], [229], [108], [51].

Observations and examples from analytic practice. (Tr:JS) SE 13: 193-198.

Fr: Observations et exemples tirés de la pratique analytique, extraits incorporés à *L'interprétation des rêves*. (Tr: Meyerson, I.; revised Berger, D.) Paris: PUF 1967, 204, 350-352.

It: Esperienze ed esempi tratti dalla pratica dell'analisi. Opere 7.

Sp: Experiencias y ejemplos de la práctica analítica. (Tr:LR) Obr Comp-BA 19:261. Obr Comp 1967/1968, 3:178-180.

90

1941c Eine erfüllte Traumahnung. GW 1941, 17:21.
(1899)
10443

A premonitory dream fulfilled. (Tr:JS) CP 1950, 5:70-73. In Devereux, G. *Psychoanalysis and the occult*, NY: IUP 1953, 49-51. SE 5:623-625.

It: Un presentimento onirico avveratosi. (Tr: Luserna, E.) Opere 2: 465-468.

Sp: Una premonición onírica cumplida. (Tr:LR) Obr Comp-BA 21:27-32. Obr Comp 1967/1968, 3:369-371.

91

1920f Ergänzungen zur Traumlehre. (Read at 6th Int Psa Congress, The
10444 Hague, 8-11 Sept 1920). Author's abstract: Z 1920, 6:397-398. [Strachey (SE 18:4) questions whether this abstract was actually written by Freud.]

Supplements to the theory of dreams. J 1920, 1:354. (Tr:JS) SE 18:4-5.

It: Complementi alla teoria del sogno. Opere 9.

Sp: Complementos a la teoría onírica. (Tr:LR) Obr Comp-BA 19:137-138. Obr Comp 1967/1968, 3:95.

92

1941f Ergebnisse, Ideen, Probleme. GW 1941, 17:149-152.
(1938)
10445

Findings, ideas, problems. (Tr:JS) SE 23:299-300.

Fr: Résultats, idées, problèmes. (Notes de l'exil). (Tr: Briand, J. B. & Green, A.) L'Arc, Aix-en-Provence 1968, (34):67-70.

It: Risultati, idee, problemi. Opere 11.

Sp: Conclusiones, ideas, problemas. (Tr:LR) Obr Comp-BA 21:135-140. Obr Comp 1967/1968, 3:446-448.

Hallazgos, ideas, problemas. Obr Comp 1967/1968, 3:339-340.

93

1929a   Ernest Jones zum 50. Geburtstag. Z 1929, 15(2-3):147-148. GS 1934,
10446   12:395-396. GW 1948, 14:554-555.

To Ernest Jones on the occasion of his fiftieth birthday. J 1929, 10(2-3): 123-124.

Dr. Ernest Jones (on his 50th birthday). (Tr:JS) SE 21:249-250.

It: Il dottor Ernest Jones (per il cinquantesimo compleanno). Opere 10.

Sp: A Ernest Jones, en su cincuenta aniversario. (Tr:LR) Obr Comp-BA 20: 215-216. Obr Comp 1967/1968, 3:333-334.

94

1919k   E. T. A. Hoffmann über die Bewusstseinsfunktion. Z 1919, 5:308.
10446A
        E. T. A. Hoffmann on the function of consciousness. (Tr:JS) SE 17: 233-234n. Included as footnote to translation of "Das Unheimliche."

95

1922f   Etwas vom Unbewussten. (Read at 7th Int Psa Congress, Berlin, 26 Sept
10446B   1922) Ābs Z 1922, 5:486.

Some remarks on the unconscious. J 1923, 4:367. (Tr:JS) SE 19:3-4 [Included with editor's introduction to "Das Ich und das Es."]

It: Qualche parola sull'inconscio. Opere 9.

Sp: Observaciones sobre el inconsciente. (Tr:LR) Obr Comp-BA 21:399. Obr Comp 1967/1968, 3:997.

96

1931d   Das Fakultätsgutachten im Prozess Halsmann. Psa B 1931, 2(1):32-34.
10447   GS 1934, 12:412-413. Psa P 1935, 9:208-209. GW 1948, 14:541-542.

The expert opinion in the Halsmann case. (Tr: Richards, A.) SE 21: 251-253.

It: La perizia della Facoltà medica nel processo Halsmann. Opere 11.

Sp: La pericia forense en el proceso Halsmann. (Tr:LR) Obr Comp-BA 21:301-304.

La peritación forense en el processo Halsmann. Obr Comp 1967/1968, 3:533-534.

97

1892-
1893
10448
Ein Fall von hypnotischer Heilung: nebst Bemerkungen über die Entstehung hysterischer Symptome durch den "Gegenwillen." Z Hypnotismus 1892-93, 1(3, Dec):102-107; (4, Jan):123-129. GS 1925, 1:258-272. GW 1952, 1:3-17.
Abs Inhalts wiss Arb 21.

A case of successful treatment by hypnotism: with some remarks on the origin of hyterical symptoms through "counter-will." (Tr:JS) CP 1950, 5:33-46.

A case of successful treatment by hypnotism: with some remarks on the origin of hysterical symptoms through "counter-will." (Tr:JS) SE 1: 117-128.
Abs (Tr:JS) SE 3:242-243.

It: Un caso di guarigione ipnotica. Con osservazioni in merito alla insorgenza di sintomi isterici da "contra-volunta." Riv Psa 1959, 5:201-210. Opere 1:122-136.

Por: Um caso de cura hipnótica e algumas observações sôbre a gênese de sintomas histéricos por "vontade contrária." (Tr:CMdeF) Obr Comp-P 2:101-118.

Sp: Un caso de curación hipnótica y algunas observaciones sobre la génesis de síntomas histéricos por "voluntad contraria." (Tr:LLBT) Obr Comp-Madrid 10:295-310. Obr Comp-BA 10:207. Obr Comp 1948, 1:167-174. Obr Comp 1967/1968, 1:167-172.

98

1909c
10449
Der Familienroman der Neurotiker. In Rank, O. *Der Mythus von der Geburt des Helden*. Leipzig/Vienna: Deuticke 1909, 64-68. 2nd ed, 1922, 82-86. Neurosenlehre und Technik 1931, 300-304. GS 1934, 12:367-371. Psa P 1934, 8:281-285. GW 1941, 7:227-231.

The family romance of neurotics. (Tr: Jelliffe, S. E. & Robbins, F.) In Rank, O. *Myth of the birth of the hero*, JNMD 1913, 40:668, 718; NY: JNMD 1914, 63-68.

Family romances. (Tr:JS) CP 1950, 5:74-78. SE 9:237-241.

Fr: Le roman familial des névrosés. (Tr:JLa) In *Névrose, psychose et perversion*. Paris: PUF 1973, 157-160.

Heb: Haroman hamishpachti shel haneurotikanim. Kitvei 3, chap. 9.

It: Il romanzo familiare dei nevrotici. (Tr:MLB) In Rank, O. *Il mito della nascita deglia eroi*, Bibliotheca psicoanalitica italiana, Nocera inferiore 1921. (Tr: Dogana, M. T.) Opere 5:471-476.

Sp: La novela familiar del neurótico. (Tr:LR) Obr Comp-BA 21:163-168. Obr Comp 1967/1968, 3:465-468.

99

1914a   Über fausse Reconnaissance ("déjà raconté") während der psychoan-
10450   alytischen Arbeit. Z 1914, 2(1):1-5. SKSN 1918, 4:149-156, 2nd ed 1922.
Technik und Metapsychol 1924, 76-83. GS 1925, 6:76-83. Neurosenlehre und Technik 1931, 352-359. GW 1946, 10:116-123.

Fausse reconnaissance ("déjà raconté") in psycho-analytic treatment.
(Tr:JS) CP 1924, 2:334-341. SE 13:201-207 [not italicized].

Fr: De la fausse reconnaissance (déjà raconté) au cours du traitement psychanalytique. (Tr:AB) In La technique psychanalytique, Paris: PUF 1953,
1967, 1970, 72-79.

It: Falso riconoscimento ("già raccontato") durante il lavoro psicoanalitico.
Opere 7.

Jap: (Tr:KO) FCW-S 1933, 8:11 p. Seishinbunseki chiryō nakani okeru
ayamareru sai ninshiki sunde ni hanashita ni tsuite. (Tr: Kosawa, H.)
SelFr-K 1959, 15:107-117. Rev ed (Tr: Okonogi, K.) SelFr-K 1969,
15:11 p.

Por: A "fausse reconnaissance" ("Déjà raconté") durante a psicanálise.
(Tr:JPP, OG & GP) Obr Comp-P 10:271-278.

Rus: (Tr:MV) In Metodika i tekhnika psikhoanaliza. Psikholog i psikhoanal,
vyp. IV, 136 p.

Sp: La "fausse reconnaissance" ("déjà raconté") durante el análisis. (Tr:
LLBT) Obr Comp-BA 14:113-118. Obr Comp 1948, 2:331-333. Obr
Comp 1967/1968, 2:423-425.

100

1935b   Die Feinheit einer Fehlhandlung. Almanach 1936, 1935:15-17. GW
10451   1950, 16:37-39.

The fineness of parapraxia. (Tr: Foxe, A. N.) R 1939, 26(2):153-154.

The subtleties of a parapraxis. (Tr:JS) CP 1950, 5:313-315.

The subtleties of a faulty action. (Tr:JS) SE 22:233-235.

Jap: (Tr: Agō, S.) SelFr-JinSh 1970, 4:3 p.

Sp: La sutileza de un acto fallido. (Tr:LR) Obr Comp-BA 21:311-314.
Obr Comp 1967/1968, 3:538-539.

101

1927e   Fetischismus. Almanach 1928, 1927:17-24. Z 1927, 13(4):373-378.
10453   GS 1928, 11:395-401. Sexualtheorie und Traumlehre 1931, 220-227.
GW 1948, 14:311-317.

Fetishism. (Tr:JRiv) J 1928, 9(2):161-166. CP 1950, 5:198-204.
(Modified tr:JS) SE 21:152-157.

Fr: Le fétichisme. (Tr: Berger, D.) In La vie sexuelle, Paris: PUF 1969,
133-138. In Nouvelle revue de psychanalyse 1970 (2):19-24.

It: Feticismo. Opere 10.

Jap: Shūbutsu byō (Tr:KO) In *Bunseki renai ron*, FCW-S 1932, 9:218-228.

Fueteshisumusu ron. (Tr: Hayashi, T.) In *Ijō seiyoku no bunseki*, CW-Ars 1933, 15:280-292. (Tr: Yamamoto, I.) SelFr-JinSh 1969, 5:6 p.

Sp: Fetischismo. (Tr:LR) Obr Comp-BA 21:237-244. Obr Comp 1967/1968, 3:505-509.

102

1926g [Footnote on] Hering, Ewald in Levine, Israel *Das Unbewusste*. Vienna:
10454A Int Psa Verlag 1926, Part I, Section 13, p 34. See [322].

Freud and Ewald Hering. (Tr:JS) SE 14:205. [Appendix A to "The Unconscious." (235)]

103

1916e [Footnote to] Jones, E. "Professor Janet über Psychoanalyse." Z 1916,
10454 4:42.

(Tr:ASt & JS) Included in editor's introduction to *Studies in hysteria*.
SE 2:xiii, note.

104

1911j [Footnote to] Putnam, J. J. "Über Ätiologie und Behandlung der Psycho-
10454B neurosen." C 1911, 1:137.

(Tr:JS) Included in editor's footnote to "James J. Putnam (obituary)"
[127]. SE 17:271-272, note.

105

1911h [Footnote to] Stekel, W. "Zur Psychologie des Exhibitionismus." C 1911,
10455 1:495. (Signed "Der Herausgeber")

(Tr:JS) Included as footnote to translation of "Das Medusenhaupt" [148].
SE 18:274, note.

106

1911b Formulierungen über die zwei Prinzipien des psychischen Geschehens.
10456 Y 1911, 3(1):1-8. SKSN 1913, 3:271-279. GS 1924, 5:409-417. Theoretische Schriften 1931, 5-14. GW 1943, 8:230-238.

Formulations regarding the two principles in mental functioning.
(Tr: Searl, M. N.) CP 1925, 4:13-21. In part in Rickman, J. (ed) *A general selection from the works of Sigmund Freud*, London: HPI 1937;
New York: Liveright 1957. (Tr, with comments: Rapaport, D.) In
Organization and pathology of thought, NY: Columbia Univ Pr 1951,
315-328.

Formulations on the two principles of mental functioning. (Revised tr:JS)
SE 12:218-226.

Fr: (Tr:MB & AB) In Metapsychologie, RFPsa 1936, 9:22-116.

Heb: Nisuchim bidwar schnei ekronot shel hahitrachshut hanafshit. Kitvei 4, chap. 2.

It: Precisazione sui duo principi dell'accadere psichico. (Tr:CLM) In *Freud con antologia freudiana*, Turin: Boringhieri 1959, 1970. Opere 6.

Jap: Seishin genshō no ni gensoku ni kansuru teishiki. (Tr: Imura, T. & Katō, M.) In *Fuan no mondai*, SelFr-K 1955, 10. Revised ed (Tr: Katō, M.) SelFr-K 1969, 10:14 p. (Tr: Imura, T.) SelFr-JinSh 1970, 6:6 p.

Por: Os dois princípios do suceder psíquico. (Tr: OG & GP) Obr Comp-P 14:7-16.

Rus: In Psikhoterapiia 1912, no. 3. (Tr:MV) In *Osnovnye psikhologicheskie teorii v psikhoanalize. Psikholog i psikhoanal*, vyp. III, 206 p.

Sp: Los dos principios del suceder psíquico. (Tr:LLBT) Obr Comp-Madrid 14:249-257. Obr Comp-BA 14:199-205. Obr Comp 1948, 2:403-406. Obr Comp 1967/1968, 2:495-498.

107

1926e   Die Frage der Laienanalyse. Unterredungen mit einem Unparteiischen.
10458   Leipzig/Vienna/Zurich: Int Psa Verlag 1926, 123 p. GS 1928, 11: 307-384. GW 1948, 14:209-286. Extract with title: Psychoanalyse und Kurpfuscherei [Psychoanalysis and quackery]. Almanach 1927, 1926 (Sept):47-59. Sonntagsblatt der New Yorker Volkszeitung 1925, Sept 19. *See also* Nachwort zu *Frage der Laienanalyse* [165].

The problem of lay-analyses. (Tr: Maerker-Branden, A. P.) (Pref:SFe) In *The problem of lay-analyses*, NY: Brentano 1927, 25-186.

The question of lay-analysis: an introduction to psycho-analysis. (Tr: Proctor-Gregg, N.) (Pref:EJ) London: IPC 1947, vi+81 p. NY: Norton 1950, 125 p.

The question of lay analysis: conversations with an impartial person. (Tr:JS) SE 20:183-250.

Arab: (Tr: Ramzi, I.) Cairo: DarOel-Ma'arif, 156 p.

Fr: Psychanalyse et médecine. (Tr:MB; revised: Freud, S.) In *Ma vie et la psychanalyse*, Paris: Gallimard 1928, 1949, 117-239. 1968, 93-184.

It: Il problema dell'analisi condotta da non medici. Opere 10. (Tr: Flescher, J. & CLM) In *La mia vita e la psicanalisi*, Milan: A.P.E.-Mursia 1956.

Jap: Hiimono no bunseki kahi no mondai. (Tr:KO) In *Bunseki byōhō ron*, FCW-S 1932, 8:207-321. (Tr: Kimura, K. & Naitō, K.) In *Shirō to bunseki no mondai*, CW-Ars 1933, 12:68-184.

Nor: Psykoanalysen i Praksis. (Tr: Schjelderup, K.) Oslo: Gyldendal Norsk Forlag 1930, 175 p.

Pers: Mafhume sādeye ravānkāvi. (Tr: Javaher-Kalam, F.) Teheran: Morvarid 1963, 1968, 144 p.

Por: Psicanálise e medicina (análise profana). (Tr:OG, IsIz, & GP) Obr Comp-P 18:141-222.

Sp: Psicoanalisis y medicina (análisis profano). (Tr:LLBT) Obr Comp-Madrid 12. Obr Comp-BA 12:9-72. Obr Comp 1948, 2:751-786. Obr Comp 1967/1968, 2:843-878.

108

1913h Fragmentarische Träume. Erf Beisp Psa Prx [89] no. 21. Z 1913,
10459 1:377-382.

Fragmentary dreams. (Tr:JS) SE 13:197-198.

109

1904a Die Freud'sche psychoanalytische Methode. In Löwenfeld, L. *Die psy-*
(1903) *chischen Zwangserscheinungen,* Wiesbaden: Bergmann 1904, 545-551.
10462 SKSN 1906, 1:218-224. 2nd ed, 1911, 213-219. 3rd ed, 1920. 4th ed,
       1922. Technik und Metapsychol 1924, 3-10. GS 1925, 6:3-10. GW 1942,
       5:3-10.

Freud's psycho-analytic method. (Tr: Bernays, J.) CP 1924, 1:264-271.

Freud's psycho-analytic procedure. (Revised tr:JS) SE 7:249-254.

Fr: La méthode psychanalytique de Freud. (Tr:AB) In *La technique psych-analytique,* Paris: PUF 1953, 1970, 1-8.

It: Il metodo psicoanalitico freudiano. Psiche 1912, 1:129-135. (Tr: Dogana, M. T.) Opere 4:407-414.

Jap: Furoido no seishinbunseki ryō. (Tr:KO) In *Bunseki byōhō ron,* FCW-S 1932, 8:1-10.

Furoido no seishinbunseki no hōhō. (Tr: Kosawa, H.) In *Seishinbunseki ryōhō,* SelFr-K 1959, 15:3-12. Rev ed (Tr: Okonogi, K.) SelFr-K 1969, 15:10 p.

Por: O método psicanalítico de Freud. (Tr:JPP, OG & GP) Obr Comp-P 10:175-182.

Rus: (Tr:MV) In *Metodika i tekhnika psikhoanaliza. Psikholog i psikhoanal,* vyp. IV, 136 p.

Sp: El método psicoanalítico de Freud. (Tr:LLBT) Obr Comp-Madrid 14. Obr Comp-BA 14:57-62. Obr Comp 1948, 2:301-303. Obr Comp 1967/1968, 2:393-395.

110

1920d Gedankenassoziation eines vierjährigen Kindes. Z 1920, 6:157. GS 1924,
10463 5:244-245. Psychoanalyse der Neurosen 1926, 85-86. Neurosenlehre
       und Technik 1931, 172-173. GW 1947, 12:305-306.

Associations of a four-year-old child. (Tr:JS) SE 18:266.

Heb: Asoziaziat machshava ezel bat arba. Kitvei 3, chap. 11.

It: Associazione d'idee di un bambino di quattro anni. Opere 9.

Por: Associação de idéias de uma criança de 4 anos. (Tr:OG, IsIz & MG) Obr Comp-P 9:171-172.

Sp: Asociación de ideas de una niña de cuatro años. (Tr:LLBT) Obr Comp-Madrid 13:131-132. Obr Comp-BA 13:107. Obr Comp 1948, 1: 1208-1209. Obr Comp 1967/1968, 1:1194-1195.

111

1910e Über den Gegensinn der Urworte. Referat über der gleichnamige
10464 Brochüre von Karl Abel. Y 1910, 2(1):179-184. SKSN 1913, 3:280-287. GS 1924, 10:221-228. GW 1943, 8:214-221.

The antithetical sense of primal words. A review of a pamphlet by Karl Abel, *Über den Gegensinn der Urworte*, 1884. (Tr: Searl, M. N.) CP 1925, 4:184-191.

The antithetical meaning of primal words. (Tr: Tyson, A.) SE 11: 155-161.

Fr: Des sens opposés dans les mots primitifs. (Tr: Marty, Mme. E. & MB) In *Essais de psychanalyse appliquée*, Paris: Gallimard 1933, 59-67.

Heb: Al mashmautan haipachit shel hamilim hakamaiot. Kitvei 4, chap. 15.

It: Significato opposto delle parole primordiali. Opere 6. In *Saggi sull'arte, la letteratura e il linguaggio*, Turin: Boringhieri 1969, vol. 1.

Jap: Genshi kotoba no aihan igi ni tsuite. (Tr:KO) In *Bunseki geijutsu ron*, FCW-S 1931, 1937, 6:208-219.

Por: O duplo sentido antitético das palavras primitivas. (Tr:ED) Obr Comp-P 11:109-116.

Sp: El doble sentido antitético de las palabras primitivas. (Tr:LLBT) Obr Comp-BA 18:59-86. Obr Comp 1948, 2:961-964. Obr Comp 1967/1968, 2:1053-1056.

112

1914d Zur Geschichte der psychoanalytischen Bewegung. Y 1914, 6:207-260.
10470 SKSN 1918, 4:1-77, 2nd ed, 1922. GS 1924, 4:411-480. Leipzig/Vienna/Zurich: Int Psa Verlag 1924, 72 p. GW 1946, 10:44-113. Munich: Werner Fritsch 1966, 72 p.

The history of the psychoanalytic movement. (Tr:AAB) R 1916, 3: 406-454. NY: NMDP 1917, no. 25, 58 p. BWSF 1938, 933-977.

On the history of the psycho-analytic movement. (Tr:JRiv) CP 1924, 1:287-359. (Modified tr:JS) SE 14:7-66. NY: Norton 1966, 79 p.

Fr: Contribution à l'histoire du mouvement psychanalytique. (Tr: Jankélévitch, S.) In *Essais de psychanalyse*, Paris: Payot 1927, 266-320. In *Cinq leçons sur la psychanalyse*, Paris: Payot 1968, 1969, 1973, 69-155.

Gr: Istoria tis psychanalysios. (Tr: Cohen, A.) Athens: Gavotsis 1932.

Heb: Letoldot hatenua hapsichoanalitit. Kitvei 3, chap. 3.

Hun: (A psychoanalytikus mozgalom története.) (Tr: Kovács, V. & Dukesz, G.) In *Önéletrajz*, Budapest: Pantheon 1936. (Tr: Ignotus) In Nuygat, Budapest, 101-135.

It: Per la storia del movimento psicoanalitico. (Tr: Fachinelli, E.; Staude, A.; & Montinari, M.) In *Psicoanalisi. Esposizione divulgative*, Turin: Boringhieri 1963, 1965. Opere 7.

Jap: Seishinbunseki rōdō shi. (Tr: KO) In *Seishinbunseki so ron*, FCW-S 1933, 10:217-312.

Seishinbunseki undō no rekishi ni tsuite. (Tr: Kakeda, K.) In Mizukara o kataru, SelFr-K 1960, 1969, 17:103-269.

Por: História do movimento psicanalítico. (Tr:OG, IsIz & GP) Obr Comp-P 18:5-72.

Rus: (Tr:MV) In *Osnovnye psikhologicheskie teorii v psikhoanalize. Psikholog i psikhoanal*, vyp. III, 206 p.

Sp: Historia del movimiento psicoanalitico. (Tr:LLBT) Obr Comp-Madrid 12. Obr Comp-BA 12:101-154. Obr Comp 1948, 2:889-920. Obr Comp 1967/1968, 2:981-1012. Madrid: Alianza Editorial 1969.

113

1918b Aus der Geschichte einer infantilen Neurose. SKSN 1918, 4:578-717.
(1914) SKSN 1922, 5:1-140. Leipzig/Vienna/Zurich: Int Psa Verlag 1924,
10471 132 p. GS 1924, 8:439-567. Neurosenlehre und Technik 1931, 37-171. GW 1947, 12:29-157.

From the history of an infantile neurosis. (Tr:ASt & JS) CP 1925, 3: 473-605. (Revised tr:JS) SE 17:7-122. In *The wolf man*, NY: Basic Books 1971, 153-262.

Cz: Z dejin pripadu detske neurosy. (Tr: Friedmann, O.) In *Psychoanalytické chorobopisy*, Prague: Julius Albert 1937.

Fr: Extrait de l'histoire d'une névrose infantile (L'homme aux loups). (Tr:MB & RL) In *Cinq psychanalyses*, Paris: Denoël & Steele 1935; PUF 1954, 1966, 1967, (Revised tr:AB) 1970, 325-420.

It: Dalla storia di una nevrosi infantile (caso clinico dell'uomo dei lupi). (Tr: Lucentini, M.) In *Casi clinici*, Turin: Boringhieri 1952, 1962. (Tr:CLM; Panaitescu, E. A.; & Lucentini, M.) In *Psicoanalisi infantile*, Turin: Boringhieri 1968, 1970. Opere 7.

Jap: Aru shō ni shinkeishō no byōreki kara. (Tr: Hayashi, T.) In *Ijō seiyoku bunseki*, CW-Ars 1933, 15:295-504.

Aru yōjiki shinkeibyō no byōreki yori. (Tr: Kumada, M. & Okonogi, K.) In *Shōrei no kenkyū*, SelFr-K 1959, 16:162 p.

Por: História de uma neurose infantil. (Tr:ED & OG) Obr Comp-P 16:177.

Sp: Historia de una neurosis infantil. (Tr:LLBT) Obr Comp-Madrid 16: 161-283. Obr Comp-BA 16:145-239. Obr Comp 1948, 2:693-750. Obr Comp 1967/1968, 2:785-842.

114

1932a   Zur Gewinnung des Feuers. Imago 1932, 18(1):8-13. Almanach 1933,
10472   1932:28-35. GS 1934, 12:141-147. GW 1950, 16:3-9.

The acquisition of fire. (Tr: Jackson, E. B.) Q 1932, 1(2):210-215.

The acquisition of power over fire. (Tr:JRiv) J 1932, 13(4):405-410. CP 1950, 5:288-294.

The acquisition and control of fire. (Revised) SE 22:187-193.

It: L'acquisizione del fuoco. Opere 11.

Jap: (Tr: Kimura, M.) SelFr-JinSh 1969, 3:15 p.

Sp: Sobre la conquista del fuego. (Tr:LR) Obr Comp-BA 19:91-98. Obr Comp 1967/1968, 3:67-72.

115

1911f   "Gross ist die Diana der Epheser." [Based on Sartiex, F. *Villes mortes*
10473   *d'Asie mineure*] C 1911, 2:158-159. GW 1943, 8:360-361.

"Great is Diana of the Ephesians." (Tr:JS) SE 12:342-344.

It: "Grande è la Diana efesia." Opere 6.

Sp: "¡Grande es Diana Efesia!" (Tr:LR) Obr Comp-BA 21:187-190. Obr Comp 1967/1968, 3:480.

116

1911e   Die Handhabung der Traumdeutung in der Psychoanalyse. C 1911,
10475   2(3):109-113. SKSN 1918, 4:378-385. Technik und Metapsychol 1924, 45-52. GS 1925, 6:45-52. Neurosenlehre und Technik 1931, 321-328. GW 1943, 8:350-357.

The employment of dream-interpretation in psycho-analysis. (Tr:JRiv) CP 1924, 2:305-311.

The handling of dream-interpretation in psycho-analysis. (Revised) SE 12:91-96.

Fr: Le maniement de l'interprétation des rêves en psychanalyse. (Tr:AB) In *La technique psychanalytique*, Paris: PUF 1953, 1967, 1970, 43-49.

It: L'impiego dell'interpretazione dei sogni nella psicoanalisi. Opere 6.

Jap: (Tr:KO) FCW-S 1933, 8:9 p. Seishinbunseki ryōhō nakani okeru yume kaishaku shiyō. (Tr: Kosawa, H.) SelFr-K 1959, 15:64-73. Rev ed (Tr: Okonogi, K.) SelFr-K 1969, 15:10 p.

Por: O emprêgo da interpretação dos sonhos na psicanálise. (Tr:JPP, OG & GP) Obr Comp-P 10:215-222.

Rus: In Psikhoterapiia 1913, no. 2.

Sp: El empleo de la interpretación de los sueños en el psicoanálisis. (Tr:LLBT) Obr Comp-BA 14:89-94. Obr Comp 1948, 2:318-320. Obr Comp 1967/1968, 2:410-412.

117

1926d Hemmung, Symptom und Angst. Leipzig/Vienna/Zurich: Int Psa
10476 Verlag 1926, 136 p. GS 1928, 11:23-115. Neurosenlehre und Technik 1931, 205-299. GW 1948, 14:113-205. Extract from Chapter I in Neue Freie Presse, Vienna 1926, 21 Feb (no. 22069):12. Braille: Vienna: Hohe Warte.

Inhibition, symptom and anxiety. (Tr: Clark, L. P.) (Pref: SFe) Stamford, Conn: Psychoanalytic Institute 1927, vi+103 p. Extract in Archives Psa 1927, 1:461-521.

Inhibitions, symptoms and anxiety. (Tr: Bunker, H. A.) Q 1935, 4(4): 616-625; 1936, 5(1):1-28; (2):261-279; (3):415-443.

The problem of anxiety. (Tr: Bunker, H. A.) NY: Psychoanalytic Quarterly Press & W. W. Norton 1936, vii+165 p. NY: W. W. Norton 1964, 127 p.

Inhibitions, symptoms and anxiety. (Tr:ASt) London: HPI 1936, 179 p. Major Works, 718-754. (Tr:JS) SE 20:87-174.

Arab: Al-qalaq. (Tr: Najātī, M.) Cairo: Maktabit al-Nahḍah al-Miṣriyyah 1962.

Fr: Inhibition, symptôme et angoisse. (Tr: Jury, P. & Fraenkel, E.) Paris: PUF 1951, viii+114 p. (Tr: Tort, M.) Paris: PUF 1965, 1968, 103 p.

Gr: Anhos kai enstikton. (Tr: Meranaios, C.) Athens: Karavias 1940.

To anhos kai i zoi ton enstikton. (Tr: Ferentinos, S.) Athens: Gavotsis 1941.

It: Inibizione, sintomo e angoscia. (Tr: Servadio, E.) Turin: G. Einaudi 1951, 112 p. Boringhieri 1951, 1966, 110 p. 7th ed. 1971, 112 p. Opere 10.

Jap: Jisei to chōkō to kiyū. (Tr: Yabe, Y.) In Seiyoku ron, kinsei ron, FCW-S 1931, 5:175-294.

Seishi, shōjō, oyobi kyōfu. (Tr: Hayashi, T.) In Choishiki shinrigaku, CW-Ars 1932, 13:169-298.

Yokushi shōjō fuan. (Tr: Imura, T. & Katō, M.) In Fuan no mondai, SelFr-K 1955, 10. Rev ed (Tr: Katō, M.) SelFr-K 1969, 10:104 p. (Tr: Imura, T.) SelFr-JinSh 1970, 6:57 p.

Por: Inibição, sintoma e angústia. (Tr:OG, IsIz & MG) Obr Comp-P 9:304.

Rus: Strakh. (Tr:MV) In Nauchnaia biblioteka "Sovremennykh problem," Moskva: Sovremennye problemy 1927, 104 p.

Sp: Inhibición, síntoma y angustia. (Tr:LLBT) Obr Comp-Madrid 11:5-114. Obr Comp-BA 11:9-84. Obr Comp 1948, 1:1235-1276. Obr Comp 1967/1968, 2:31-72.

118

1896a L'hérédité et l'étiologie des névroses. [In French] Rev neurologique 1896,
10477 4(6, 30 Mar):161-169. SKSN 1906, 1:135-148. GS 1925, 1:388-403. GW 1952, 1:407-422. In *Névrose, psychose et perversion*, Paris: PUF 1973, 47-57.
Abs Inhalts wiss Arb 37.

Heredity and the aetiology of the neuroses. (Tr: Meyer, M.) CP 1924, 1:138-154. (Tr:JS) SE 3:143-156.
Abs (Tr:JS) SE 3:255.

It: L'ereditarietà e l'etiologia delle nevrosi. (Tr: Campione, A.) Opere 2: 289-304.

Por: A herança e a etiologia das neuroses. (Tr:CMdeF) Obr Comp-P 2: 209-228.

Sp: La herencia y la etiología de las neurosis. (Tr:LLBT) Obr Comp-Madrid 11:196-213. Obr Comp-BA 11:145-158. Obr Comp 1967/1968, 1:204-210.

La herencia y la teoría de las neurosis. (Tr:LLBT) Obr Comp 1948, 1:205-211.

119

1927d Der Humor. [Read by Anna Freud at 10th Int Psa Congress, Innsbruck,
10478 1 Sept 1927.] Almanach 1928, 1927:9-16. Imago 1928, 14(1):1-6. GS 1928, 11:402-408. GW 1948, 14:383-389.

Humour. (Tr:JRiv) J 1928, 9(1):1-6. CP 1950, 5:215-221. (Tr:JS) SE 21:161-166.

Fr: L'humour. (Tr:MB & Nathan, M.) In *Variétés*, special no. "Le surréalisme en 1929." In *Le mot d'esprit et ses rapports avec l'inconscient*, Paris: Gallimard 1930, 1969, 367-376.

Heb: Hahumur. Kitvei 2, chap. 11.

It: L'umorismo. Opere 10. In *Saggi sull'arte, la letteratura e il linguaggio*, Turin: Boringhieri 1969, vol. 1.

Jap: Fumoru. (Tr:KO) In *Bunseki geijutsu ron*, FCW-S 1931, 1937, 6: 134-142.

Fumōru-yūmoa. (Tr:YT) In *Geijutsu ron*, SelFr-K 1953, 7:14 p. Rev ed (Tr:YT & Ikeda, K.) SelFr-K 1970, 7:14 p. (Tr:YT) SelFr-JinSh 1969, 3:6 p. (Tr: Kikumori, H.) Tokyo: Kawade Shobō Shinsha Pr 1972.

Sp: El humor. (Tr:LR) Obr Comp-BA 21:245-252. Obr Comp 1967/1968, 3:510-513.

120

1908a Hysterische Phantasien und ihre Beziehung zur Bisexualität. Z Sexualwiss
10481 1908, 1(1, Jan):27-34. SKSN 1909, 2:138-145. GS 1924, 5:246-254.
GW 1941, 7:191-199.

Hysterical fancies and their relation to bisexuality. (Tr:AAB) SPH 1909,
194-200. 2nd ed, 1912. 3rd ed, 1920. In *Major Works* 1952, 115-118.

Hysterical phantasies and their relation to bisexuality. (Tr:DB) CP 1924,
2:51-58. (Revised tr:JS) SE 9:159-166.

It: Fantasie isteriche e loro rapporto con la bissualità. (Tr: Dogana, M. T.)
Opere 5:389-398.

Jap: Hisuteribyō no kūsō to ryōsei kanken. (Tr: Konuma, M.) In *Ijo seiyoku
bunseki*, CW-Ars 1933, 15:56-58.

Hisuteri kūsō to ryōsei guyūsei ni taisuru sono kanken. (Tr:KO) In
Bunseki renai ron, FCW-S 1932, 9:99-110.

Hisuterishōsha no kūsō to sono ryōsei guyū ni taisuru kankei. (Tr: YT)
In *Aijō no shinrigaku*, SelFr-K 1960, 14:14 p.

Por: Fantasias históricas e sua relação com a bissexualidade. (Tr:OG & MG)
Obr Comp-P 5:139-148.

Sp: Fantasías históricas y su relación con la bisexualidad. (Tr:LLBT) Obr
Comp-Madrid 13:133-141. Obr Comp-BA 13:108-114. Obr Comp 1948,
1:965-968. Obr Comp 1967/1968, 1:954-957.

121

1923b Das Ich und das Es. [Preliminary draft at 7th Int Psa Congress, Berlin,
10482 26 Sept 1922] Leipzig/Vienna/Zurich: Int Psa Verlag 1923, 77 p.
GS 1925, 6:351-405. Theoretische Schriften 1931, 338-391. GW 1940,
13:237-289. Braille: Vienna: Hohe Warte

The Ego and the Id. (Tr:JRiv) London: HPI 1927, 88 p. Extracts. In
Rickman, J. (ed) *A general selection from the works of Sigmund Freud*,
London: HPI 1937, 245-274.

The Ego and the Id. (Tr:JS) SE 19:12-66.

Arab: Al-dhāt wal-gharā'iz. (Tr: Najātī, M.) Cairo: Maktabit al-Nahdah al-
Misriyyah 1961.

Fr: Le moi et le ça. (Tr: Jankélévitch, S.) In *Essais de psychanalyse*, Paris:
Payot 1927, 1951, 163-218. (Revised tr: Hesnard, A.) Paris: Payot 1970,
177-234.

Gr: To ego kai to ekino. (Tr: Meranaios, C.) Athens: Gavotsis 1933, 76 p.
(Tr: Syrros, P.) Athens: Panekdotiki 1966.

Heb: Haani vehastam. Kitvei 4, chap. 8.

Hun: Az ősvalami és az én. (Tr: Hollós, I. & Dukesz, G.) Budapest: Pantheon
Kiadas 1937, 78 p. In Buda, B. *A pszichoanalizis és modern irányzatai*,
Budapest: Gondolat 1971, 139-161.

It: L'Io e l'Es. (Tr: Barbaro, U.) In *Nuovi saggi di psicoanalisi*, Rome: O.E.T. 1946. Opere 9.

Jap: Jiga to esu. (Tr: Kubo, Y.) In *Kaikan gensoku higan*, CW-Ars 1930, 6:211-283. (Tr: Yabe, Y.) FCW-S 1932, 7:1-66. (Tr: Imura, T.) SelFr-K 1954, 4:243-316. Rev ed: 1970, 4:64 p.

Por: O Ego e o Id. (Tr:OG, IsIz & MG) Obr Comp-P 9:181-303.

Rus: IA i ono. (Tr: Polianskiĭ, V. F.) In *Sovremennaia kul'tura*, Leningrad: Academia 1924, 63 p.

Sp: El "Yo" y el "Ello." (Tr:LLBT) Obr Comp-Madrid 9:237-296. Obr Comp-BA 9:191-238. Obr Comp 1948, 1:1213-1234. Obr Comp 1967/ 1968, 2:9-30.

122

1940e   Die Ichspaltung im Abwehrvorgang. Z 1940, 25(3/4):241-244. GW
(1938)   1941, 17:59-62.
10483

Splitting of the ego in the defensive process. (Tr:JS) J 1941, 22(1):65-68. CP 1950, 5:372-375.

Splitting of the ego in the process of defence. (Revised tr:JS) SE 23: 275-278.

Fr: Le clivage du moi dans le processus de défense. (Tr: Lewinter, R. & Pontalis, J. B.) Nouvelle Revue de psychanalyse 1970, (2):25-28.

It: La scissione dell'Io nel processo di difesa. Opere 11.

Jap: Boei katei ni okeru jiga no bunretsu. (Tr: Kosawa, H.) In *Seishinbunseki ryoho*, SelFr-K 1959, 15:300-305. Rev ed (Tr: Okonogi, K.) SelFr-K 1969, 15:6 p.

Sp: La escisión del yo en el proceso defensivo. (Tr:LR) Obr Comp-BA 21: 61-66. Obr Comp 1967/1968, 3:389-391.

123

1923e   Die infantile Genitalorganisation. (Eine Einschaltung in die Sexual-
10484   theorie). Z 1923, 9(2):168-171. GS 1924, 5:232-237. Psychoanalyse
der Neurosen 1926, 140-146. Sexualtheorie und Traumlehre 1931, 188-193. GW 1940, 13:291-298.

The infantile genital organization of the libido: a supplement to the theory of sexuality. (Tr:JRiv) J 1924, 5:125-129. CP 1924, 2:244-249.

The infantile genital organization (an interpolation into the theory of sexuality). (Tr:JS) SE 19:141-145.

Fr: L'organisation génitale infantile. (Tr:JLa) In *La vie sexuelle*, Paris: PUF 1969, 113-116.

It: L'organizzazione genitale infantile. (Tr: Campione, A.; Candreva, S.; Montinari, M.; CLM; & Sagittario, E.) In *La vita sessuale*, Turin: Boringhieri 1970. Opere 9.

Por: Organização genital infantil. (Tr:OG, IsIz & MG) Obr Comp-P 9: 173-180.

Rus: (Tr:MV) In *Ocherki po psikhologii seksual 'nosti. Psikholog i psikhoanal,* vyp. VIII, 188 p.

Sp: La organizatión genital infantil (Adición a la teoría sexual). (Tr:LLBT) Obr Comp-BA 13:97-101. Obr Comp 1948, 1:1209-1212. Obr Comp 1967/1968, 1:1195.

124

1908c   Über infantile Sexualtheorien. Mutterschutz (neue Folge): Sexual-
10485   Probleme 1908, 4(12, Dec):763-779. SKSN 1909, 2:159-174. 2nd ed, 1912. 3rd ed, 1921. GS 1924, 5:168-185. Sexualtheorie und Traumlehre 1931, 43-61. GW 1941, 7:171-188.

On the sexual theories of children. (Tr:DB) CP 1924, 2:59-75. (Revised tr:JS) SE 9:209-226.

Fr: Les théories sexuelles infantiles. (Tr: Pontalis, J. B.) In *La vie sexuelle,* Paris: PUF 1969, 14-27.

It: Teorie sessuali dei bambini. (Tr: Panaitescu, E. A.) Opere 5:451-454. (Tr: CLM; Panaitescu, E. A.; & Lucentini, M.) In *Psicoanalisi infantile,* Turin: Boringhieri 1968, 1970.

Jap: (Tr: Kakeda, K.) SelFr-JinSh 1969, 5:14 p.

Por: Teorias sexuais infantis. (Tr:OG, IsIz & MG) Obr Comp-P 9:119-136.

Sp: Teorías sexuales infantiles. (Tr:LLBT) Obr Comp-BA 13:47-60. Obr Comp 1948, 1:1185-1192. Obr Comp 1967/1968, 1:1171-1178.

125

1913j   Das Interesse an der Psychoanalyse. Scientia, Bologna, 1913, 14(31):
10486   240-250; (32):369-384. GS 1924, 4:313-343. GW 1943, 8:390-420.

The claims of psycho-analysis to scientific interest. (Tr:JS) SE 13: 165-190.

Fr: L'intérêt de la psychanalyse. (Tr: Horn, M. W.) Scientia, Bologna 1913, 14(suppl. no. 31):151-167; (no 32):236-251.

Heb: Hainyan shebapsichoanalisa. Kitvei 3, chap. 4.

It: L'interesse per la psicoanalisi. (Tr: Fachinelli, E.; Staude, A.; & Montinari, M.) In *Psicoanalisi. Esposizioni divulgative,* Turin: Boringhieri 1963, 1965. Opere 7.

Jap: Bunseki no kyōmi. (Tr: Kubo, Y.) In *Kaikan gensoku higan,* CW-Ars 1930, 6:289-325. (Tr:KO) FCW-S 1930, 4:40 p.

Por: Múltiplo interêsse da psicanálise. (Tr:GP) Obr Comp-P 17:193.

Sp: Múltiple interés del psicoanálisis. (Tr:LLBT) Obr Comp-BA 12:73-100. Obr Comp 1948, 2:875-888. Obr Comp 1967/1968, 2:967-980.

Sw: Den psykoanalytiska interessesfären. (Tr: Bjerre, P.) In Bjerre, P. *Psykoanalysen. Dess uppkomst, omvandlingar och tillämpning.* Stockholm: Natur och Kultur 1924, 11-34.

126

1919c   Internationaler psychoanalytischer Verlag und Preiszuteilungen für
10487   psychoanalytische Arbeit. Z 1919, 5:137-138. GW 1947, 12:333-336.

A note on psycho-analytic publications and prizes. (Tr:JS) SE 17: 267-269.

It: Publicazione e premiazione di lavori psicoanalitici. Opere 9.

Sp: La Editorial Psicoanalítica Internacional y los premios para trabajos psicoanalíticos. (Tr:LR) Obr Comp-BA 20:227-229. Obr Comp 1967/ 1968, 3:343-344.

127

1919b   James J. Putnam. (obituary) [Signed "Der Herausgeber."] Z 1919, 5:136. GS 1928, 11:276-277. GW 1947, 12:315.

James J. Putnam. (Tr:JS) SE 17:271-272. Includes translation of [104].

It: Necrologio di J. J. Putnam. Opere 9.

Sp: En memoria de James J. Putnam. (Tr:LR) Obr Comp-BA 20:199-200. Obr Comp 1967/1968, 3:323.

128

1920g   Jenseits des Lustprinzips. Leipzig/Vienna/Zurich: Int Psa Verlag 1920,
10490   60 p; 1921, 64 p; 1923, 94 p. GS 1925, 6:191-257. Theoretische Schriften 1931, 178-247. GW 1940, 13:3-69.

Beyond the pleasure principle. (Tr:CJMH) (Pref:EJ) London/Vienna: Int Psa Pr 1922, viii+90 p. NY: Boni & Liveright 1924. In Rickman, J. (ed) *A general selection from the works of Sigmund Freud,* London: HPI 1937, 162-194. London: HPI 1942, viii+90 p. *Major Works* 639-663. (Tr:JS) London: HPI 1950, vi+97 p. SE 18:7-64.

Dut: Het levensmysterie en de psychoanalyse. (Tr: Querido, A.) Amsterdam: Em. Querido 1922, 138 p. Amsterdam: Wereldbibliotheek 1952, 1953, 1955, 1957, 1962, 110 p.

Fr: Au delà du principe du plaisir. (Tr: Jankélévitch, S.) In *Essais de psychanalyse,* Paris: Payot 1927, 1951, 5-75. (Revised tr: Hesnard, A.) Paris: Payot 1970, 7-81.

Gr: Peran tis idonis. (Tr: Kyprianos, C.) Athens: Gavotsis 1930, 88 p.

Peran tis archis tis idonis. (Tr: Zographou, M.) Athens: Tzongas 1950.

Pera apo tin archi tis idonis. (Tr: Varsamis, N.) Athens: Karanikolas 1971.

Heb: Meever leekaron haoneg. Kitvei 4, chap. 7.

Hun: A halálösztön és az életösztönök. (Tr: Kovács, V.) Budapest: Világirodalom 1923, 64 p.

It: Al di là del principio di piacere. (Tr: Barbaro, U.) In *Nuovi saggi di psicoanalisi*, Rome: O.E.T. 1946. Opere 9.

Jap: Kai no genri o koete. (Tr: Kubo, Y.) In *Kaikan gensoku higan*, CW-Ars 1930, 6:1-88.

Kai fukai gensoku o koete. (Tr: Tsushima, K.) FCW-S 1930, 4:1-88. (Tr:KO) Tokyo: Shunyodo 1940.

Kaikan gensoku no higan. (Tr: Imura, T.) In *Jiga ron*, SelFr-K 1937, 4:3-81. Rev ed (Tr: Okonogi, K.) SelFr-K 1970, 4:82 p. SelFr-JinSh 1970, 6:45 p.

Por: Mais além do principio do prazer. (Tr:CMdeF & IsIz) Obr Comp-P 8:255.

Rus: Po tu storonu printsipa udovol'stviia. (Tr: Vygotskiĭ, L. S. & Luriia, A. R.) In *Nauchnaia biblioteka "Sovremennykh problem,"* Moskva: Kn-vo Sovremennye Problemy 1925, 110 p.

Sp: Más allá del principio del placer. (Tr:LLBT) Obr Comp-Madrid 2: 299-377. Obr Comp-BA 2:217. Obr Comp 1948, 1:1111-1140. Obr Comp 1967/1968, 1:1097-1126. Madrid: Aliana Editorial 1969.

129

1925g Josef Breuer (obituary). Z 1925, 11(2):255-256. GS 1928, 11:281-283.
10491 GW 1948, 14:562-563.

Josef Breuer. J 1925, 6(4):459-460. (Tr:JS) SE 19:279-280.

It: Necrologio di Josef Breuer. Opere 10.

Sp: En memoria de José Breuer. (Tr:LR) Obr Comp-BA 20:209-211. Obr Comp 1967/1968, 3:330-331.

130

1923f Josef Popper-Lynkeus und die Theorie des Traumes. Zeitschrift des
10492 Allgemeine Nährpflicht, Vienna 1923, 6. GS 1928, 11:295-297. GW 1940, 13:357-359.

Josef Popper-Lynkeus and the theory of dreams. (Tr:JS) SE 19:261-263.

Heb: In Doryon, I. *Lynkeus' new state.* Jerusalem, 1939, 1940, 163-173.

It: Josef Popper-Lynkeus e la teoria del sogno. In Robert, M. *La rivoluzione psicoanalitica*, Turin: Boringhieri 1967, 163. Opere 9.

Sp: Josef Popper-Lynkeus y la teoría onírica. (Tr:LR) Obr Comp-BA 19: 179-184. Obr Comp 1967/1968, 3:126-127.

131

1926b Karl Abraham (obituary). [Signed "Der Herausgeber:" Sigm Freud]

10494 Z 1926, 12(1):1-2. GS 1928, 11:283-284. GW 1948, 14:564.

  Karl Abraham. J 1926, 7:1. (Modified tr:JS) SE 20:277-278.

  It: Necrologio di Karl Abraham. Opere 10.

  Sp: En memoria de Karl Abraham. (Tr:LR) Obr Comp-BA 20:213-214.
      Obr Comp 1967/1968, 3:332.

132

1919j   Kell-e az egyetemen a psychoanalysist tantitani? [First published in
(1918) Hungarian] (Tr from German:SFe) Gyógyászat 1919, 59(13):192.
10494A [In a personal communication, dated 5 Aug 1971, Dr. Imre Hermann in-
        dicated that in his opinion and that of Dr. L. Lévy, former editor of
        Gyógyászat, this manuscript was actually written by Dr. Ferenczi.]

  No German text extant.

  On the teaching of psycho-analysis in universities. (Tr: O'Donovan, J. F.
  & LR; revised tr:JS & Balint, M.) SE 17:171-173. J 1956, 37:14-15.

  It: Bisogna insegnare la psicoanalisi nell'università? Opere 9.

  Sp: Sobre la ensenanza del psicoanálisis en la Universidad. (Tr:LR) Rev
      Psicoanál 1955, 12:111-114. Obr Comp-BA 21:395-398. Obr Comp
      1967/1968, 3:994-996.

133

1919e   "Ein Kind wird geschlagen." Beitrag zur Kenntnis der Entstehung
10495 sexueller Perversionen. Z 1919, 5(3):151-172. SKSN 1922, 5:195-228.
        GS 1924, 5:344-373. Psychoanalyse der Neurosen 1926, 50-84. Sexual-
        theorie und Traumlehre 1931, 124-155. GW 1947, 12:197-226.

  "A child is being beaten." A contribution to the study of the origin of
  sexual perversions. (Tr:ASt & JS) J 1920, 1:371-395. CP 1924, 2:
  172-201. (Revised tr:JS) SE 17:179-204. In Ruitenbeek, H. M. *Psychotherapy of perversions*, NY: Citadel Pr 1967, 70-98.

  Fr: "On bat un enfant." (Tr: Hoesli, H.) RFPsa 1933, 6(3-4):274-297.

      "Un enfant est battu." Contribution à la connaissance de la genèse des
      perversions sexuelles. (Tr: Guérineau, D.) In *Névrose, psychose et
      perversion*. Paris: PUF 1973, 219-243.

  It: "Un bambino viene picchiato." Contributo alla conoscenza dell'origine
      delle perversioni sessuale. Riv Psa 1963, 9:3-21. Opere 9.

  Jap: Shōni ga chō chaku sareru. (Tr: Konuma, M.) In *Ijō seiyoku bunseki*,
       CW-Ars 1933, 15:208-276.

  Por: Surram uma criança. (Tr:OG, IsIz & MG) Obr Comp-P 9:143-170.

  Sp: Pegan a un niño. Aportación al conocimiento de la génesis de las
      perversiones sexuales. (Tr:LLBT) Obr Comp-Madrid 13:232-262.
      Obr Comp-BA 13:185-207. Obr Comp 1948, 1:1195-1207. Obr Comp
      1967/1968, 1:1181-1193.

134

1917b Eine Kindheitserinnerung aus *Dichtung und Wahrheit*. (Presented to
10496 Vienna Psa Soc. First part, 13 Dec 1916; second part, 18 Apr 1917)
Imago 1917, 5(2):49-57. SKSN 1918, 4:564-577. GS 1924, 10:357-368.
Dichtung und Kunst 1924, 87-98. GW 1947, 12:15-26.

A childhood recollection from *Dichtung und Wahrheit*. (Tr:CJMH)
CP 1925, 4:357-367. (Revised tr:JS) SE 17:147-156.

Fr: Un souvenir d'enfance dans "Fiction et Vérité" de Goethe. (Tr: Marty,
Mme. E. & MB) In *Essais de psychanalyse appliquée*, Paris: Gallimard
1933, 149-162; 1971, 149-161.

Heb: Sichron yaldut mitoch "Shira veemet" legate (Goethe). Kitvei 2, chap. 6.

It: Un ricordo di infanzia tratto da "poesia e verità" di Goethe. Opere 9.
In *Saggi sull'arte, la letteratura e il linguaggio*, Turin: Boringhieri 1969,
vol. 1.

Jap: Shisaku to shinjutsu ni arawareta Géte no shōniki kioku. (Tr: Shinoda,
H. & Hamano, O.) In *Geijutsu no bunseki*, CW-Ars 1933.

Gete no yōjiki kioku. (Tr:KO) In *Bunseki geijutsu ron*, FCW-S 1931,
1937, 6:284-300.

"Shi to shinjutsu" no naka no yōnenjidai no ichi kioku. (Tr:YT) SelFr-K
1953, 7:18 p. Rev ed (Tr:YT & Ikeda, K.) SelFr-K 1970, 7:18 p.

"Shi to shinjutsu" chu no yōji jidai no ichi kioku. (Tr:YT) In *Sei no
seishin bunseki*, Tokyo: Kawade Shobō Shinsha 1957. SelFr-JinSh 1969,
3:9 p. (Tr: Kikumori, H.) Tokyo: Kawade Shobō Shinsha 1972, 10 p.

Por: Um recordação infantil de Goethe em "Poesia e Verdade." (Tr:ED)
Obr Comp-P 11:281-292.

Sp: Un recuerdo infantil de Goethe en "Poesía y Verdad." (Tr:LLBT)
Obr Comp 1948, 2:1037-1041. Obr Comp 1967/1968, 2:1128-1133.
(Tr:LR) Obr Comp-BA 18:139-150.

135

1910c Eine Kindheitserinnerung des Leonardo da Vinci. Leipzig/Vienna:
10497 Deuticke 1910, 71 p (Schriften zur angewandten Seelenkunde, 7). 2nd
ed, 1919, 76 p. 3rd ed, 1923, 78 p. GS 1925, 9:371-454. GW 1943,
8:128-211.

Leonardo da Vinci. A psychosexual study of infantile reminiscence.
(Tr:AAB) NY: Moffat, Yard 1916, 130 p. (Pref:EJ) London: Kegan
Paul 1922, v+130 p. NY: Dodd, Mead 1932, 138 p. NY: Norton 1964,
101 p.

Leonardo da Vinci and a memory of his childhood. (Tr: Tyson, A.)
SE 11:63-137.

Cz: Vzpomínka z dětství Leonarda da Vinci. (Tr: Kratochvíl, L.) Prague:
Orbis 1933, 135 p.

Fr: Un souvenir d'enfance de Léonard de Vinci. (Tr:MB) *Les Documents Bleus*, (32) Paris: Gallimard 1927, 216 p, 1952, 217 p.

Gr: Paidiki ilikia toy nta sintsi. (Tr: Franghias, A.) Athens: Atlas 1955.

Heb: Sichron yaldut shel Leoanardo da Vinci. Kitvei 2, chap. 7.

It: Un ricordo d'infanzia di Leonardo da Vinci. Opere 6. In *Saggi sull'arte, la letteratura e il linguaggio*, Turin: Boringhieri 1969, vol. 1.

Jap: Reonarudo dabinchi no seishin bunseki. (Tr: Yasuda, T.) In *Geijutsu to seishinbunseki*, Tokyo: Logos 1929, 3-112.

Reonarudo no yōjiki kioku. (Tr:KO) In *Bunseki geijutsu ron*, FCW-S 1931, 1937, 6:160-206. (Tr: Shinoda, H. & Hamano, O.) In *Geijutsu no bunseki*, Tokyo: Ars 1933.

Reonarudo dabinchi no yōnenki no ichi kioku. (Tr:YT) In *Geijutsu ron*, SelFr-K 1953, 7:110 p. Rev ed (Tr:YT & Ikeda, K.) SelFr-K 1970, 7:118 p.

(Tr:YT) SelFr-JinSh 1969, 3:58 p. (Tr: Kikumori, H.) Tokyo: Kawade Shobō Shinsha Pr 1972, 69 p.

Jug: Jedna uspomena iz detinjstva Leonarda da Vinčija. (Tr: Matić, V.; Jeretić, V.; & Bogičević, D.) In *Iz kulture i umetnosti*, [Collected Works, vol. 5] Novi Sad: Matica Srpska 1969.

Por: Uma recordação de infância de Leonardo de Vinci. (Tr:ED) Obr Comp-P 11:5-82. Rio de Janeiro: Delta.

Rus: Leonardo da Vinchi. (Tr: E.S.G.) Moskva: Izd. Kn-va Sovremennyia problemy 1912, 119 p.

Leonardo da-Vinchi. Vospominaniia dietstva. Sanktpeterburg: Prometeĭ 1912, 98 p.

Sp: Un recuerdo infantil de Leonardo de Vinci. (Tr:LLBT) Obr Comp-Madrid 8:241-334. Obr Comp-BA 8:169-236. Obr Comp 1948, 2:365-402. Obr Comp 1967/1968, 2:457-494.

136

1913l   Kindheitsträume mit spezieller Bedeutung. Z 1913, 1:79. (Continuation
10498   of "Paragraph in *Offener Sprechsaal*" [178].) Included in *Aus der Geschichte einer infantilen Neurose* [113] q.v. for other languages.

Childhood dreams of special importance. (Tr:JS) SE 17:4.

137

1937d   Konstruktionen in der Analyse. Z 1937, 23(4):459-469. GW 1950, 16:
10499   43-56.

Constructions in analysis. (Tr:JS) J 1938, 19(4):377-387. (Revised tr:JS) CP 1950, 3:358-371. Psa Clin Interpret, 65-78. (Corrected tr:JS) SE 23:257-269.

It: Costruzioni nell'analisi. Opere 11.

Jap: Bunseki gihō ni okeru kōsei no shigoto. (Tr: Kosawa, H.) In *Seishin-bunseki ryōhō*, SelFr-K 1959, 15:217-236. Rev ed (Tr: Okonogi, K.) SelFr-K 1969, 15:20 p.

Sp: Construcciones en el análisis. (Tr:LR) Obr Comp-BA 21:353-368. Obr Comp 1967/1968, 3:573-584.

138

1895f Zur Kritik der "Angstneurose." Wien klin Rdsch 1895, 9(27, 7 July):
10504 cols 417-419; (28, 14 July):cols 435-437; (29, 21 July):cols 451-452. SKSN 1906, 1:94-111. 2nd ed, 1911. 3rd ed, 1920. 4th ed, 1922. GS 1925, 1:343-362. GW 1952, 1:357-376.
Abs Inhalts wiss Arb 33.

A reply to criticisms on the anxiety-neurosis. (Tr:JR) CP 1924, 1: 107-127.

A reply to criticisms of my paper on anxiety neurosis. (Revised tr:JS) SE 3:123-139.
Abs (Tr:JS) SE 3:252.

It: A proposito di una critica della "nevrosi d'angoscia." (Tr: Campione, A.) Opere 2:177-194.

Por: Crítica da neurose de angústia. (Tr:CMdeF) Obr Comp-P 2:229-250.

Sp: Crítica de las neurosis de angustia. (Tr:LLBT) Obr Comp-Madrid 11:214-235. Obr Comp-BA 11:159-174. Obr Comp 1948, 1:212-219. Obr Comp 1967/1968, 1:211-218.

139

1908d Die "kulturelle" Sexualmoral und die moderne Nervosität. Mutterschutz
10505 (neue Folge): Sexual-Probleme 1908, 4(3, Mar):107-129. SKSN 1909, 2:175-196. 2nd ed, 1912. 3rd ed, 1921. GS 1924, 5:143-167. Sexual-theorie und Traumlehre 1931, 17-42. GW 1941, 7:143-167.

Modern sexual morality and modern nervousness. (Incomplete) Amer J Urol 1915, 11:391-405.

"Civilized" sexual morality and modern nervousness. (Tr:EBH & ECM) CP 1924, 2:76-99. In *The case of Dora and other papers*, NY: Norton 1952.

"Civilized" sexual morality and modern nervous illness. (Revised tr:JS) SE 9:181-204.

Dut: De sexueele beschavingsmoraal als oorzaak der moderne zenuwzwakte. (Tr: Stärcke, A.) Baarn: Hollandia Drukkerij 1914, 9-32.

Fr: La morale sexuelle civilisée et la maladie nerveuse des temps moderne. (Tr: Berger, D.) In *La vie sexuelle*, Paris: PUF 1969, 28-46.

It: La morale sessuale "civile" e il nervosismo moderno. (Tr: Dogana, M.) In *Il disagio della civiltà e altri saggi*, Turin: Boringhieri 1971. Opere 5: 411-432.

Il nervosismo moderno. In Zolla, E. *La psicanalisi*, Milan: Garzanti 1960, 223-241.

Jap: (Tr: Kimura, K.) CW-Ars n.d., 5. Bummeiteki sei dōtoku to kindai no shinkeibyō. (Tr:KO) In *Bunseki renai ron*, FCW-S 1932, 9:65-98.

"Bunkateki" moraru to gendai no shinkeishitsu. (Tr: Yasuda, T. & Yasuda, I.) In *Sei to aijō no shinri*, Tokyo: Kadaokawa Shoten 1955. (Tr: Imura, T. & YT) In *Sei no seishin bunseki*, Tokyo: Kawade Shobō Shinsha 1957.

"Bunkateki" sei dōtoku to gendaijin no shinkei kabin. (Tr:YT) In *Aijō no shinrigaku*, SelFr-K 1960, 14:36 p.

Por: A moral sexual "cultural" e o nervosismo moderno. (Tr:OG & MG) Obr Comp-P 5:115-138.

Rus: "Kul'turnaia" seksual'naia moral' i sovremennaia nervoznost'. In *Psikhologicheskie ètiudy. Biblioteka "Psikhoterapiia"* no. 1. Izd. 2-e. Moskva: Red. zhurnala "Psikhoterapiia" 1912, 55 p.

Sp: La moral sexual "cultural" y la nervosidad moderna. (Tr:LLBT) Obr Comp-BA 13:27-46. Obr Comp 1948, 1:954-964. Obr Comp 1967/1968, 1:943-953.

Tur: (Tr: Hilav, S.) In *Ciniyet ve psikanaliz*, Istanbul: Varlik Yayinevi 1963.

140

1915g [Letter to Dr. Frederik van Eeden, 28 Dec 1914.] In De Amsterdammer
(1914) 1915, No. 1960 (17 Jan):3.
10512

Jones 2. (Tr:JS) SE 14:301-302.

141

1929b Lettre à Maxime Leroy sur "Quelques rêves de Descartes." [First
10419 published in French] In Leroy, M. *Descartes, le philosophe au masque*, Paris: Editions Rieder 1929, 1:89-90. With title *Descartes, l'homme au masque*, Paris: Editions Rieder 1930, 1:89-90.

Brief an Maxime Leroy: über einen Traum des Cartesius. GS 1934, 12:403-405. GW 1948, 14:558-560.

Some dreams of Descartes'. A letter to Maxime Leroy. (Tr: Richards, A.) SE 21:203-204.

No German text extant.

It: Un sogno di Cartesio: lettera a Maxime Leroy. In Robert, M. *La rivoluzione psicoanalitica*, Turin: Boringhieri 1967, 335. Opere 10.

Sp: Carta a Maxim Leroy sobre un sueño de Descartes. (Tr:LR) Obr Comp-BA 19:203-208. Obr Comp 1967/1968, 3:137-138.

142

1931a Über libidinöse Typen. Z 1931, 17(3):313-316. Almanach 1933, 1932:
10525 9-13. GS 1934, 12:115-119. GW 1948, 14:509-513.

Libidinal types. (Tr: Jackson, E. B.) Q 1932, 1(1):3-6. (Tr:JRiv) J 1932, 13(3):277-280. CP 1950, 5:247-251. (Corrected tr:JS) SE 21:217-220.

Fr: Des types libidinaux. (Tr: Berger, D.) In *La vie sexuelle*, Paris: PUF 1969, 156-159.

It: Tipi libidici. (Tr: Campione, A.; Candreva, S.; Montinari, M.; CLM; & Sagittario, E.) In *La vita sessuale*, Turin: Boringhieri 1970. Opere 11.

Jap: (Tr: Kakeda, K.) SelFr-K 1953, 5:10 p. (Tr: Kakeda, K. & Shimura, H.) SelFr-JinSh 1969, 5:4 p.

Sp: Sobre los tipos libidinales. (Tr:LR) Obr Comp-BA 21:273-278. Obr Comp 1967/1968, 3:514-517.

143

1937a Lou Andreas-Salomé (obituary). Z 1937, 23(1):5. GW 1950, 16:270.
10526

Lou Andreas-Salomé. (Tr:JS) SE 23:297-298.

It: Necrologio di Lou Andreas-Salomé. Opere 11.

Sp: En memoria de Lou Andreas-Salomé. (Tr:LR) Obr Comp-BA 20: 222-224. Obr Comp 1967/1968, 3:338.

144

1939a Der Mann Moses und die monotheistische Religion: Drei Abhandlungen.
(1937- Amsterdam: Verlag Allert de Lange 1939, 241 p. GW 1950, 16:101-246.
1939) Includes *Moses ein Ägypter* [155]; *Wenn Moses ein Ägypter war* ...
10527 [254]. Section C, Part II [Read by Anna Freud at Paris International Psycho-Analytic Congress, 2 Aug 1938]; with title: "Der Fortschritt in der Geistigkeit," Z 1939, 24(1/2):6-9.

Moses and monotheism. (Tr: Jones, K.) London: HPI 1939, 223 p. NY: Knopf 1939, viii+218 p. (Tr:JS) SE 23:7-137.

Dut: Moses en het monotheisme. (Tr: Houwaard, C.) Amsterdam: G. W. Breughel 1947, 186 p.

Fr: Moïse et le monothéisme. (Tr:AB) Paris: Gallimard 1948, 208 p.; 1967, 186 p.

Gr: O Moissis kai o monotheismos. (Tr: Meranaios, C.) Athens: Maris 1942.

Hun: Mózes és az egyistenhit. (Tr: Ozorai, G.) Budapest: Biblioteca 1946, 189 p.

It: Mosè e il monoteismo: tre saggi. (Tr: Ballardini, A.) Milan: L. Pepe Diaz 1952, 219 p. Opere 11.

Jap: Ningen Mose to ichi shinkyō. (Tr: Doi, M. & Yoshida, M.) In *Genso no mirai*, SelFr-K 1955, 8:218 p.

Sp: Moisés y la religión monoteísta. (Tr:LR) Obr Comp-BA 20:7-132. Obr Comp 1967/1968, 3:181-286.

Sw: Moses och monoteismen. Tre avhandlingar. (Tr: Törngren, P. H.) Stockholm: Bonniers 1939, 187 p.

145

1913h Der Mantel als Symbol. Erf Beisp Psa Prx [89] no. 10. Z 1913, 1:377-382.
10528 GS 1925, 3:73. GW 1942, 2-3:361.

Overcoat as symbol. In *The interpretation of dreams*. (Tr:JS) SE 5:365.
SE 13:196.

FOR OTHER LANGUAGES, see under *Der Traumdeutung* [227].

146

1913d Märchenstoffe in Träumen. Z 1913, 1(2):147-151. SKSN 1918, 4:
10529 168-176. GS 1925, 3:259-266. Traumlehre 1925, 3-10. Sexualtheorie
und Traumlehre 1931, 308-315. GW 1946, 10:2-9. 2nd example in [113].

The occurrence in dreams of material from fairy tales. (Tr:JS) CP 1925,
4:236-243. SE 12:281-287.

Heb: Motivim mebdayot bachalomot. Kitvei 3, chap. 13.

It: Materiale fiabesco nei sogni. Opere 7.

Jap: Yume ni okeru dōwa no yōso. (Tr: Ishinaka, S.) In *Sensō to shi no
seishinbunseki*, CW-Ars 1932, 14:223-234.

Yume to dowa. (Tr:KO) In *Bunseki geijutsu ron*, FCW-S 1931, 6:
354-364.

(Tr: Kikumori, H.) Tokyo: Kawade Shobō Shinsha Pr 1972, 7 p.

Sp: Sueños con temas de cuentos infantiles. (Tr:LR) Obr Comp-BA 19:
125-134. Obr Comp 1967/1968, 3:88-93.

147

1921c Massenpsychologie und Ich-Analyse. Leipzig/Vienna/Zurich: Int Psa
10530 Verlag 1921, iii+140 p. 2nd ed, 1923, iv+120 p. GS 1925, 6:261-349.
Theoretische Schriften 1931, 248-337. GW 1940, 13:71-161.

Group psychology and the analysis of the ego. (Tr:JS) London/Vienna:
Int Psa Pr 1922, viii+134 p. London: HPI; NY: Liveright 1940. (Revised
tr:JS) SE 18:69-143. *Major Works* 664-696. NY: Bantam Books 1960,
xvii+108 p. Extracts in Rickman, J. (ed) *A general selection from the
works of Sigmund Freud*, London: HPI 1937, 195-244.

Dut: Het ik en de psychologie der massa. (Tr: Suchtelen, N. van) Amsterdam:
Wereldbibliotheek 1924, 1932, 1947, 1948, 1952, 1954, 1957, 95 p.

Fr: Psychologie collective et analyse du moi. (Tr: Jankélévitch, S.) Paris:
Payot 1924, 1950. In *Essais de psychanalyse*, Paris: Payot 1927, 1948,
1951, 1963, 76-162.(Revised tr: Hesnard, A.) Paris: Payot 1970, 83-175.

Gr: Psychologia omadiki kai analysis tou ego. (Tr: Athanassopoulos, G.)
Athens: Elefteroudaki 1925.

Omadiki kai atomiki psychologhia. (Tr: Panaglos, A.) Athens: Gavotsis
1934; Maris 1949.

Omadiki psychologhia kai analissis tou ego. (Tr: Franghias, A.) Athens: Atlas 1957.

Heb: Hapsichologia shel hehamon vehaanalisa shel haani. (Tr: Dvossis, I.) Jerusalem 1928, 84 p. (Tr: Baer, A.) Kitvei 5, 19-77.

It: Psicologia delle masse e analisi dell'Io. (Tr: Barbaro, U.) In *Nuovi saggi di psicoanalisi,* Rome: O.E.T. 1946. (Tr: Panaitescu, E. A.) In *Il disagio della civiltà e altri saggi,* Turin: Boringhieri 1971. Opere 9.

Jap: Shūdan shinri to jiga no bunseki. (Tr: Imura, T.) In *Jiga ron,* SelFr-K 1929, 4:85-189. Rev ed SelFr-K 1970, 4:106 p. (Tr: Hasegawa, M.) In *Kaisō-shūkyō-bummei,* FCW-S 1931, 3:3-133.

Shūdan shinrigaku to jiga no bunseki. (Tr: Kubo, Y.) In *Kaikan gensoku higan,* CW-Ars 1930, 6:91-208.

(Tr: Okonogi, K.) SelFr-JinSh 1970, 6:59 p.

Por: Psicologia das massas e análise do eu. (Tr:OG, IsIz, & MG) Obr Comp-P 9:7-108.

Rus: Psikhologiia mass i analiz chelovecheskogo "IA". (Tr: Kogan, IA. M.) In *Nauchnaia biblioteka "Sovremennykh problem,"* Moskva: Kn-vo "Sovremennye problemy" 1925, 98 p.

Sp: Psicología de las masas. (Tr:LLBT) Obr Comp-Madrid 9:3-106. Obr Comp-BA 9:7-90. Obr Comp 1948, 1:1141-1180. Obr Comp 1967/1968, 1:1127-1166. Madrid: Alianza Editorial 1969.

Yid: Die psichologie fun die massen un der analise fun mentschlechen "ich." (Tr: Lerman, S.) Warsaw: M. Jeruchamsohn 1928, 113 p.

148

1940c Das Medusenhaupt. Z 1940, 25:105-106. GW 1941, 17:47-48.
(1922)
10531

Medusa's head. (Tr:JS) J 1941, 22:69-70. CP 1950, 5:105-106. SE 18: 273-274. Includes translation of [105].

It: La testa di Medusa. Opere 9.

Sp: La cabeza de Medusa. (Tr:LR) Obr Comp-BA 21:51-54. Obr Comp 1967/1968, 3;385-386.

149

1906a Meine Ansichten über die Rolle der Sexualität in der Ätiologie der
(1905) Neurosen. In Löwenfeld, L. *Sexualleben und Nervenleiden,* Wiesbaden:
10532 Bergmann 1906 (4th ed); 1914 (5th ed), 313-322. SKSN 1906, 1:225-234. GS 1924, 5:123-133. GW 1942, 5:149-159.

My views on the role of sexuality in the etiology of the neuroses. (Tr: AAB) SPH 1909, 186-193. 1912. 1920. In *Major Works* 1952, 111-115.

My views on the part played by sexuality in the aetiology of the neuroses. (Tr: Bernays, J.) CP 1924, 1:272-283. (Tr:JS) SE 7:271-279.

It: Le mie opinioni sul ruolo della sessualità nell'etiologia delle nevrosi. (Tr:CLM) In *Freud con antologia freudiana*, Turin: Boringhieri 1959, 1970. Opere 5:217-228. (Tr: Campione, A.; Candreva, S.; Montinari, M.; CLM; & Sagittario, E.) In *La vita sessuale*, Turin: Boringhieri 1970.

Jap: Shūdan shinri to jiga no bunsekigaku zenshū. (Tr: Hasegawa, S. & KO) In *Shakai, shūkyō, bunmei*, Tokyo: Shunyodo 1931, 361 p.

Por: A sexualidade na etiologia das neuroses. (Tr:CMdeF) Obr Comp-P 2:47-64. (Tr:OG & MG) Obr Comp-P 5:103-114.

Sp: La sexualidad en la etiologia da las neurosis. (Tr:LLBT) Obr Comp-BA 12:185-204. Obr Comp-BA 13:9-18. Obr Comp 1948, 1:146-156, Obr Comp 1948, 1:949-953. Obr Comp 1967/1968, 1:146-156. Obr Comp 1967/1968, 1:939-942.

150

1932c Meine Berührung mit Josef Popper-Lynkeus. In "Festschrift des Vereines"
10533 (Gedenknummer zum zehnjährigen Todestag von Josef Popper-Lynkeus), Allgemeine Nährpflicht, Vienna 1932, 15. Psa B 1932, 4:113-118. GS 1934, 12:415-420. GW 1950, 16:261-266.

My contact with Josef Popper-Lynkeus. (Tr:JS) J 1942, 23(2):85-87. CP 1950, 5:295-301. (Revised) SE 22:219-224.

It: I miei rapporti con Josef Popper-Lynkeus. Opere 11.

Sp: Mi relación con Josef Popper-Lynkeus. (Tr:LR) Obr Comp-BA 19: 209-216. Obr Comp 1967/1968, 3:139-143.

151

1955c Memorandum on the electrical treatment of war neurotics. [Published in
(1920) English] A memorandum written to the Kommission zur Erhebung
10474 militärischer Pflichtverletzungen (Commission for Enquiry into Violations of Military Duty). Dated by Freud: Vienna, 23 Feb 1920. Official stamp of the Commission shows receipt of the memorandum on 25 Feb 1920. (Tr:JS) SE 17:211-215. J 1956, 37:16-18.

Gutachten über die elektrische Behandlung der Kriegsneurotiker von Prof. Dr. Sigm. Freud, Wien, 23.2.20. [The heading, in Freud's handwriting, on the original document.] Original German text unpublished.

It: Promemoria sul trattamenti elettico dei nevrotici gi guerra. Opere 9.

Sp: Informe sobre la electroterapia de los neuróticos de guerra. Rev Psicoanál 1956, 13:277-280.

152

1917d Metapsychologische Ergänzung zur Traumlehre. Z 1917, 4(6):277-287.
(1915) SKSN 1918, 4:339-355. 2nd ed, 1922. GS 1924, 5:520-534. Technik und
10534 Metapsychol 1924, 242-256. Theoretische Schriften 1931, 141-156. GW 1946, 10:412-426.

Metapsychological supplement to the theory of dreams. (Tr: CMB) CP 1925, 4:137-151. (Tr: JS) SE 14:222-235.

Fr: Complément métapsychologique à la science des rêves. (Tr: MB & AB) In Métapsychologie, RFPsa 1936, 9(1):90-102. Paris: Gallimard 1940, 162-188.

Complément métapsychologique à la théorie des rêves. (Tr: JLa & Pontalis, J. B.) In Métapsychologie, Paris: Gallimard 1968, 125-146.

Heb: Hashlama meta-psichologit leinyan torat hachalom. Kitvei 4, chap. 10.

It: Integrazione metapsicologica della dottrine del sogno. (Tr: Veltri, P.) Riv Psa 1956, 2:91-100.

Supplemento metapsicologico alla teoria del sogno. Opere 8.

Jap: Yumegaku ni kansuru chōishiki shinrigakuteki hosoku. (Tr: Hayashi, T.) In Chōishiki shinrigaku, CW-Ars 1932, 13:120-166.

Por: Adendo metapsicológicao à teoria dos sonhos. (Tr: CMdeF & IsIz) Obr Comp-P 8:221-234.

Rus: (Tr: MV) In Osnovnye psikhologicheskie teorii v psikhoanalize. Psikholog i psikhoanal, vyp. III, 206 p.

Sp: Adición metapsychológica a la teoría de los sueños. (Tr: LLBT) Obr Comp 1948, 1:1081-1086. Obr Comp 1967/1968, 1:1069-1074.

153

1924h   Mitteilung des Herausgebers. Z 1924, 10:373.
10535

Announcement by the Director: editorial changes in the Zeitschrift. (Tr: JS) SE 19:293.

It: Communicazione del direttore sui mutamenti nella direzione della "Zeitschrift." Opere 10.

154

1915f   Mitteilung eines der psychoanalytischen Theorie widersprechenden
10536   Falles von Paranoia. Z 1915, 3(6):321-329. SKSN 1918, 4:125-138. 2nd ed, 1922. GS 1924, 5:288-300. Psychoanalyse der Neurosen 1926, 23-37. Neurosenlehre und Technik 1931, 23-36. GW 1946, 10:234-246.

A case of paranoia running counter to the psychoanalytical theory of the disease. (Tr: EG) CP 1924, 2:150-161.

A case of paranoia running counter to the psycho-analytic theory of the disease. (Revised tr: JS) SE 14:263-272.

The woman who felt persecuted. In Greenwald, H. Great cases in psychoanalysis, NY: Ballantine 1959, 25-37.

Fr: Un cas de paranoïa qui contredisait la théorie psychanalytique de cette affection. (Tr: Jury, P.) RFPsa 1935, 8(1):2-11.

Communication d'un cas de paranoïa en contradiction avec la théorie psychanalytique. (Tr: Guérineau, D.) In *Névrose, psychose et perversion*. Paris: PUF 1973, 209-218.

It: Communicazione di un caso di paranoia in contrasto con la teoria psicoanalitica. Opere 8.

Jap: Seishinbunsekigaku setsu ni haichiseru paranoia shō no furei. (Tr: Konuma, M.) In *Ijō seiyoku bunseki*, CW-Ars 1933, 15:82-100.

Por: Communicação de um caso de paranóia que contradiz a teoria psicanalítica. (Tr:OG & MG) Obr Comp-P 5:233-244.

Sp: Communicación de un caso de paranoia contrario a la teoría psicoanalítica. (Tr:LLBT) Obr Comp-BA 13:141-150. Obr Comp 1948, 1:1006-1010. Obr Comp 1967/1968, 1:994-998.

155

1937b   Moses ein Ägypter. Imago 1937, 23(1):5-13. Almanach 1938, 1937:
10537   9-22. Part I of *Der Mann Moses und die monotheistische Religion* 9-25. GW 1950, 16:103-113.

Moses an Egyptian. (Tr: Jones, K.) J 1938, 19(3):291-298. (Tr:JS) SE 23:7-16.

Cz: Czechosl psa annual 1948.

Fr: Un Égyptien: Moïse. (Tr:AB) Part I of *Moïse et le monothéisme*, Paris: Gallimard 1967, 5-19.

Sp: Moisés, egipcio. (Tr:LR) Obr Comp-BA 20:13-22. Obr Comp 1967/1968, 3:181-187.

FOR OTHER LANGUAGES, see under *Der Mann Moses und die monotheistische Religion* [144].

156

1914b   Der Moses des Michelangelo. Imago 1914, 3(1):15-36. (anonymously)
10538   GS 1924, 10:257-286. *Dichtung und Kunst* 1924, 29-58. GW 1946, 10:172-201. *See also* "Nachtrag zur Arbeit über den Moses des Michelangelo" [162].

The Moses of Michelangelo. (Tr:ASt) CP 1925, 4:257-287. (Corrected tr:JS) SE 13:211-236.

Fr: Le Moïse de Michel-Ange. (Tr: Marty, Mme. E.; revised:MB) RFPsa 1927, 1(1):120-147. In *Essais de psychanalyse appliquée*, Paris: Gallimard 1933, 1971, 9-41.

Heb: Moshe shel michael angelo. Kitvei 2, chap. 2.

It: Il Mosè di Michelangelo. (Tr: Servadio, E.) In Riv ital psicoanal 1932, 1:353-380. In *Saggi sull'arte, la letteratura e il linguaggio*, Turin: Boringhieri 1969, vol. 1. Opere 7. Naples: V. Idelson, 34 p.

Jap: Mikeruangero no Mōze. (Tr:KO) In *Bunseki geijutsu ron*, FCW-S 1931, 1937, 6:243-282. (Tr:YT) In *Geijutsu ron*, SelFr-K 1953, 7:42 p. Rev ed (Tr:YT & Ikeda, K.) SelFr-K 1970, 7:44 p.

Mikeranzero no mōzesu. (Tr: Shinoda, H. & Hamano, O.) In *Geijutsu no bunseki*, Tokyo: Ars 1933, 10. (Tr: Chino, S.) Tokyo: Ars, 10.

(Tr:YT) SelFr-JinSh 1969, 3:22 p. (Tr: Kikumori, H.) Tokyo: Kawade Shobō Shinsha Pr 1972, 26 p.

Jug: Mikelandelo v Mojsije. (Tr: Matić, V.; Jeretić, V.; & Bogičević, D.) In *Iz kulture i umetnosti*, [Collected Works, Vol 5] Novi Sad: Matica Srpska 1969.

Por: O "Moisés" de Miguel Ângelo. (Tr:ED) Obr Comp-P 11:147-176.

Rus: (Tr:MV) Moscow: Staatsverlag.

Sp: El "Moisés" de Miguel Angel. (Tr:LLBT) Obr Comp 1948, 2:977-989. Obr Comp 1967/1968, 2:1069-1081. (Tr:LR) Obr Comp-BA 18:83-108.

157

1913f Das Motiv der Kästchenwahl. Imago 1913, 2(3):257-266. SKSN 1918,
10539 4:470-485. 2nd ed, 1922. GS 1924, 10:243-256. *Dichtung und Kunst* 1924, 15-28. GW 1946, 10:24-37.

The theme of the three caskets. (Tr:CJMH) CP 1925, 4:244-256. SE 12: 291-301. In Manheim, L. F. & Manheim, E. B. *Hidden patterns*, NY: Macmillan 1966, 79-92.

Fr: Le choix des trois coffrets. (Tr: Marty, Mme. E.; revised:MB) RFPsa 1927, 1(3):549-561. In *Essais de psychanalyse appliquée*, Paris: Gallimard 1933, 1971, 87-103.

Heb: Motiv bechirat hateva. Kitvei 2, chap. 5.

It: La fiaba dei tre scrigni. (Tr: Veltri, P.) Riv Psa 1958, 4:83-92.

Il motivo della scelta edgli scrigni. In *Saggi sull'arte, la letteratura e il linguaggio*, Turin: Boringhieri 1969, vol. 1. Opere 7.

Jap: Hakoerami no dōki. (Tr:KO) In *Bunseki geijutsu ron*, FCW-S 1931, 1937, 6:222-241.

Kobako erami no shushi. (Tr: Shinoda, H. & Hamano, O.) In *Geijutsu no bunseki*, Tokyo: Ars 1933.

Kobako erabi no mochifu. (Tr:YT) In *Geijutsu ron*, SelFr-K 1953, 7:22 p. SelFr-JinSh 1969, 3:10 p. Rev ed (Tr:YT & Ikeda, K.) SelFr-K 1970, 7:22 p.

(Tr: Kikumori, H.) Tokyo: Kawade Shobō Shinsha Pr 1972, 12.

Por: O tema de escolha do confrezinho. (Tr:ED) Obr Comp-P 11:133-146.

Sp: El tema de la elección de cofrecillo. (Tr:LLBT) Obr Comp 1948, 2: 971-976. (Tr:LR) Obr Comp-BA 18:69-82. Obr Comp 1967/1968, 2:1063-1068.

158

1916b Mythologische Parallele zu einer plastischen Zwangsvorstellung. Z 1916,

10540   4(2):110-111. SKSN 1918, 4:195-197. GS 1924, 10:240-242. GW 1946, 10:398-400.

A mythological parallel to a visual obsession. (Tr:CJMH) CP 1925, 4:345-346. (Revised) SE 14:337-338.

Fr: Parallèles mythologiques à une représentation obsessionnelle plastique. (Tr: Marty, Mme. E. & MB) In *Essais de psychanalyse appliquée*, Paris: Gallimard 1933, 1971, 83-85.

It: Parallelo mitologico con una rappresentazione ossessiva plastica. Opere 8.

Por: Um paralelo mitológico a uma representação obsessiva plástica. (Tr:ED) Obr Comp-P 11:129-132.

Sp: Símil mitólogica de una representación obsesiva plástica. (Tr:LR) Obr Comp-BA 18:135-138.

Un paralelo mitológico a una representación obsesiva plástica. (Tr: LLBT) Obr Comp 1948, 2:970. Obr Comp 1967/1968, 2:1062.

159

1912h Nachfrage des Herausgebers über Kindheitsträume. C 1912, 2:680.
10540A
Request for examples of childhood dreams. (Tr:ASt & JS) SE 17:4.

160

1935a   Nachschrift 1935 zur *Selbstdarstellung*. Almanach 1936, 1935:9-14.
10541 In *Selbstdarstellung*, 2nd ed, Vienna: Int Psa Verlag 1936, 102-107. London: HPI 1946, 102-107. GW 1950, 16:31-34. See *Selbstdarstellung* [209].

Postscript 1935 to *An autobiographical study*. (Tr:JS) In *An autobiographical study*, London: HPI 1935. SE 20:71-74.

Fin: Omaelämäkerrallinen tutkielma. (Tr: Nousiainen, P. & Nousiainen, T.) Helsinki: Kustannusosakeyhtiö Otava 1962.

It: La finezza di un'azione sbagliata. (Tr: Flescher, J.) Rome: Editrice Scienza Moderna 1948. Opere 11.

Sp: Apéndice al "Estudio autobiográfico." (Tr:LR) Obr Comp-BA 21: 305-310. Obr Comp 1967/1968, 3:535-537.

161

1922c   Nachschrift zur Analyse des kleinen Hans. Z 1922, 8(3):321. GS 1924,
10542 8:264-265. *Vier Krankengeschichten* 1932, 282-283. GW 1940, 13: 431-432. See "Analyse der Phobie eines fünfjährigen Knaben" [45].

Postscript (1922) to "Analysis of a phobia in a five-year-old boy." (Tr:ASt & JS) CP 1925, 3:288-289. SE 10:148-149.

Fr: Épilogue (1922) à l'analyse du petit Hans. (Tr:MB) In *Cinq psychanalyses*, Paris: PUF 1954, 1970, 198.

Por: Apêndice: análise da fobia de um minino de cinco anos. (Tr:OG) Obr Comp-P 15:265.

Sp: Apéndice al análisis de Juanito. (Tr:LR) Obr Comp-BA 21:191-194. Obr Comp 1967/1968, 3:481.

162

1927b Nachtrag zur Arbeit über den Moses des Michelangelo. Imago 1927,
10544 13(4):552-553. GS 1928, 11:409-410. GW 1948, 14:321-322. See "Der Moses des Michelangelo" [156].

Postscript to my paper on the Moses of Michelangelo. (Tr:ASt) J 1951, 32:94. (Corrected tr:JS) SE 13:237-238.

Fr: Appendice 1927. (Tr: Marty, Mme. E.; revised:MB) RFPsa 1927, 1(1):148. In Essais de psychanalyse appliquée, Paris: Gallimard 1933, 41-42; 1971, 43-44.

Heb: Nispach lemoshe shel Michael angelo. Kitvei 2, chap. 3.

Sp: Apéndice al estudio sobre el Moisés de Miguel Angel. (Tr:LR) Obr Comp-BA 18:109-110.

163

1912a Nachtrag zu dem autobiographisch beschriebenen Fall von Paranoia
(1911) (Dementia paranoides). [Read at 3rd Psa Congress, Weimar, Sept 1911].
10543 Y 1912, 3(2):588-590. SKSN 1913, 3:267-270. GS 1924, 8:432-435. Vier Krankengeschichten 1932, 460-463. GW 1943, 8:317-320. See "Psychoanalytische Bemerkungen über einen autobiographisch beschriebenen Fall von Paranoia (Dementia paranoides)" [192].

Postscript to the case of paranoia. (Tr:ASt & JS) CP 1925, 3:467-470. SE 12:80-82.

Fr: Appendice (1912) à l'autobiographie d'un cas de paranoïa. (Tr:MB & RL) In Cinq psychanalyses, Paris: PUF 1954, 1970, 321-324.

164

1911a Nachträge zur Traumdeutung. C 1911, 1:187-192. Without the intro-
10545 ductory paragraphs which were never reprinted in German. In Die Traumdeutung 1911 (3rd ed). GS 1925, 3:77 ff. GW 1942, 2-3:365-370, 412-413.

Additions to the interpretation of dreams. (Tr:AAB) The interpretation of dreams, 3rd ed, London: Allen & Unwin, 341-346, 382-383. Complete paper, including the unreprinted portions. (Tr:JS) SE 5:360-366, 408-409.

Fr: Suppléments à l'interprétation des rêves. (Tr: Meyerson, I.; revised tr: Berger, D.) In L'interprétation des rêves, Paris: PUF 1967, 309-314, 349-350.

FOR OTHER LANGUAGES, see under "Die Traumdeutung" [227].

165

1927a   Nachwort zur *Frage der Laienanalyse.* Z 1927, 13(3):326-332. GS 1928,
10546   11:385-394. GW 1948, 14:287-296. See *Die Frage der Laienanalyse*
[107].

Concluding remarks on the question of lay analysis. J 1927, 8(3):392-398.

Postscript to a discussion on lay analysis (Tr:JS) CP 1950, 5:205-214.
(Revised tr:JS) SE 20:251-258.

Jap: (Tr: Kimura, K. & Naito, K.) In *Shirō to bunseki no mondai*, CW-Ars
1933, 12:68-184.

Hiimono no bunseki kahi no mondai no fugen. (Tr:KO) In *Bunseki
byōhō ron*, FCW-S 1932, 8:322-334.

Sp: Apéndice a la discusión sobre "El análisis profano." (Tr:LR) Obr Comp-
BA 21:227-236. Obr Comp 1967/1968, 3:498-504.

166

1933a   Neue Folge der Vorlesungen zur Einführung in die Psychoanalyse.
(1932)   Vienna: Int Psa Verlag 1933, 255 p. GS 1934, 12:149-345. GW 1940,
10547   15:iv+207 p. Part of Lectures 30 and 31: Almanach 1933, 1932:9-30;
35-58. Part of Lecture 34: Psa B 1932, 4:481-497.

New introductory lectures on psycho-analysis. (Tr: Sprott, W. J. H.)
London: HPI 1933, xi+240 p. NY: Norton 1933, xi+257 p. In *Major
Works* 1952, 807-884. (Tr:JS) SE 22:5-182. NY: Norton 1965, 202 p.
In *The complete introductory lectures on psychoanalysis*, NY: Norton
1966. Lecture 30: "Dreams and occultism" in Devereux, G. *Psycho-
analysis and the occult*, NY: IUP 1953, 91-109.

Chin: Ching shen fen hsi ying shin pien. (Tr: Fu, Kao Chio) Shanghai: The
Commercial Press 1933, 179 p.

Dan: Nye forelaesninger til indføring i psykoanalysen. (Tr: Boisen, M.)
Copenhagen: Hans Reitzel 1959, 1966, 152 p.

Fin: In *Johdatus psykoanalyysiin.* (Tr: Puranen, E.) Jyväskylä: K. J.
Gummerus Osakeyhtiö 1964.

Fr: Nouvelles conférences sur la psychanalyse. (Tr:AB) Paris: Gallimard
1936, 1952, 249 p. 1971, 243 p.

Gr: Ypostasis tis psychikis prossopikotitos. (Tr: Meranaios, C.) Athens:
Koronzis 1944.

Heb: Mavo lepsichoanalisa—sidra chadasha. (Tr: Baer, A.) Kitvei 5, 185-322.
Excerpt in *Hatarbut vehadat*, Merchavia: Hakibut Haarzi 1943.

Hun: A lélekelemzés legujabb eredményei. (Tr: Lengyel, J.) Debrecen:
Pannonia nyomda 1943, 216 p.

It: Introduzione alla psicoanalisi: nuove lezioni. (Tr: Weiss, E.) Rome:
Cremonese 1934, 168 p. In *Introduzione allo studio della psicoanalisi
(prima serie e nuova serie)*, Rome: Astrolabio, 1947, 1965.

Introduzione alla psicoanalisi (nuova serie di lezioni). (Tr: Dogana, F. & Sagittario, E.) In *Introduzione alla psicoanalisi. Prima e seconda serie di lezioni*, Turin: Boringhieri 1969, 1970, 1972. Opere 11.

Jap: Zoku seishinbunseki nyūmon. (Tr: Kosawa, H.) SelFr-K 1953, 3:3-286 [contains lectures #29-#35]. (Tr: Kakeda, K. & YT) SelFr-JinSh 1971, 1:150 p.

Jug: Nova predavanja za uvodenje u psihoanalizu. (Tr: Jerotić, V. & Volf, N.) [Collected Works, Vol. 8] Novi Sad: Matica Srpska 1969.

Nor: Nytt i psykoanalysen. (Tr: Schjelderup, K.) Oslo: Gyldendal Norsk Forlag 1934, 194 p; 1967, 146 p.

Por: Novas contribuições à psicanálise. (Tr:GP) Obr Comp-P 17:5-192.

Sp: Nuevas aportaciones al psicoanálisis. Madrid: Biblioteca Nueva 1934. (Tr:LLBT) Obr Comp-Madrid 17:5-236. Obr Comp-BA 17:7-162. Obr Comp 1948, 2:787-874. Obr Comp 1967/1968, 2:879-966.

Sw: (Tr: Asker, A.) In *Orientering i psykoanalysen*, Stockholm: Natur och Kultur 1955.

167

1924b Neurose und Psychose. Z 1924, 10(1):1-5. GS 1924, 5:418-422. Psycho-
(1923) analyse der Neurosen 1926, 163-168. Neurosenlehre und Technik 1931,
10548 186-191. GW 1940, 13:387-391.

Neurosis and psychosis. (Tr:JRiv) CP 1924, 2:250-254. (Tr:JS) SE 19: 149-153.

Fr: Névrose et psychose. (Tr: Guérineau, D.) In *Névrose, psychose et perversion*. Paris: PUF 1973, 283-296.

It: Nevrosi e psicosi. (Tr:CLM) In *Freud con antologia freudiana*, Turin: Boringhieri 1959, 1970. Opere 9.

Jap: Shinkei-shō to seishinbyō. (Tr: Imura, T. & Katō, M.) In *Fuan no mondai*, SelFr-K 1955. Rev ed (Tr: Katō, M.) SelFr-K 1969, 10:8 p.

Por: Neurose e psicose. (Tr:OG & GP) Obr Comp-P 14:17-22.

Sp: Neurosis y psicosis. (Tr:LLBT) Obr Comp-Madrid 14:258-262. Obr Comp-BA 14:206-209. Obr Comp 1948, 2:407-408. Obr Comp 1967/ 1968, 2:499-500.

168

1912c Über neurotische Erkrankungstypen. C 1912, 2(6):297-302. SKSN 1913,
10549 3:306-313. GS 1924, 5:400-408. GW 1943, 8:322-330.

Types of neurotic nosogenesis. (Tr:ECM) CP 1924, 2:113-121. Excerpts in Rickman, J. (ed) *A general selection from the works of Sigmund Freud*, London: HPI 1937.

Types of onset of neurosis. (Tr:JS) SE 12:231-238.

Fr: Sur les types d'entrée dans la névrose. (Tr:JLa) In *Névrose, psychose et perversion*. Paris: PUF 1973, 175-182.

It: Modi tipici di ammalarsi nevrosamente. Opere 6.

Jap: Shinkeishō no hatsubyō no kata. (Tr: Imura, T. & Katō, M.) In *Fuan no mondai*, SelFr-K 1955. Rev ed (Tr: Katō, M.) SelFr-K 1969, 10:12 p.

Por: Sôbre os tipos de aquisição da neurose. (Tr:OG & MG) Obr Comp-P 5:211-220.

Rus: In Psikhoterapiia 1913, no. 5.

Sp: Sobre los tipos de adquisición de las neurosis. (Tr:LLBT) Obr Comp-Madrid 13:291-300. Obr Comp-BA 13:230-239. Obr Comp 1948, 1:997-1000. Obr Comp 1967/1968, 1:985-988.

169

1904d [Note on] "Magnetische Menschen." In Thomas, T., "Magnetische
10550 Menschen." Neue Freie Presse 1904, 6 Nov (Morgenblatt):10.

170

1912g A note on the unconscious in psycho-analysis. [In English] (Revised by
10551 Ernest Jones) Proceedings of the Society for Psychical Research 1912, 26(66):312-318. CP 1925, 4:22-29. In Rickman, J. (ed) *A general selection from the works of Sigmund Freud*. London: HPI 1937, 54-62. SE 12:260-266.

Einige Bemerkungen über den Begriff des Unbewussten in der Psychoanalyse. (Tr from English: Sachs, H.) Z 1913, 1(2):117-123. SKSN 1918, 4:157-167. 2nd ed, 1922. GS 1924, 5:433-442. Technik und Metapsychol 1924, 155-164. Theoretische Schriften 1931, 15-24. GW 1943, 8:430-439.

Fr: Quelques observations sur le concept d'inconscient en psychanalyse. (Tr:MB & AB) In *Métapsychologie*, RFPsa 1936, 9(1):22-28; Paris: Gallimard 1940, 9-24.

Note sur l'inconscient en psychanalyse. (Tr:JLa & Pontalis, J. B.) In *Métapsychologie*, Paris: Gallimard 1968, 175-187.

Heb: Hearot achadot al halo muda hapsichoanalisa. Kitvei 4, chap. 6.

It: Nota sull'inconscio in psicoanalisi. (Tr:CLM) In *Freud con antologia freudiana*, Turin: Boringhieri 1959, 1970. Opere 6.

Jap: Seishinbunsekigaku ni okeru muishiki no gainen. (Tr: Hayashi, T.) In *Chōishiki shinrigaku*, CW-Ars 1932, 13:3-14. (Tr: Okonogi, K.) SelFr-JinSh 1970, 6:7 p.

Por: Algumas observações sôbre o conceito do inconsciente na psicanálise. (Tr:CMdeF & IsIz) Obr Comp-P 8:129-138.

Rus: In Psikhoterapiia 1913, no. 5.

Sp: Algunas observaciones sobre el concepto de lo inconsciente en el psicoanálisis. (Tr:LLBT) Obr Comp-Madrid 9. Obr Comp-BA 9. Obr Comp 1948, 1:1043-1046. Obr Comp 1967/1968, 1:1031-1034.

171

1925a Notiz über den "Wunderblock." Z 1925, 11(1):1-5. GS 1925, 6:415-420.
(1924) Theoretische Schriften 1931, 392-398. GW 1948, 14:3-8.
10552
A note upon the "mystic writing-pad." (Tr:JS) J 1940, 21(4):469-474. CP 1950, 5:175-180. SE 19:227-232. (Tr, condensed, with comments: Rapaport, D.) Organ Path Thought 329-337.

Heb: Reshima al dafdefet hapele. Kitvei 4, chap. 13.

It: Nota sul "notes magico." Opere 10.

Por: O "bloco maravilhoso." (Tr:OG & GP) Obr Comp-P 14:37-42.

Sp: El "block maravilloso." (Tr:LLBT) Obr Comp-Madrid 14:277-282. Obr Comp-BA 14:221-225. Obr Comp 1948, 2:414-416. Obr Comp 1967/1968, 2:506-508.

172

1941b Notiz "III." GW 1941, 17:17-18.
(1892)
10553
Draft "III." (Tr:JS) CP 1950, 5:31-32. (Revised tr:JS) SE 1:149-150.

It: III. Opere 1:141-142.

Sp: Nota "III." (Tr:LR) Obr Comp-BA 21:24-26. Obr Comp 1967/1968, 3:368.

173

1895c Obsessions et phobies. Leur méchanisme psychique et leur étiologie.
(1894) [In French] Rev neurol 1895, 3(2, 30 Jan):33-38. SKSN 1906, 1:86-93.
10554 2nd ed, 1911. 3rd ed, 1920. 4th ed, 1922. GS 1925, 1:334-342. GW 1: 345-353. In Névrose, psychose et perversion. Paris: PUF 1973, 39-45.
Abs Inhalts wiss Arb 30.

Zwangsvorstellungen und Phobien. Ihr psychischer Mechanismus und ihre Ätiologie. (Tr: Schiff, A.) Wien klin Rdsch 1895, 9(17, 28 Apr): 262-263; (18, 5 May):276-278.

Obsessions and phobias. (Tr: Meyer, M.) CP 1924, 1:128-137. (Revised tr:JS) SE 3:74-84.
Abs (Tr:JS) SE 3:250.

It: Ossessioni e fobie: loro meccanismo psichico e loro etiologia. (Tr: Campione, A.) Opere 2:139-148.

Por: Obsessões e fobias. Seu mecanismo psíquico e sua etiologia. (Tr:CMdeF) Obr Comp-P 2:195-208.

Sp: Obsesiones y fobias: su mecanismo psíquico y su etiología. (Tr:LLBT)
Obr Comp-Madrid 11:185-195. Obr Comp-BA 11:137-144. Obr Comp
1948, 1:200-204. Obr Comp 1967/1968, 1:200-203.

174

1924c   Das ökonomische Problem des Masochismus. Z 1924, 10(2):121-133.
10555   GS 1924, 5:374-386. Psychoanalyse der Neurosen 1926, 147-162.
Neurosenlehre und Technik 1931, 193-207. GW 1940, 13:371-383.

The economic problem in masochism. (Tr:JRiv) CP 1924, 2:255-268.

The economic problem of masochism. (Tr:JS) SE 19:159-170.

Fr: Le problème économique du masochisme. (Tr: Pichon, E. & Hoesli, H.)
RFPsa 1928, 2(2):211-223. (Tr:JLa) In Névrose, psychose et perversion.
Paris: PUF 1973, 287-297.

It: Il problema economico del masochismo. Opere 10.

Jap: Mazohisumusu ni okeru ribido keizai no mondai. (Tr: Hayashi, T. &
Konuma, M.) In Ijō seiyoku no bunseki, CW-Ars 1933, 15.

Masokisumusu ron. (Tr:KO) In Bunseki renai ron, FCW-S 1932,
9:198-216.

Mazokisumu no kaizai-teki mondai. (Tr:YT) In Aijō no shinrigaku,
SelFr-K 1960, 14:20 p.

(Tr: Aoki, H.) SelFr-JinSh 1970, 6:10 p.

Por: O problema econômico do masoquismo. (Tr:OG & MG) Obr Comp-P
5:297.

Sp: El problema económico del masoquismo. (Tr:LLBT) Obr Comp-Madrid
13:263-276. Obr Comp-BA 13:208-218. Obr Comp 1948, 1:1036-1042.
Obr Comp 1967/1968, 1:1023-1030.

175

1912f   Zur Onanie-Diskussion. Einleitung; Schlusswort. In Die Onanie (Dis-
10556   kussionen der Wiener Psychoanalytischen Vereinigung, 2) Wiesbaden:
Bergmann 1912, iii-iv, 132-140. GS 1925, 3:324-337. Sexualtheorie und
Traumlehre 1931, 228-239. GW 1934, 8:332-345.

Masturbation. (Tr: Paul, E.) Medical Critic and Guide 1921, 24(Sept):
327-334. [Possibly pirated translation; omits Introduction.]

Contributions to a discussion on masturbation. (Introduction; Conclu-
sion) (Tr:JS) SE 12:243-254.

It: Contributi a una discussioni sull'onanismo. Opere 6.

Jap: Jiiron. (Tr:YT) In Aijō no shinrigaku, SelFr-K 1960, 14:22 p.

Sp: Contribuciones al simposio sobre la masturbación. (Tr:LR) Obr Comp-
BA 21:173-186. Obr Comp 1967/1968, 3:470-479.

176

1925c   To the opening of the Hebrew University. [First published in English.]
10557   The New Judea 1925, 1(14, 27 Mar):227. GS 1928, 11:298-299.
GW 1948, 14:556-557.

On the occasion of the opening of the Hebrew University. SE 19:292.
Quarterly Review of the Harefuah 1959, (4):115.

No German text extant.

It: In occasione dell'inaugurazione dell'Università ebraica. Opere 10.

Sp: Mensaje para la inauguración de la Universidad Hebrea. (Tr:LR) Obr
Comp-BA 19:258. Obr Comp 1967/1968, 3:176.

177

1955a   Original record of the case of obsessional neurosis (The Rat Man). [First
(1907-   published in English] (Tr:ASt & JS) SE 10:259-318.
1908)
10558
For German text see French below.

Fr: L'Homme aux rats. Journal d'une analyse. (Tr: Hawelka, E. R. &
Hawelka, P.) Paris: PUF 1974, 287 p. Includes German text and
contains, both in French and German, the first sessions omitted in SE.

178

[Paragraph on observations of coitus] in *Offener Sprechsaal* [Open
10559   Forum]. C 1912, 2:680.

(Tr:JS) SE 17:4.

179

1913h   Position beim Erwachen aus einem Traum. Erf Beisp Psa Prx [89] no. 4.
10560
Position when waking from a dream. (Tr:JS) SE 13:195.

180

1922d   Preisausschreibung. Z 1922, 8:527.
10568
Prize offer. (Tr:JS) SE 17:270.

181

1921d   Preiszuteilungen. Z 1921, 7:381.
10569
Award of prizes. (Tr:JS) SE 17:269-270.

182

1904e   Professor S. Hammerschlag: obituary. Neue Freie Presse 1904, 11 Nov
10570   (Morgenblatt):8.

Obituary of Professor S. Hammerschlag. (Tr: Richards, A.) SE 9: 255-256.

It: Necrologio del professor Samuel Hammerschlag. (Tr: Dogana, M. T.) In Noterelle sulla "Neue freie Presse" (1903-1904). Opere 4:421.

183

1890a Psychische Behandlung (Seelenbehandlung). In Kossmann, R. & Weiss, 10572 J. *Die Gesundheit, ihre Erhaltung, ihre Störung, ihre Wiederherstellung,* Stuttgart/Berlin/Leipzig: Union Deutsche Verlagsgesellschaft 1905, 1(6):368-384. Psa P 1937, 11:133-147. GW 1942, 5:289-315.

Psychical (or mental) treatment. (Tr:JS) SE 7:283-302.

It: Trattamento psichico (Trattamento dell'anima). (Tr: Luserna, E.) Opere 1:93-111.

Sp: Psicoterapie (tratamiento por el espíritu). (Tr:LR) Obr Comp-BA 21: 141-162. Obr Comp 1967/1968, 3:449-464.

184

1898b Zum psychischen Mechanismus der Vergesslichkeit. Mschr Psychiatr 10573 Neurol 1898, 4(6, Dec):436-443. GW 1952, 1:519-527.

The psychical mechanism of forgetfulness. (Tr:ASt) SE 3:289-297.

Heb: Leinyan hamechanism hanafshi shel hashachechanut. Kitvei 4, chap. 12.

It: Meccanismo psichico della dimenticanza. (Tr: Campione, A.) Opere 2: 423-432.

Sp: Sobre el mecanismo psíquico del olvido. (Tr:LR) Obr Comp-BA 22: 447-483.

185

1893a (& Breuer, Josef) Über den psychischen Mechanismus hysterischer
(1892) Phänomene: Vorläufige Mitteilung. Sections I-II, Neurol Zbl 1893,
10574 12(1, 1 Jan):4-10. Sections III-V, Neurol Zbl 1898, 12(2, 15 Jan):43-47.
Sections I-II, Wien med Blätter 1893, 16(3, 19 Jan):33-35. Sections
III-V, Wien med Blätter 1893, 16(4, 26 Jan):49-51. In *Studien über
Hysterie* 1895, 1-14. SKSN 1906, 1:14-29. 2nd ed, 1911. 3rd ed, 1920.
4th ed, 1922. GS 1925, 1:7-24. GW 1952, 1:81-98.
   Abs Inhalts wiss Arb 24.

The psychic mechanism of hysterical phenomena (preliminary communication). (Tr:AAB) SPH 1909, 1-13. 2nd ed, 1912. 3rd ed, 1920. In *Studies in hysteria*, NY/Wash: NMDP 1936, 1-13. *Major Works*, 25-31.

On the psychical mechanism of hysterical phenomena. (Tr:JR) CP 1924, 1:24-41.

On the psychical mechanism of hysterical phenomena (preliminary communication). (Tr:JS & ASt) SE 2:3-17.
   Abs (Tr:JS) SE 3:244.

Cz: In *Studie o hysterii*. (Tr: Dosužkov, B.) Prague: Albert 1947.

Fr: Les mécanismes psychiques des phénomènes hystériques: communication préliminaire. (Tr:AB) In *Etudes sur l'hystérie*, Paris: PUF 1967, 1-13.

Hun: Pri la psijala mekanismo di histeriala fenomeni. (Privozora kommikajo). (Tr: Bekonyi, S.) Budapest: Ido-Editerio, 36 p.

It: Meccanismo psichico dei fenomeni isterici. (Tr: Schwarz, L.) Opere 2: 89-102.

Jap: (Tr: Yasuda, T.) In *Furoido seishinbunseki taiken*, CW-Ars 1931, 1:6-26.

Hisuteri no shinri ryōho. (Tr: Kakeda, K. & Yoshida, M.) In *Hisuteri kenkū*, SelFr-K 1955, 9.

Sp: El mecanismo psíquico de los fénomenos histéricos. Gaceta Médica de Granada 1893, 11(232):105-111; (233):129-135. (Tr:LLBT) Obr Comp 1948, 1:25-32. Obr Comp-BA, 10:9-22. Obr Comp 1967/1968, 1:25-32.

186

1910a Über Psychoanalyse: fünf Vorlesungen gehalten zur zwanzigjährigen
(1909) Gründungsfeier der Clark University in Worchester, Mass, Sept. 1909.
10575 Leipzig/Vienna: Deuticke 1910, 62 p. 2nd ed, 1912. 3rd ed, 1916. 4th ed, 1919. 5th ed, 1920. 6th ed, 1922. 7th ed, 1924. 8th ed, 1930. 9th ed, 1946. 10th ed, 1947. (Slightly changed) GS 1924, 4:349-406. GW 1943, 8:3-60. Frankfurt/M: Fischer Bücherei 1953.

The origin and development of psychoanalysis: five lectures delivered Sept 1909, Clark University, Worchester, Mass. (Tr: Chase, H. W.) Am J Psychol 1910, 21(2-3):181-218. In *Lectures and addresses delivered before the departments of psychology and pedagogy in celebration of the twentieth anniversary of the opening of Clark University*, Worcester, Mass. 1910, Part I:1-38. In Van Teslaar (ed) *An outline of psychoanalysis*, NY: Boni & Liveright 1924, 21-70. *Major Works* 1952, 1-20. Extracts in Rickman, J. (ed) *A general selection from the works of Sigmund Freud*, London: HPI 1937, 3-43. (Pref: Allers, R.) Chicago: Gateway Editions 1955, 59 p.

Five lectures on psycho-analysis: delivered on the occasion of the celebration of the twentieth anniversary of the foundation of Clark University, Worcester, Massachusetts, September 1909. (Tr:JS) SE 11: 9-55.

Arab: M'älem el tahīl el nafsani. (Tr: Najātī, M.) Al qāhirah maktabit el nahdah el misriyyah, 3rd ed, 1958.

Dan: Om psykoanalyse. (Tr: Gelsted, O.) In *Det ubevidste*, Copenhagen: Martins 1920, 123 p. (Introd: Brüel, Oluf) 1944, 142 p.

Dut: Over psychoanalyse. (Tr: Emden, J. E. G. van) Leiden: S. C. van Doesburgh 1912; Tweede Druk 1922, vii+65 p.

Fr: Origine et développement de la psychanalyse. (Tr: Le Lay, Y.) La Revue de Genève 1920 (Dec):865-875; 1921 (Jan):80-87; (Feb):195-220.

La psychanalyse. (Tr: LeLay, Y.) Geneva: Sonor 1921, 73 p.

Cinq leçons sur la psychanalyse. (Tr: LeLay, Y.) Paris: Payot 1921, 1926, 1966, 1968, 1969, 1973, 157 p. In *Psychologie collective et analyse du moi*, Paris: Payot 1950.

Gr: Eisagoge eis ten psuchanalusin. (Tr: Pherentinou, S.) Athens: Gkoboste, 60 p.

Pente mathimata psychanalysseos. (Tr: Syrros, P.) Athens: Panekdotiki 1968.

Heb: Al hapsichoanalisa. Kitvei 3, chap. 2.

Hun: Pszichoanalizis. Öt előadás. (Tr:SFe) Budapest: Nyugat 1912, 62 p. Manó Dick 1915, 91 p; 1919, 93 p.

It: Sulle psicoanalisi: cinque conferenze. (Tr:MLB) Il Manicomio: Nocera Superiore 1915, 68 p.

Cinque conferenze sulla psicoanalisi. (Tr: Fachinelli, E.; Staude, A.; & Montinati, M.) In *Psicoanalisi. Esposizioni divulgative*, Turin: Boringhieri 1963, 1965. Opere 6.

Jap: Seishin bunseki go kō. (Tr:KO) In *Seishinbunseki sō ron*, FCW-S 1933, 10:5-79. (Tr: Kakeda, K.) SelFr-K 1959, 1969, 17:68 p.

Nor: Psykoanalysen. (Tr: Brøgger, W.) Oslo: Cappelen 1965, 135 p.

Pol: O psychoanalizie. (Tr: Jekels, L.) Lwów: Altenberg 1911, 72 p.

Por: Cinco licoes de psicanalise. (Tr: Marcondes, D. & Corrêa, J. B.) São Paulo: Companhia Editora Nacional 1931, 123 p.

Psicoanalisis. (Tr:JPP, OG & GP) Obr Comp-P 10:118-172.

Rus: O psikhoanalizie. Piat' lektsiĭ prochitannykh na prazdnikie po povodu 20-lietiia sushchestvovaniia Clark University, Worcester, Mass. v sentiabrie, 1909 g. (Tr: Osipov, N. E. & Fel'tsman, O. ?) In *Psikhoterapevticheskaia biblioteka*, vyp. I, Moskva: Nauka 1912, viii+68 p.

Sp: Cinco conferencias sobre la psicoanálisis. (Tr:LLBT) Obr Comp-Madrid 2:145-216. Obr Comp-BA 2:207-158. Obr Comp 1948, 2:32-58. Obr Comp 1967/1968, 2:125-150.

187

1923a "Psychoanalyse" und "Libidotheorie." In Marcuse, M. *Handwörterbuch*
10576 *der Sexualwissenschaft*, Bonn: Marcuse & Weber 1923, 296-298, 377-383. GS 1928, 11:201-223. GW 1940, 13:211-233.

Two encyclopaedia articles: (a)Psycho-analysis and (b)The libido theory. (Tr:JS) J 1942, 23:97-107. CP 1950, 5:107-135. SE 18:235-259.

It: La psicoanalisi. In Zolla, E. *La psicoanalisi*, Milan: Garzanti 1960, 5-29.

Due articoli: "Psicoanalisi" e "Teoria della libido." (Tr: Fachinelli, E.; Staude, A.; & Montinari, M.) In *Psicoanalisi. Esposizione divulgative*, Turin: Boringhieri 1963, 1965. Opere 9.

Jap: "Seishinbunsekigaku" to "ribido gakusetsu." (Tr: Hayashi, T.) In *Chōishiki shinrigaku*, CW-Ars 1932, 13:301-338.

Por: Sistemática. Teoria de la libido. (Tr:JPP, OG & GP) Obr Comp-P 10: 90-117.

Sp: La psicoanálisis y la teoría de la libido. (Tr:LLBT) Obr Comp-Madrid 17:265-298. Obr Comp-BA 17:183-204.

Sistemica. Teoría de la libido. Obr Comp 1948, 2:19-31. Obr Comp 1967/1968, 2:121-123.

188

1941d Psychoanalyse und Telepathie. (MS dated 2 Aug 1921) GW 1941,
(1921) 17:27-44.
10577
Psychoanalysis and telepathy. (Tr: Devereux, G.) In Devereux, G. *Psychoanalysis and the occult*, NY: IUP 1953, 56-68. (Tr:JS) SE 18: 177-193.

It: Psicoanalisi e telepatia. Opere 9.

Sp: Psicoanálisis y telepatía. (Tr:LR) Obr Comp-BA 21:33-50. Obr Comp 1967/1968, 3:372-384.

189

1913m On psycho-analysis. [Presented in Sydney, New South Wales, Sept 1911.]
(1911) Australasian Medical Congress, Transactions of the Ninth Session 1913,
10578 2(8):839-842. (Revised tr:JS) SE 12:207-211.

No German text extant.

It: Sulla psicoanalisi. Opere 6.

190

1924f Psychoanalysis: exploring the hidden recesses of the mind. [First
10506 published in English] (Tr:AAB) In *These eventful years: the twentieth century in the making as told by many of its makers*, London/NY: Encyclopaedia Britannica Publishing Co. 1924, vol. 2, chap. 73:511-523.

A short account of psycho-analysis. (Tr:JS) SE 19:191-209.

Kurzer Abriss der Psychoanalyse. GS 1928, 11:183-200. GW 1940, 13:403-427.

Hun: A pszichoanalizis rövid vázlata. (Tr: Buda, B.) In Buda, B. *A pszicho-analizis és modern irányzatai*, Budapest: Gondolat 1971, 71-89.

It: Breve compendio di psicoanalisi. Opere 9.

Jap: Seishinbunsekigaku no kōgai. (Tr: Hayashi, T.) In *Chōishiki shinri-gaku*, CW-Ars 1932, 13:341-372.

Seishinbunseki yō ryō. (Tr: KO) In *Seishinbunseki sō ron*, FCW-S 1933, 10:83-114.

Seishinbunsekigaku gaisetsu. (Tr: Kosawa, H.) In *Seishinbunseki ryōhō*, SelFr-K 1959, 15:306-408.

Por: História. (Tr:JPP, OG & GP) Obr Comp-P 10:67-89.

Sp: Historia. (Tr:LLBT) Obr Comp-Madrid 17:237-264. Obr Comp-BA 17:165-182. Obr Comp 1948, 2:9-19. Obr Comp 1967/1968, 2:101-110.

Tur: (Tr: Hilav, S.) In *Ciniyet ve psikanaliz*, Istanbul: Varlikyayinevi 1963.

191

1926f   Psycho-analysis: Freudian school. (Tr:JS) *Encyclopaedia Brittanica*
10579   1926, 13th ed, new vol. 3:253-255. 1929, 14th ed, 18:672-674. (Revised tr:JS) SE 20:263-270.

Psychoanalyse. GS 1934, 12:372-380. Almanach 1935, 1934:9-17 (without bibliography). Psa P 1935, 9(2):73-80 (with bibliography). GW 1948, 14:299-307.

Fr: Psychanalyse: école freudienne. (Tr: Lauzun, G.) In Lauzun, G. *Sigmund Freud et la psychanalyse*, Paris: Seghers 1966, 163-171.

Hin: Manovisleshan. (Tr: Vedalankar, D.) Delhi: Rajpal 1958.

It: Psicoanalisi. Opere 10.

Sp: Psicoanálisis: escuela freudiana. (Tr:LR) Obr Comp-BA 21:217-226. Obr Comp 1967/1968, 3:492-497.

192

1911c   Psychoanalytische Bemerkungen über einen autobiographisch be-
10580   schriebenen Fall von Paranoia (Dementia paranoides). Y 1911, 3(1): 9-69. SKSN 1913, 3:198-266. GS 1924, 8:355-431. *Vier Krankengeschichten* 1932, 377-460. GW 1943, 8:240-316. See also "Nachtrag zu dem autobiographisch beschriebenen Fall von Paranoia (Dementia paranoides)" [163].

Psycho-anaiytic notes upon an autobiographical account of a case of paranoia (dementia paranoides). (Tr:ASt & JS) CP 1925, 3:387-466. (With additions and corrections) SE 12:9-79.

Cz: Psychoanalyticke poznamky k autobiograficky vylicenému pripadu paranoje. (Tr: Friedmann, O.) In *Psychoanalytické chorobopisy*, Prague: Julius Albert 1937.

Fr: Remarques psychanalytiques sur l'autobiographie d'un cas de paranoïa (Dementia paranoides) (Le président Schreber). (Tr:MB & RL) RFPsa 1932, 5(1):2-70. In *Cinq psychanalyses*, Paris: Denoël & Steele 1935; PUF 1954, 1966, 1967, 1970, 263-324.

[Schreber, D. P.; "Mémoires d'un névropathe." (Tr: Duquenne, P.) *Cahiers pour l'analyse*, Le Seuil, Paris 1966-67, (5):65-116; (6):139-152; (7):97-121; (8):120-133.]

It: Osservazioni psicoanalitiche su un caso di paranoia (dementia paranoides) descritto autobiograficamente (caso clinico del presidente

Schreber). (Tr: Lucentini, M.) In *Casi clinici*, Turin: Boringhieri 1952, 1962. Opere 6.

Jap: Jidenteki ni kijutsu sareta paranoia (mōsōsei chinō) no ichi shōrei ni kansuru seishin bunsekigakuteki kōsatsu. (Tr: Kumada, M. & Okonogi, K.) In *Shōrei no kenkyū*, SelFr-K 1959, 16:100 p.

Por: Considerações psicanalíticas sôbre um caso de paranóia (dementia paranoides) autobiogràficamente descrito. (Tr:ED & OG) Obr Comp-P 16:95-176.

Sp: Observaciones psicoanalíticas sobre un caso de paranoia (dementia paranoides) autobiográficamente descrito. (Tr:LLBT) Obr Comp-BA 16:81-144. Obr Comp 1948, 2:661-692. Obr Comp 1967/1968, 2: 752-784.

193

1910i Die psychogene Sehstörung in psychoanalytischer Auffassung. Ärztliche
10581 Fortbildung supplement to Ärztliche Standeszeitung, Vienna 1910, 9(9, 1 May):42-44. SKSN 1913, 3:314-321. GS 1924, 5:301-309. GW 1943, 8:94-102.

Psychogenic visual disturbance according to psycho-analytic conceptions. (Tr:ECM) CP 1924, 2:105-112.

The psycho-analytic view of psychogenic disturbance of vision. (Tr:JS & ASt) SE 11:211-218.

Fr: Le trouble psychogène de la vision dans la conception psychanalytique. (Tr: Guérineau, D.) In *Névrose, psychose et perversion*. Paris: PUF 1973, 167-173.

It: I disturbi visivi psicogeni nell'interpretazione psicoanalitica. Opere 6.

Por: Conceito psicanalítico das perturbações psicógenas da visão. (Tr:OG & MG) Obr Comp-P 5:203-210.

Sp: Concepto psicoanalítico de las perturbaciones psicógenas de la visión. (Tr:LLBT) Obr Comp-Madrid 13:188-196. Obr Comp-BA 13:151-157. Obr Comp 1948, 1:993-996. Obr Comp 1967/1968, 1:982-984.

194

1920a Über die Psychogenese eines Falles von weiblicher Homosexualität.
10582 Z 1920, 6(1):1-24. SKSN 1922, 5:159-194. GS 1924, 5:312-343. Psychoanalyse der Neurosen 1926, 87-124. Sexualtheorie und Traumlehre 1931, 155-188. GW 1947, 12:271-302.

The psychogenesis of a case of homosexuality in a woman. (Tr: Low, B. & Gabler, R.) J 1920, 1:125-149. CP 1924, 2:202-231. In Krich, A. M. *The homosexuals as seen by themselves and thirty authorities*, NY: Citadel Pr 1954, 262-285. (Revised tr:JS) SE 18:147-172.

Fr: Psychogénèse d'un cas d'homosexualité féminine. (Tr: Hoesli, H.) RFPsa 1933, 6(2):130-154. (Tr: Martet, P.) In Krich, A. M. *Les homo-*

sexuels, Paris: Correa 1955, 249-278. (Tr: Guérineau, D.) In *Névrose, psychose et perversion*. Paris: PUF 1973, 245-270.

It: Psicogenesi di un caso di omosessualità femminile. Opere 9.

Jap: Dōseiai ni ochi itta aru josei no shinri jōsei ni tsuite. (Tr: Konuma, M.) In *Ijō seiyaku bunseki*, CW-Ars 1933, 15:104-154.

Aru fujin dōseiaisha no shinriteki genkon. (Tr:KO) In *Bunseki renai ron*, FCW-S 1934, 9:132-175.

Josei dōseiai no ichi keisu no seiritsu shi ni tsuite. (Tr:YT) SelFr-K 1960, 14:44 p.

Por: Sôbre a psicogènese de um caso de homossexualidade feminina. (Tr:OG & MG) Obr Comp-P 5:255-284.

Sp: Sobre la psicogénesis de un caso de homosexualidad femenina. (Tr: LLBT) Obr Comp-Madrid 13:199-231. Obr Comp-BA 13:160-184. Obr Comp 1948, 1:1016-1029. Obr Comp 1967/1968, 1:1004-1017.

195

1914f Zur Psychologie des Gymnasiasten. In *Festschrift* celebrating the 50th
10583 anniversary of foundation of K.k. Erzherzog-Rainer Realgymnasium Vienna 1914, Oct. Almanach 1927, 1926:43-46. GS 1928, 11:287-290. Psa P 1935, 9:307-310. GW 1946, 10:204-207.

Some reflections on schoolboy psychology. (Tr:JS) SE 13:241-244.

It: Psicologia del ginnasiale. Opere 7.

Sp: Sobre la psicología del colegial. (Tr:LR) Obr Comp-BA 19:249-252. Obr Comp 1967/1968, 3:169-171.

196

1942a Psychopathic characters on the stage. [Published in English.] (Tr from
(1905- handwritten original manuscript: Bunker, H. A.) Q 1942, 11(4, Oct):
1906) 459-464. (Tr:JS) SE 7:305-310.
10584

Ger: Original text unpublished.

It: Personaggi psicopatici sulla scena. (Tr: Dogana, M. T.) Opere 5: 231-238.

Jap: (Tr: Kikumori, H.) Tokyo: Kawade Shobō Shinsha Pr 1972, 6 p.

Sp: Personajes psicopáticos en el teatro. (Tr:LR) Rev Psicoanál 1955, 12:115-121. Obr Comp-BA 21:388-394. Obr Comp 1967/1968, 3: 988-993.

197

1901b Zur Psychopathologie des Alltagslebens (Über Vergessen, Versprechen,
10585 Vergreifen, Aberglaube und Irrtum). Mschr Psychiatr Neurol 1901,

10(1 July):1-32; (2 Aug):95-143. Berlin: Karger 1904, 92 p. 2nd ed (enlarged), 1907, 132 p. 3rd ed (enlarged), 1910, 149 p. 4th ed (enlarged), 1912, 198 p. 5th ed (enlarged), 1917, iv+232 p. 6th ed (enlarged), Leipzig/Vienna: Int Psa Verlag 1919, iv+312 p. 7th ed (enlarged), Leipzig/Vienna/Zurich: Int Psa Verlag 1920, iv+334 p. 8th ed, 1920, 9th ed, 1923, iii+324 p. 10th ed (enlarged), 1924, 310 p. 11th ed, 1929, 310 p. 12th ed, IPC 1947. GS 1924, 4:1-310. GW 1941, 4:iv+322 p. Frankfurt/M: Fischer Bücherei 1954, 233 p.

Psychopathology of everyday life. (Tr, intro:AAB) London: Fisher Unwin; NY: Macmillan 1914, vii+342 p. London: Penguin Books 1938; NY 1939, 218 p. BWSF 1938, 35-178. London: Ernest Benn 1949, vii+239 p. London: Collins 1958, viii+180 p.

The psychopathology of everyday life. Forgetting, slips of the tongue, bungled actions, superstitions and errors. (Tr: Tyson, A.) SE 6:1-279. NY: Norton 1965, 1966, xii+310 p. London: Benn 1966, x+310 p.

Arab: Hayati wa al tahil al nafsy. (Tr: Zewar, M. & Abd El Monheim Al Meleigy) Al Qāhirah: Dār El M'āref 1957.

Cz: Psychopathologie všedního žιvota. (Tr: Friedmann, O.) Prague: Julius Albert 1938, 234 p.

Dan: Hverdagslivets psykopatologi. (Tr: Boisen, M.) Copenhagen: Hans Reitzel 1959, 220 p; 1965, 224 p.

Dut: De invloed van ons onbewusste in ons dagelijksch leven. Over vergeten, zich verspreken, zich vergissen, onhandigheid. (Tr: Stärcke, J.) Amsterdam: Mij voor goede en goedkoope lectuur 1916, 1921, viii+ 308 p. De Wereldbibliotek 1931, 408 p.

Fin: Arkielämämme psykopatologiaa. Unohtamisesta, virhesanonnoista, virheteoista, taikauskosta ja erehdyksistä. (Tr: Takala, M. & Santala, M.) (Intro: Kaila, E.) Helsinki: Otava 1954, 293 p; (Intro: Ikonen, P.) 1961, 254 p. Shortened ed in Koskennieme, M. *Jokamiehen korkeakoulu,* Helsinki: Kustannusosakeyhtiö Otava 1961.

Fr: Psychopathologie de la via quotidienne. (Tr: Jankélévitch, S.) Paris: Payot 1922, 1967, 1969, 297 p.

Gr: Psychopathologia tis kathimerinis zois. (Tr: Meranaios, C.) Athens: Gavotsis 1935. (Tr: Meranaios, C. & Zographou, M.) Athens: Maris 1948. (Tr: Syrros, P.) Athens: Panekdotiki 1963.

Heb: Psichopatologia shel chave yom-yom. (Tr: Vojslavsky, Z.) Tel-Aviv: Massadah 1942, 1944, 1967.

Hun: A mindennapi élet pszichopathológiája. Az elfelejtés, elszólás, elirás, babona és tévedés. (Tr: Takács, M.) Budapest: Világirodálom 1923, 196 p. In Ferenczi, S. & Storfer, A. *Collected papers of Sigmund Freud,* Vol. 2, Vienna: Int Psa Verlag; Budapest: Somló 1932, 281 p.

A mindennapi élet pszichopathológiája. Elfelejtésröl, elszólásról, elvétésröl, babonáról és tévedésröl. (Tr: Gergely, E. & Lukács, K.) Budapest: Bibliotheca 1958, 335 p.

It: Psicopatologia della vita quotidiana. Applicazione della psico-analisi all'interpretazione degli atti della vita corrente. Rome: Astrolabio 1948, 311 p.

Psicopatologia della vita quotidiana. Dimenticanza, lapsus, sbadataggini, superstizioni ed errori. (Tr: Piazza, C. F.; Ranchetti, M.; & Sagittario, E.) (Pref:CLM) Turin: Boringhieri 1965, xi+251 p. 1971, 300 p. Opere 4:57-301.

Jap: Nichijo no seikatsu seishinbunseki. (Tr:KO) In *Furoido seishinbunsekigaku zenshū*, FCW-S 1930, 2:1-402.

Nichijō seikatsu no ijo shinri. (Tr: Marui, K.) Tokyo: Ars 1930, 430 p. CW-Ars 1941, 4:430 p.

Nichijō seikatsu ni okeru seishin byōri. (Tr: Marui, K.) In *Nichijō seikatsu ni okeru seishin byōri*, Tokyo: Iwanami Shoten 1941, 415 p. 1954.

Seikatsu shinri no sakugo. (Tr: Hamakawa, S.) SelFr-K 1959, 13:3-370.

(Tr: Ikemi, T. & YT) SelFr-JinSh 1970, 4:232 p.

Jug: Psihopatologija svakodnevnog života. (Intro & tr: Klajn, H.) Beograd: Kosmos 1937, 337 p. Novi Sad: Matica Srpska 1961, 321 p. [Collected Works, Vol. 1] Novi Sad: Matica Srpska 1969.

Pol: Psychopatologia zycia godziennego. (Tr: Jekels, L. & Ivanka, H.) Lwów: Altenberg 1912, 239 p.

Por: Psicopatologia da vida quotidiana. (Tr:ED) Rio de Janeiro: Guanabara, Waissman, Koogan 1933, 301 p. Obr Comp-P 6:5-317. (Tr: Cabral, A.) Rio de Janeiro: Zahar 1963.

Rus: Psikhopatologiia obydennoǐ zhini. (Tr: Medem, V.) In *Nauchnaia biblioteka "Sovremennykh problem,"* Moskva: Izd-vo "Sovremennye problemy" 1910, 162 p. 2nd ed Moskva: Kn-vo "Sovremennye problemy" 1916. 3rd ed Moskva: Izd-vo "Sovremennye problemy" 1923, 256 p. 4th ed Moskva: Kn-vo "Sovremennye problemy" 1926, 256 p.

Sp: Psicopatologia de la vida cotidiana. (Tr:LLBT) Obr Comp-Madrid 1. Obr Comp-BA 1:9-276. Obr Comp 1948, 1:635-778. Obr Comp 1967/ 1968, 1:629-770.

Sw: Vardagslivets psykopatologie. (Tr: Groddek, E. & Landquist, J.) Stockholm: Bonniers 1924, 255 p. (Tr: Landquist, J. & Landquist, S.) Stockholm: Forum 1957, 292 p; Bonniers 1964, 1967, 224 p.

198

1905a Über Psychotherapie. (Read before Wiener medizinisches Doktoren-
(1904) kollegium, 12 Dec 1904) Wien med Presse 1905, 1 Jan:9-16. SKSN 1906,
10586 1:205-217. 2nd ed, 1911. 3rd ed, 1920. 4th ed, 1922. Technik und Metapsychol 1924, 11-24. GS 1925, 6:11-24. GW 1942, 5:13-26.

On psychotherapy. (Tr:AAB) SPH 1909, 175-185. 2nd ed, 1912. 3rd ed,

1920. In *Major Works* 1952, 106-111. (Tr: Bernays, J.) CP 1924, 1:249-263. (Tr:JS) SE 7:257-268.

Fr: De la psychothérapie. (Tr:AB) In *La technique psychanalytique*, Paris: PUF 1953, 1970, 9-22.

It: Psicoterapia. (Tr: Dogana, M. T.) Opere 4:429-442.

Jap: (Tr:KO) FCW-S 1933, 8:19 p. Seishin ryōhō tsuite. (Tr: Kosawa, H.) SelFr-K 1959, 15:13-32.

Por: Sôbre psicoterapia. (Tr:JPP, OG & GP) Obr Comp-P 10:183-194.

Rus: (Tr:MV) In Metodika i tekhnika psikhoanaliza. *Psikholog i psikhoanal*, vyp. IV, 136 p.

Sp: Sobre psicoterapia. (Tr:LLBT) Obr Comp-BA 14:63-72. Obr Comp 1948, 2:304-309. Obr Comp 1967/1968, 2:396-401.

199

1917a A pszihoanalizis egy nehézségéröl. [First published in Hungarian]
10595 Nyugat, Budapest 1917, 10(1):47-52.

Eine Schwierigkeit der Psychoanalyse. Imago 1917, 5(1):1-7. SKSN 1918, 4:553-563. GS 1924, 10:347-356. GW 1947, 12:3-12.

One of the difficulties of psycho-analysis. (Tr:JRiv) J 1920, 1:17-23. JMS 1921, 67:34-40. CP 1925, 4:347-356.

A difficulty in the path of psycho-analysis. (Tr:JS) SE 17:137-144.

Fr: Une difficulté de la psychanalyse. (Tr: Marty, Mme. E. & MB) In *Essais de psychanalyse appliquée*, Paris: Gallimard 1933, 137-147. (Tr: Buchet, E.) In Waelder, R. *Les pages immortelles de Freud*, Paris: Correa 1948, 173-181.

It: Una difficoltà della psicoanalisi. (Tr:CLM) In *Freud con antologia freudiana*, Turin: Boringhieri 1959, 1970. Opere 8.

Jap: Seishinbunseki no konnan. (Tr: Kikuchi, E.) In *Sensō to shi seishinbunseki*, CW-Ars 1932, 14:149-161.

Por: Uma dificuldade da psicanálise. (Tr:ED) Obr Comp-P 11:235-244.

Rus: In [Psychological theories]. Moscow: Staatsverlag 1923.

Sp: Una dificultad del psicoanálisis. (Tr:LR) Obr Comp-BA 18:13-22. (Tr:LLBT) Obr Comp 1948, 2:1016-1019. Obr Comp 1967/1968, 2:1108-1111.

200

1893c Quelques considérations pour une étude comparative des paralysies
10588 motrices organiques et hystériques. [In French] Arch Neurol 1893, 26(77:July):29-43. SKSN 1906, 1:30-44. GS 1925, 1:273-289. GS 1952, 1:39-55.
Abs Inhalts wiss Arb 28.

Some points in a comparative study of organic and hysterical paralyses. (Tr: Meyer, M.) CP 1924, 1:42-58.

Some points for a comparative study of organic and hysterical motor paralyses. (Tr:JS) SE 1:160-172.
Abs (Tr:JS) SE 3:248.

It: Alcune considerazioni per uno studio comparato delle paralisi motorie organiche e isteriche. (Tr: Campione, A.) Opere 2:71-86.

Por: Estudo comparatico das paralisias motoras organicas e histéricas. (Tr:CMdeF) Obr Comp-P 2:173-195.

Sp: Estudio comparativo de las parálisis motrices orgánicas e histéricas. (Tr:LLBT) Obr Comp-Madrid 11:165-184. Obr Comp-BA 11:123-136. Obr Comp 1948, 1:193-199. Obr Comp 1967/1968, 1:192-199.

201

1912e   Ratschläge für den Arzt bei der psychoanalytischen Behandlung. C 1912,
10589   2(9):483-489. SKSN 1918, 4:399-411. 2nd ed, 1922. Technik und Metapsychol 1924, 64-75. GS 1925, 6:64-75. Neurosenlehre und Technik 1931, 340-351. GW 1943, 8:376-387.

Recommendations for physicians on the psycho-analytic method of treatment. (Tr:JRiv) CP 1924, 2:323-333.

Recommendations to physicians practising psycho-analysis. (Modified tr:JS) SE 12:111-120.

Fr: Conseils aux médecins sur le traitement psychanalytique. (Tr:AB) In *La technique psychanalytique*, Paris: PUF 1953, 1967, 1970, 61-71.

It: Consigli al medico nel trattamento psicoanalitico. Opere 6.

Jap: (Tr:KO) FCW-S 1933, 8:16 p. Bunseki i ni kansuru bunseki chiryōjō no chui. (Tr: Kosawa, H.) In *Seishinbunseki ryōhō*, SelFr-K 1959, 15: 91-106. Rev ed (Tr: Okonogi, K.) SelFr-K 1969, 15:16 p.

Por: Conselhos as médico para o tratamento psicanalíticao. (Tr:JPP, OG & GP) Obr Comp-P 10:235-246.

Rus: In Psikhoterapiia 1913, no. 2.

Sp: Consejos al médico en el tratamiento psicoanalítico. (Tr:LLBT) Obr Comp-BA 14:104-112. Obr Comp 1948, 2:326-330. Obr Comp 1967/1968, 2:418-422.

202

1924e   Der Realitätsverlust bei Neurose und Psychose. Z 1924, 10(4):374-379.
10590   GS 1925, 6:409-414. Psychoanalyse der Neurosen 1926, 178-184. Neurosenlehre und Technik 1931, 199-204. GW 1940, 13:363-368.

The loss of reality in neurosis and psychosis. (Tr:JRiv) CP 1924, 2: 277-282. (Tr:JS) SE 19:183-187.

Fr: La perte de la réalité dans la névrose et dans la psychose. (Tr: Guérineau, D.) In *Névrose, psychose et perversion*. Paris: PUF 1973, 299-303.

It: La perdita di realtà nella nevrosi e nella psicosi. (Tr:CLM) In *Freud con antologia freudiana*, Turin: Boringhieri 1959, 1970. Opere 10.

Jap: Shinkei-shō to seishinbyō no genjutsu sōshitsu. (Tr: Imura, T. & Katō, M.) In *Fuan no mondai*, SelFr-K 1955, 10:8 p. Rev ed (Tr: Katō, M.) SelFr-K 1969, 10:10 p. (Tr: Imura, T.) SelFr-JinSh 1970, 6:4 p.

Por: A perda da realidade na neurose e na psicose. (Tr:OG & GP) Obr Comp-P 14:31-36.

Sp: La pérdida de realidad en la neurosis y en la psicosis. (Tr:LLBT) Obr Comp-BA 14:216-220. Obr Comp 1948, 2:412-413. Obr Comp 1967/1968, 2:504-505.

203

1928a Ein religiöses Erlebnis. Imago 1928, 14(1):7-10. GS 1928, 11:467-470.
(1927) Almanach 1929, 1928:9-12. GW 1948, 14:393-396.
10591

A religious experience. J 1929, 10(1):1-4. (Tr:JS) CP 1950, 5:243-246. SE 21:169-172. In Strunk, O. *Readings in the psychology of religion*, NY: Abingdon Pr 1959, 117-119.

Fr: Un événement de la vie religieuse. (Tr:MB) In *L'avenir d'une illusion*, Paris: Denoël & Steele 1932; PUF 1971, 95-100.

It: Un'esperienza religiosa. Opere 10.

Por: Uma experiência religiosa. (Tr:OG & GP) Obr Comp-P 14:43-48.

Sp: Una experiencia religiosa. (Tr:LLBT) Obr Comp-BA 14:226. Obr Comp 1948, 2:417-418. Obr Comp 1967/1968, 2:509-510.

204

1956a Report on my studies in Paris and Berlin. Carried out with the assistance
(1886) of a travelling bursary granted from the University Jubilee Fund
10408 (October, 1885—end of March, 1886). [First published in English.] (Tr:JS) J 1956, 37(1):2-7. SE 1:5-15.

Bericht über meine mit Universitäts-Jubiläums Reisestipendium unternommene Studienreise nach Paris und Berlin. In Gicklhorn, J. & Gicklhorn, R. *Sigmund Freuds akademische Laufbahn im Lichte der Dokumente*, Vienna: Urban & Schwarzenbach 1960, 82.

Fr: Rapport sur mes études à Paris et à Berlin. (Tr:AB) RFPsa 1956, 20(3): 299-306.

It: Relazione sui miei viaggi di studio a Parigi e a Berlino. (Tr: Schwarz, L.) Opere 1:5-16.

205

1925e Résistances à la psychanalyse. [First published in French] La Revue
10650 Juive, Geneva 1925, 1(2, 15 Mar):209-219.

Die Widerstände gegen die Psychoanalyse. Imago 1925, 11(3):222-233.

Almanach 1926, 1925:9-21. Psychoanalyse der Neurosen 1926, 185-198. GS 1928, 11:224-235. GW 1948, 14:99-110.

The resistances to psycho-analysis. (Tr:JS) CP 1950, 5:163-174. SE 19: 213-224.

Heb: Hahitnagduyot lapsichoanalisa. Kitvei 3, chap. 7.

It: Le resistenze alla psicoanalisi. Opere 10.

Nor: (Tr: Schjelderup, K.) In *Psykoanalysen i praksis*, Oslo: Gyldendal Norsk Forlag 1930.

Sp: Las resistencias contra el psicoanálisis. (Tr:LR) Obr Comp-BA 19: 99-110. Obr Comp 1967/1968, 3:73-80.

206

1926a An Romain Rolland (zum 60. Geburtstag). In *Liber amicorum Romain*
10592 *Rolland*, Zurich/Leipzig: Rotapfel 26 Jan 1926, 152. GS 1928, 11: 275-276. GW 1948, 14:553. *Briefe.*

To Romain Rolland. (Tr:JS) SE 20:279. *Letters.*

It: A Romain Rolland. Opere 10.

Sp: A Romain Rolland. (Tr:LR) Obr Comp-BA 20:212. Obr Comp 1967/ 1968, 3:332.

207

1913h Rücksicht auf Darstellbarkeit. Erf Beisp Psa Prx [89] no. 19. Z 1913,
10593 1:377-382. GW 1942, 2-3:413.

Considerations of representability. (Tr:JS) SE 13:197. In *The interpretation of dreams*, SE 5:409.

FOR OTHER LANGUAGES, see under *Die Traumdeutung* [227].

208

1933c Sándor Ferenczi (obituary). Z 1933, 19(3):301-304. GS 1934, 12:
10594 397-399. GW 1950, 16:267-269.

Sándor Ferenczi. J 1933, 14(3):297-299. (Tr:JS) SE 22:227-229.

Hun: (Tr: Szilágyi, G.) In *Lélekelemzési Tanulmányok. Dolgozatok a pszichoanalizis főbb kérdéseiről* by Members of the Hungarian Psychoanalytic Society, Budapest: Somló 1933, 5-8.

It: Necrologio di Sándor Ferenczi. Opere 11.

Sp: En memoria de Sándor Ferenczi. (Tr:LR) Obr Comp-BA 20:217-220. Obr Comp 1967/1968, 3:335-336.

209

1925d "Selbstdarstellung." In Grote, L. R.: *Die Medizin der Gegenwart in*

(1924) *Selbstdarstellungen*, Leipzig: Meiner 1925, 4:1-52. GS 1928, 11:
10596 119-182. GW 1948, 16:33-96.

Selbstdarstellung. Leipzig/Vienna/Zurich: Int Psa Verlag 1934, 52 p. Including *Nachschrift 1935* [160], 1936, 107 p. London: IPC 1946, 107 p. Braille: Vienna: Hohe Warte.

An autobiographical study. (Tr:JS) In *The problem of lay-analyses*, NY: Brentano 1927, 189-316. Including *Postscript 1935*, London: HPI 1935, 137 p. SE 20:7-70.

Autobiography. (Tr:JS) NY: Norton 1935, 153 p. In Fabricant, N. *Why we become doctors*, NY: Grune & Stratton 1953, 42-43.

Cz: O sobě psychoanalyse. (Tr: Friedmann, O.) Prague: "Orbis" 1936, 1937, 80 p.

Fin: Omaelämäkerrallinen tutkielma. (Tr: Nousiainen, P. & Nousiainen, T.) Helsinki: Kustannusosakeyhtiö Otava 1962, 161 p.

Fr: Ma vie et la psychanalyse. (Tr:MB; revised: Freud, S.) Paris: Gallimard 1928, 1949, 1968, 184 p.

Gr: I zoi moy kai i psychoanalyssi. (Tr: Zographou, M.) Athens: Tsongas 1950.

Istoria tou psychoanalytikou kinimatos. (Tr: Syrros, P.) Athens: Panekdotiki 1970.

Heb: Deyokan asmo. (Tr: Golan, S. & Sohar, Z.) Merchavia 1947. Kitvei, chap. 8.

Hun: Önéletrajz. (Tr: Ignotus) Nyugat 1925, 2:101-138. (Tr: Kovacs, V.) Budapest: Pantheon Kiadás 1936, 128 p.

It: Mia vita ed opera. (Tr: Flescher, J.) Rome: Editore Scienza moderna 1948, 146 p.

La mia vita e la psicoanalisi. (Tr: Flescher, J. & CLM) Milan: Mursia 1956, 1966, 240 p.

Autobiografia. Opere 10. (Tr:CLM) Excerpts in *Freud con antologia freudiana*, Turin: Boringhieri 1959, 1970.

Jap: Ji den. (Tr: Kimura, K. & Naitō, K.) In *Seishinbunseki nyūmon*, CW-Ars 1932, 12:185-272. (Tr:KO) In *Seishinbunseki sō ron*, FCW-S 1933, 10:117-213.

Jira o hanaseru. (Tr: Kakeda, K.) In *Jira o hanaseru*, SelFr-K 1960, 17:3-100. Rev ed SelFr-K 1969, 17:100 p. SelFr-JinSh 1970, 4:55 p.

Furoito jiden. (Tr: Ikumatsu, K.) Tokyo: Shinchosha 1959, 100 p.

(Tr: Kikumori, H.) Tokyo: Kawade Shobō Shinsha Pr 1967, 106 p.

Jug: Autobiografija. (Tr: Jerotić, V. & Volf, N.) [Collected Works, Vol. 8] Novi Sad: Matica Srpska 1969.

Pol: Wizerunek wlasny. (Tr: Zalszupin, H.) Warsaw: Wydawnictwo J. Przeworskiego 1936, 97 p.

Por: Autobiografia. (Tr:OG, IsIz & GP) Obr Comp-P 18:73-140.

Sp: Autobiografía. (Tr:LLBT) Obr Comp 1948, 2:921-950. Obr Comp
1967/1968, 2:1013-1042. Madrid: Alianza Editorial 1969. (Tr: Romero,
H.) Santiago: Edicion Pax.

210

1913h Selbstkritik der Neurotiker. Erf Beisp Psa Prx [89] no. 15. Z 1913, 1:377-
10596A 382. GS 1928, 11:301-303. Neurosenlehre und Technik 1931, 306-308.
GW 1946, 10:40-42.

Self-criticism by neurotics. (Tr:JS) SE 13:196-197.

211

1898a Die Sexualität in der Ätiologie der Neurosen. Wien klin Rdsch 1898,
10598 12(2, 9 Jan):21-22; (4, 23 Jan):55-57; (5, 30 Jan):70-72; (7, 13 Feb):
103-105. SKSN 1906, 1:181-204. GS 1925, 1:439-464. GW 1952,
1:491-516.

Sexuality in the aetiology of the neuroses. (Tr: Bernays, J.) CP 1924,
1:220-248. (Revised tr:JS) SE 3:263-285.

It: La sessualità nell'etiologia delle nevrosi. (Tr: Campione, A.) Opere 2:
397-420. In *La vita sessuale*, Turin: Boringhieri 1970.

Jap: Shinkeibyō no genin toshite no sei. (Tr: Imura, T. & Katō, M.) In *Fuan
no mondai*, SelFr-K 1955, 10. Rev ed (Tr: Katō, M.) SelFr-K 1969,
10:30 p.

Sp: La sexualidad en la etiologia de las neurosis. (Tr:LLBT) Obr Comp-
Madrid 13:7-17. Obr Comp-BA 13:9-19.

212

1907c Zur sexuellen Aufklärung der Kinder (offener Brief an Dr. M. Fürst).
10599 Soz Med Hyg 1907, 2(6, June):360-367. SKSN 1909, 2:151-158. 2nd ed,
1912. 3rd ed, 1921. GS 1924, 5:134-142. Sexualtheorie und Traumlehre
1931, 7-16. GW 1941, 7:19-27.

The sexual enlightenment of children. An open letter to Dr. M. Fürst
editor of Soziale Medizin und Hygiene. (Tr: E. B. H.) CP 1924, 2:36-44.
In *Major Works* 1952, 119-122. (Revised tr:JS) SE 9:131-139.

Fr: Les explications sexuelles données aux enfants. (Tr: Berger, D.) In
La vie sexuelle, Paris: PUF 1969, 7-13.

Heb: Leinyan hahasbara haminit leyeladim. Kitvei 3, chap. 10.

It: Istrusione sessuale dei bambini. (Tr:CLM) In *Freud con antologia
freudiana*, Turin: Boringhieri 1959, 1970. In *Psicoanalisi infantile*,
Turin: Boringhieri 1968, 1970. Opere 5:355-364.

Jap: (Tr: Yamamoto, Y.) SelFr-JinSh 1969, 5:6 p.

Nor: (Tr: Schjelderup, K.) In *Psykoanalysen i praksis*, Oslo: Glydendal Norsk
Forlag 1930.

Por: A educação sexual da criança. (Tr:OG, IsIz & MG) Obr Comp-P 9: 109-118.

Sp: La ilustración sexual del niño. Carta abierta al doctor M. Fürst. (Tr: LLBT) Obr Comp-BA 13:19-26. Obr Comp 1948, 1:1181-1184. Obr Comp 1967/1968, 1:1167-1170.

213

1940b Some elementary lessons in psycho-analysis. [In German with English
(1938) title] In part as footnote to *Abriss der Psychoanalyse*, Z 1940, 25(1):
10600 21-22. Complete in GW 1941, 17:141-147.

Some elementary lessons in psycho-analysis. (Tr:JS) In part as appendix to *Outline of psycho-analysis*, J 1940, 21(1):83-84. Complete in CP 1950, 5:376-382. (Revised tr:JS) SE 23:281-286.

It: Alcune lezioni elementari di psicoanalisi. (Tr: Lucentini, M.) In *Casi clinici*, Turin: Boringhieri 1952, 1962. (Tr: Fachinelli, E.; Staude, A.; & Montinari, M.) In *Psicoanalisi. Esposizione divulgative*, Turin: Boringhieri 1963, 1965. Opere 11.

Sp: Algunas lecciones elementales de psicoanálisis. (Tr:LR) Obr Comp-BA 21:127-134. Obr Comp 1967/1968, 3:441-445.

214

1895d (& Breuer, Josef) Studien über Hysterie. Leipzig/Vienna: Deuticke
10601 1895, v+269 p. 2nd ed, 1909, vii+269 p. 3rd ed, 1916. 4th ed, 1922. Without Breuer's contributions: GS 1925, 1:3-238. GW 1952, 1:77-213. All editions include "Über den psychischen Mechanismus hysterischer Phänomene: vorläufige Mitteilung" [185].
Abs Inhalts wiss Arb 31.

Studies in hysteria. [In part: omits case histories of Fräulein Anna O., Frau Emmy von N. and Katharina, and Breuer's chapter on theory.] (Tr:AAB) SPH 1909, 1-120. 2nd ed, 1912. 3rd ed, 1920. 4th ed, 1922.

Studies in hysteria. [Complete text. Does not include Freud's footnotes added in 1925.] (Tr:AAB) NY: NMDP 1936, ix+241 p.

Studies on hysteria. [Complete. Includes Breuer's contributions and Freud's added footnotes of 1925.] (Tr:JS & ASt) SE 2:xxix-xxxi+305 p. London: Hogarth Pr 1956; NY: Basic Books 1957, xxxi+335 p. Boston: Beacon Pr 1958. London: Mayflower 1960.
Abs (Tr:JS) SE 3:250-251.

Cz: Studie o hysterii. (Tr: Budínský, J.; Dosužkov, B.; Havelková, M.; Kopřiva, K.; Kučera, O.; & Wiškowský, E.) Prague, J. Albert 1947, 187 p.

Fr: Etudes sur l'hystérie. (Tr:AB) Paris: PUF 1956, 247 p; 1967, 255 p.

It: Studi sull'isteria. [Includes Breuer's contributions] (Tr: Piazza, C. F.) Opere 1:171-440.

Jap: Hisuteri. [Breuer's cases omitted] (Tr: Yasuda, T.) In *Furoido seishin-bunseki taiken*, CW-Ars 1931, 1:6-335. (Tr: Kakeda, K. & Yoshida, M.) SelFr-K 1955, 9. Includes "On the psychical mechanism of hysterical phenomena" [185].

Por: A histeria. [Breuer's cases omitted] (Tr: CMdeF) Obr Comp-P 1:17-238.

Sp: La histeria. [Breuer's cases omitted] (Tr: LLBT) Obr Comp-Madrid 10: 7-249. Obr Comp-BA 10:9-194. Obr Comp 1948, 1:25-130. Obr Comp 1967/1968, 1:25-130.

Agregados a *Estudio sobre la histeria*. (Tr: LR) Obr Comp-BA 22: 484-488. Obr Comp 1967/1968, 3:969-972.

215

1918a Das Tabu der Virginität. (Beiträge zur Psychologie des Liebeslebens III).
(1917) (Read at Vienna Psa Soc, 12 Dec 1917) SKSN 1918, 4:229-251. GS 1924,
10602 5:212-231. In *Beiträge zur Psychologie des Liebeslebens* [56], Leipzig/Vienna/Zurich: Int Psa Verlag 1924, 29-48. Sexualtheorie und Traumlehre 1931, 95-115. GW 1947, 12:161-180.

The taboo of virginity. (Contributions to the psychology of love III). (Tr: JRiv) CP 1925, 4:217-235. (Tr: Richards, A.) SE 11:193-208.

Fr: Le tabou de la virginité. (Contribution à la psychologie de la vie amoureuse III). (Tr: AB) RFPsa 1933, 6(1):2-17. (Tr: Berger, D.) In *La vie sexuelle*, Paris: PUF 1969, 66-80.

It: Il tabù della verginità. (Tr: Campione, A.; Candreva, S.; Montinari, M.; CLM; & Sagittario, E.) In *La vita sessuale*, Turin: Boringhieri 1970. Opere 6.

Jap: Shojosei no tabū. Renai no seikatsu no shinri—dai san rumbun. (Tr: KO) In *Bunseki renai ron*, FCW-S 1932, 9:36-64.

Por: O tabu de virgindade. (Tr: OG & MG) Obr Comp-P 5:184-202.

Sp: El tabú de la virginidad. (Tr: LLBT) Obr Comp-Madrid 13. Obr Comp-BA 13:81-96. Obr Comp 1948, 1:985-992. Obr Comp 1967/1968, 1:973-981.

216

1913h Tageszeiten im Trauminhalt. Erf Beisp Psa Prx [89] no. 2. Z 1913,
10603 1:377-382. GS 1925, 3:127. GW 1942, 2-3:413-414.

Times of day in the content of dreams. (Tr: AAB) In *The interpretation of dreams*, 3rd ed, 1931, 383. (Tr: JS) SE 5:409. SE 13:194.

FOR OTHER LANGUAGES, see under *Die Traumdeutung* [227].

217

1906c Tatbestandsdiagnostik und Psychoanalyse. (Lecture delivered to Pro-
10604 fessor Löffler's seminar at the University of Vienna, June 1906) Arch

Krim Anthrop 1906, 26(1, 21 Dec):1-10. SKSN 1909, 2:111-121. GS 1924, 10:197-209. GW 1941, 7:3-15.

The testimony of witnesses and psychoanalysis. (Tr:AAB) SPH 1920, 216-225.

Psycho-analysis and the ascertaining of truth in courts of law. (Tr:EBH) CP 1924, 2:13-24.

Psycho-analysis and the establishment of the facts in legal proceedings. (Tr:JS) SE 9:103-114.

Fr: La psychanalyse et l'établissement des faits en matière judiciaire par une méthode diagnostique. (Tr: Marty, Mme. E. & MB) In *Essais de psychanalyse appliquée*, Paris: Gallimard 1933, 43-57.

Heb: Ivchun mazavim vehapsichoanalisa. Kitvei 4, chap. 14.

It: Diagnostica del fatto e psicoanalisi. Opere 5:241-252.

Por: O diagnóstico dos fatos e a psicanálise. (Tr:ED) Obr Comp-P 11:85-96.

Sp: El diagnóstico de los hechos y el psicoanálisis. (Tr:LLBT) Obr Comp 1948, 2:951-955. Obr Comp 1967/1968, 2:1043-1047.

El psicoanálisis y la instrucción forense. (Tr:LR) Obr Comp-BA 18: 23-34.

218

1923d Eine Teufelsneurose im siebzehnten Jahrhundert. Imago 1923, 9(1):1-34.
10605 GS 1924, 10:409-445. Leipzig/Vienna/Zurich: Int Psa Verlag 1924, 43 p; 1928, 81 p. GW 1940, 13:317-353.

A neurosis of demoniacal possession in the seventeenth century. (Tr:EG) CP 1925, 4:436-472.

A seventeenth-century demonological neurosis. (Revised tr:JS) SE 19: 72-105.

Dan: En djaevleneurose fra det 17 århundrede. (Tr: Boisen, M.) In *Totem og tabu*, Copenhagen: Hans Reitzel 1961.

Fr: Une névrose démoniaque au XVIIᵉ siècle. (Tr: Marty, Mme. E. & MB) RFPsa 1927, 1(2):337-369. In *Essais de psychanalyse appliquée*, Paris: Gallimard 1933, 213-254.

It: Una nevrosi demoniaca nel secolo decimosettimo. Opere 9.

Jap: Jūnana seki no akuma tsuki shinkeishō. (Tr: Kikuchi, E.) In *Sensō to shi no seishinbunseki*, CW-Ars 1932, 14:165-219.

Por: Uma neurose demoníaca no século XVII. (Tr:ED) Obr Comp-P 11: 245-280.

Sp: Una neurosis demoníaca en el siglo XVII. (Tr:LLBT) Obr Comp 1948, 2:1020-1036. (Tr:LR) Obr Comp-BA 18:187-218. Obr Comp 1967/ 1968, 2:1112-1127.

219

1940d   (& Breuer, Josef) Zur Theorie des hysterischen Anfalls. Z 1940, 25:
(1892)   107-110. GW 1941, 17:9-13.
10606

On the theory of hysterical attacks. (Tr:JS) CP 1950, 5:27-30. (Revised
tr:JS) SE 1:151-154.

It: Sulla teoria dell'attacco isterico. Opere 1:143-148.

Sp: Sobre la teoría del acceso histérico. (Tr:LR) Obr Comp-BA 21:20-23.
Obr Comp 1967/1968, 3:364-367.

220

1966b   (& Bullitt, William C.) *Thomas Woodrow Wilson, twenty-eighth*
(1938)   *president of the United States: a psychological study.* [Strachey (SE 24:
73593   466) comments that the book was clearly influenced by Freud's ideas but
questions whether any portion of it, except the introduction, was actually
written by Freud.] (Foreword: Bullitt, W. C.) (Intro: Freud, S.) Boston:
Houghton Mifflin 1967, 307 p; London: Weidenfeld & Nicolson 1967,
265 p.

Dut: *Thomas Woodrow Wilson, President van 1913-1921. Een psychologische
studie.* (Tr: Kraak-de Looze, E. M. A.) Meppel: J. A. Boom & Zoon
1967, 256 p.

Fr: *Le président Thomas Woodrow Wilson, portrait psychologique.* (Tr:
Tadié, M.) Paris: Albin Michel 1968.

It: *Il caso Thomas Woodrow Wilson, ventottesimo presidente degli Stati
Uniti. Uno studio psicologico.* (Tr: Sorani, R. & Petrillo, R.) Milan:
Feltrinelli 1967, xvii+249 p.

221

1912-   Totem und Tabu. Über einige Übereinstimmungen im Seelenleben der
1913   Wilden und der Neurotiker. Part I: Die Inzestscheu. Imago 1912,
10608   1(1):17-33. Pan Vienna 1912, (11, 18 Apr). Neues Wiener Journal 1912,
18 Apr. Part II: Das Tabu und die Ambivalenz der Gefühlsregungen.
(Presented to Vienna Psycho-Analytical Society 15 May 1912) Imago
1912, 1(3):213-227, (4):301-333. Part III: Animismus, Magie und
Allmacht der Gedanken. (Presented to Vienna Psycho-Analytical Society,
15 Jan 1913) Imago 1913, 2(1):1-21. Part IV: Die infantile Wiederkehr
des Totemismus. (Presented to Vienna Psycho-Analytical Society, 4 June
1913) Imago 1913, 2(4):357-408. In book form: Leipzig/Vienna: Heller
1913, v+149 p. Leipzig/Vienna/Zurich: Int Psa Verlag, 2nd ed, 1920.
3rd ed, 1922, vii+216 p. 5th ed, 1934, 194 p. GS 1924, 10:3-194.
GW 1940, 9:1-205. *See also* "Vorrede zur hebräischen Ausgabe von
Totem und Tabu" [269].

Totem and taboo. Resemblances between the psychic lives of savages
and neurotics. (Tr:AAB) NY: Moffat, Yard 1918, xi+265 p. London:

Routledge 1919, xi+265 p. London/NY: Penguin Books 1938, 159 p. BWSF 1938, 807-930.

Totem and taboo. Some points of agreement between the mental lives of savages and neurotics. (Tr:JS) London: Routledge & Kegan Paul 1950, 1960. NY: Norton 1952, xi+172 p. SE 13:1-161.

Dan: Totem og tabu. Nogle overensstemmelser mellam sjae lelivet hos de vilde og hos neurotikerne. (Tr: Boisen, M.) Copenhagen: Reitzel 1961.

Dut: Totem en taboe. Enige parallellen tussen het zieleleven der wilden en der neurotici. (Tr: Sauvage Nolting, W. J. J.) Amsterdam: Wereld-bibliotheek 1951, 199 p; (Intro: Westerman Holstijn, A. J.) 1961, 157 p.

Fr: Totem et tabou. (Tr: Jankélévitch, S.) Paris: Payot 1923, 1947, 1965, 1968, 186 p.

Gr: Totem kai tabou. (Tr: Meranaios, C.) Athens: Gavotsis 1930. (Tr: Meranaios, K. L. & Zographou, M.) Athens: Tsongas-Photopoulos 1949. Athens: Daremas 1962. (Tr: Syrros, P.) Athens: Panekdotiki 1965.

Heb: Totem vetabu. (Tr: Dvossis, I.) Jerusalem: Kirjeith Zefer 1939. Kitvei 3, chap. 1.

Hun: Totem és tabu. A vadnépek és neurotikusok lelki életének némely megegyezése. (Tr: Pártos, Z.; revised:SFe) Budapest: Manó Dick 1918, 174 p.

It: Totem e tabù. Di alcune concordanze nella vita psichica dei selvaggi e dei nevrotici. (Tr: Weiss, E.) (Pref: Servadio, E.) Bari: G. Laterza e Figli 1930, 1946, 1952, xx+180 p.

Totem e tabù. (Tr: Daniele, S.) Turin: Boringhieri 1969, 1970, 1972, 218 p. Opere 7.

Jap: Totemu to tabū. (Tr: Yoshioka, N.) Tokyo: Keimeisha 1926, vi+300 p. (Tr: Tsushima, K.) FCW-S 1932, 7:69-313. (Tr: Seki, E.) CW-Ars 1933, 11:3-287. (Tr: Doi, M.) In Bunka ron, SelFr-K 1953, 6:282 p. Rev ed (Tr: Yoshida, M.) SelFr-K 1970, 6:264 p.

Jug: Totem i tabu. (Tr: Milekić, P.) [Collected Works, Vol. 4] Novi Sad: Matica Srpska 1969.

Pers: Ravānkāvi va tahrime zanāshu'i ba mahārem. (Tr: Saheboz-Zamani, M. H. N.) Tehran: Ata'i Publications 1959, 124 p.

Por: Totem e tabu. (Tr:JPP) Rio de Janeiro: Guanabara Waissman, Koogan 1934, 285 p. Obr Comp-P 14:49-239.

Rus: Totem i tabu. Psikhologiia pervobytnoǐ kul'tury i religii. (Tr:MV) In Psikholog i psikhoanal, vyp. VI, 170 p.

Slo: Totem a tabu. (Tr: Münz, T.) Bratislava: Verlag der Slovenská akadémia vied 1966, 187 p.

Sp: Totem y tabú. (Tr:LLBT) Obr Comp-Madrid 8:7-240. Obr Comp-BA 8:9-168. Obr Comp 1948, 2:419-508. Obr Comp 1967/1968, 2:511-600. Madrid: Alianza Editorial 1970.

222

1917e   Trauer und Melancholie. Z 1917, 4(6):288-301. SKSN 1918, 4:356-377.
(1915) GS 1924, 5:535-553. Technik und Metapsychol 1924, 257-275. Theo-
10609   retische Schriften 1931, 157-177. GW 1946, 10:428-446.

Mourning and melancholia. (Tr:JRiv) CP 1925, 4:152-170. Extracts in
Rickman, J. (ed) *A general selection from the works of Sigmund Freud*,
London: HPI 1937, 142-161. (Revised tr:JS) SE 14:243-258.

Fr: Deuil et mélancholie. (Tr:MB & AB) In *Métapsychologie*, RFPsa 1936,
9(1):102-116. Paris: Gallimard 1940, 189-222. 1952. (Tr:JLa & Pontalis,
J. B.) In *Métapsychologie*, Paris: Gallimard 1968, 147-174.

It: Lutto e melanconio. (Tr: Molinari, E.) Riv Psa 1955, 1(3):3-15. Opere 8.

Jap: Hiai to yūutsu. (Tr: Hayashi, T.) In *Chōishiki shinrigaku*, CW-Ars 1932,
13:141-166.

Hiai to merankori. (Tr: Imura, T. & Katō, M.) In *Fuan no mondai*,
SelFr-K 1955, 10. Rev ed (Tr: Katō, M.) SelFr-K 1969, 10:24 p. (Tr:
Imura, T.) SelFr-JinSh 1970, 6:13 p.

Por: A tristeza e a melancolia. (Tr:CMdeF & IsIz) Obr Comp-P 8:235-254.

Rus: (Tr:MV) In *Osnovnye psikhologicheskie teorii v psikhoanalize. Psikholog
i psikhoanal*, vyp. III, 206 p.

Sp: La aflicción y la melancholía. (Tr:LLBT) Obr Comp-Madrid 9. Obr
Comp-BA 9:202-226. Obr Comp 1948, 1:1087-1096. Obr Comp 1967/
1968, 1:1075-1082.

223

1901a   Über den Traum. In Löwenfeld, L. & Kurella, H. *Grenzfragen des
10610   Nerven- und Seelenlebens*, Wiesbaden: Bergmann 1901, 307-344.
2nd ed (enlarged & published separately) 1911, 44 p. 3rd ed, Munich/
Wiesbaden: Bergmann 1921, 44 p. GS 1925, 3:189-256. Sexualtheorie
und Traumlehre 1931, 246-307. GW 1942, 2-3:643-700.

On dreams. (Tr: Eder, M. D.) (Intro: Mackenzie, W. L.) London:
Heinemann; NY: Rebman 1914, xxxii+110 p. (Tr:JS) London: HPI
1952, viii+80 p; NY: Norton 1952, 120 p. (Revised) SE 5:633-686.

Dan: Om drømmen. (Tr: Gelsted, O.) (Intro: Brüel, O.) In *Det ubevidste*,
Copenhagen: Martins 1920, 1944.

Dut: De droom als uiting van het onbewuste zieleleven. (Tr: Stärcke, J.)
Leiden: S. C. van Doesburgh 1913, 1917, x+74 p.

Fr: Le rêve et son interprétation. (Tr: Legros, H.) Paris: Gallimard 1925,
173 p; 1969, 118 p.

Heb: Al ha-holom. (Tr: Berachyahu, M.) Jerusalem: Ever 1954.

Hun: Az álómrol. (Tr:SFe) Budapest: Manó Dick 1915, 60 p; 1919.

It: Il sogno. (Tr:MLB) Naples: Nocera Superiore 1919, 64 p. (Tr: Luserna,

E.) Opere 4:5-52. (Tr:CLM) Excerpts in *Freud con antologia freudiana*, Turin: Boringhieri 1959, 1970.

Jap: (Tr:KO) Tokyo: Shunyodo 1929.

Jug: O snu. (Tr: Vilhar, A.) In *Tumačenje snova II*. [Collected Works, Vol. 7] Novi Sad: Matica Srpska 1969. *See* [227].

Pers: Ro'yā. (Tr: Hejazi, M.) Tehran: Ebne-sina 1947, 100+10 p.

Pol: O marzeniu seunem. (Tr: Rank, B.) Miedzynarodowy Naklad Psychoanalityczny 1923, 108 p.

Rus: Psikhologiia sna. Moskva: Tip. Pechatnoe dielo 1912, 64 p. In *Nauchnaia biblioteka "Sovremennykh problem,"* Moskva: Kn-vo "Sovremmenye problemy" 1924, 83 p.

Sp: Los sueños. (Tr:LLBT) Obr Comp-Madrid 2:217-298. Obr Comp-BA 2:159-216.

Sw: Om drömmen. (Tr: Bjerre, P.) In Bjerre, P. *Psykoanalysen. Dess uppkomst, omvandlingar och tillämpning*. Stockholm: Natur och Kultur 1924, 35-81.

224

1913a Ein Traum als Beweismittel. Z 1913, 1(1):73-78. SKSN 1918, 4:177-188.
10611 2nd ed, 1922. GS 1925, 3:267-277. Traumlehre 1925, 11-21. Sexualtheorie und Traumlehre 1931, 316-326. GW 1946, 10:12-22.

A dream which bore testimony. (Tr: Glover, E.) CP 1924, 2:133-143.

An evidential dream. (Revised tr:JS) SE 12:269-277.

Fr: Un rêve utilisé comme preuve. (Tr: Guérineau, D.) In *Névrose, psychose et perversion*. Paris: PUF 1973, 199-207.

It: Un sogno come mezzo di prova. Opere 7.

Sp: Un sueño como testimonio. (Tr:LR) Obr Comp-BA 19:113-124. Obr Comp 1967/1968, 3:81-87.

225

1913h Traum ohne kenntlichen Anlass. Erf Beisp Psa Prx [89] no. 1. GS 1925,
10612 3:41. GW 1942, 2-3:238. Longer version in *Die Traumdeutung* [227], from 3rd ed on.

"Pope is dead" dream. (Tr:AAB) Longer version in *The interpretation of dreams*, from 3rd ed, 1932, 227-228 on. (Tr:JS) SE 4:232.

Dream with an unrecognized precipitating cause. (Tr:JS) SE 13:194.

FOR OTHER LANGUAGES, see under *Die Traumdeutung* [227].

226

1922a Traum und Telepathie. Imago 1922, 8(1):1-22. GS 1925, 3:278-304.

10613   Traumlehre 1925, 22-48. Sexualtheorie und Traumlehre 1931, 326-354.
          GW 1940, 13:165-191.

          Dreams and telepathy. (Tr:CJMH) J 1922, 3:283-305. CP 1925,
          4:408-435. (Revised tr:JS) SE 18:197-220. In Devereux, G. *Psycho-*
          analysis and the occult, NY: IUP 1953, 69-86.

   It: Sogno e telepatia. Opere 9.

   Sp: El sueño y la telepatía. (Tr:LR) Obr Comp-BA 19:139-164. Obr Comp
          1967/1968, 3:96-115.

                                        227

1900a   Die Traumdeutung. Leipzig/Vienna: Deuticke 1900, iv+375 p. 2nd ed
(1899)   (enlarged & revised) 1909, vi+389 p. 3rd ed (enlarged & revised) 1911,
10614 x+418 p. 4th ed (enlarged & revised) 1914, x+498 p. 5th ed (enlarged &
         revised) 1919, ix+474 p. 6th ed, 7th ed (reprints of 5th ed with new
         preface & revised bibliography) 1921, 1922, vii+478 p. 8th ed (enlarged
         & revised from 7th ed) 1930, x+435 p. GS 1925, 2:1-543; 3:1-185.
         (Reprint of 8th ed) GW 1942, 2-3:xv+642 p.

         The interpretation of dreams. (Tr, intro:AAB) London: George Allen &
         Co; NY: Macmillan 1913, xiii+510 p. 2nd ed, London: Allen & Unwin
         1915; NY: Macmillan 1915, 1916, 1919, 1920, 1921, 1922, 1923, 1927,
         xiii+510 p. 3rd ed (revised in accordance with 8th German ed) London:
         Allen & Unwin; NY: Macmillan 1932, 1937, 1942, 1945, 1950, 600 p.
         Modern Library reprint of 3rd ed, NY: Random House 1950, 477 p.
         Reprint of 3rd ed with most of Chapter 1 omitted: BWSF 1938, 181-549.
         In *Major Works* 1952, 1955, 135-387.

         The interpretation of dreams. (Tr:JS) SE 4:xxiii-xxxii+1-338; SE 5:
         v-vi+339-627. London: Allen & Unwin & Hogarth Pr; NY: Basic Books
         1955, ix-xxxii+692 p.

  Arab: Tafsīr el ahlām. (Tr: Safouan, M.) Al Qāhirah: Dār El M'āref 1958.

         Tafsīr al-ahlām. (Tr: Lūqā, N.) Cairo: Dār al-Hilāl 1962.

    Cz: Výklad snu. (Tr: Friedmann, O.; revised: Pachta, J.) Prague: Julius
         Albert 1936, 1937, 1938, 1945, 382 p.

   Dan: Drømmetydning. (Tr: Boisen, M.) Copenhagen: Hans Reitzel 1960,
         2 vols: 515 p; 1966, 524 p.

   Fin: Unien tulkinta. (Tr: Puranen, E.) Jyväskylä: K. J. Gummerus
         Osakeyhtiö 1968, 526 p.

    Fr: La science des rêves. (Tr: Meyerson, I.) Paris: Alcan 1926; PUF 1950,
         1963, 350 p.

         L'Interprétation des rêves. (Tr: Berger, D.) Paris: PUF 1967, 573 p.

    Gr: Erminia ton oniron. (Tr: Meranaios, C.) Athens: Gavotsis 1935. (Tr:
         Zographou, M.) Athens: Maris 1950; Panekdotiki 1967.

   Heb: Pesher hachalomot. (Tr: Berachyahu, M.) 1950. Tel-Aviv: Yavne 1959.

Hun: Az alomfejtés. (Tr: Hollós, I.; revised:SFe) Budapest: Somló 1915, 1919, 1935.

It: L'interpretazione dei sogni. (Tr: Bazlen, R.) Rome: Ed. Astrolabio 1948, 1952, 510 p. (Tr: Fachinelli, E. & Fachinelli, H. T.) Turin: Boringhieri 1966; rev ed 1969, 1971, 637 p. Opere 3.

Il sogno e la sua interpretazione. Milan: Editore Dall'Oglio 1951, 135 p; 1963, 129 p.

Jap: Yume no chūshaku. (Tr:KO) FCW-S 1929, 1:1-298.

Yume handan. (Tr: Niizeki, R.) CW-Ars 1930, 2-3. (Tr:YT) 2 vols, SelFr-K 1954-1955, 11-12:322 p; 399 p. In *Sei no seishin bunseki*, Tokyo: Kawade Shobō Shinsha 1957. Tokyo: Shinchōsa 1964. (Tr:YT) SelFr-JinSh 1968, 2:503 p. Tokyo: Shinchōsha Pr 1969, vol. 1, 400 p; vol. 2, 396 p. Rev ed (Tr:YT & Kikumori, H.) SelFr-K 1969, 11:328 p; 12:401 p.

Jug: Tumačenje snova I/II. (Tr: Vilhar, A.) [Collected Works, Vol. 6/7] Novi Sad: Matica Srpska 1969, 350 p/351 p.

Kor: Ggum eui haeseog. (Tr: Yi, Yong-ho) Seoul: Baegjochulpansa 1963.

Pers: Ta'bire xāb va bimārihāye ravāni. (Tr: Pur-Bager, I.) Tehran: Asia Publications 1963, 462 p.

Por: Interpretação dos sonhos. (Tr:OG) Obr Comp-P 3-4. Rio de Janeiro: Editora Delta 1958.

Rus: Tolkovanie snovidieniĭ. (Tr: Kotik, M.) Moskva: Izd-vo "Sovremennye problemy" 1912, vii+448 p.

Sp: La interpretación de los sueños. (Tr:LLBT) Obr Comp-Madrid 6-7: 7-418. Obr Comp-BA 6:7-278; 7:7-316. Obr Comp 1948, 1:233-588. Obr Comp 1967/1968, 1:231-584. Madrid: Alianza Editorial 1968. (In part) Obr Comp 1967/1968, 3:150-157.

Agregados y modificaciones de *La interpretación de los sueños*. (Tr:LR) Obr Comp-BA 19:217-246. Obr Comp 1967/1968, 3:144-168.

Prólogo para la tercera edición inglesa de *La interpretación de los sueños*. (Tr:LR) Obr Comp-BA 20:195-196. Obr Comp 1967/1968, 3:321-322.

Sw: Drömtydning. (Tr: Landquist, J.) Stockholm: Bonniers 1927, 2 vols: 290 p, 227 p. (Tr: Landquist, J.; Andersson, O.; & Schedin, G.) Stockholm: Aldus/Bonniers 1958, 388 p. (Tr: Landquist, J.) Stockholm: Aldus/Bonniers 1958, 1960, 1962, 1964, 1968, 1971. 388 p.

228

1957a (& Oppenheim, David Ernst) Träume im Folklore. In *Dreams in*
(1911) *folklore*, Part II, NY: IUP 1958, 69-111.
46264
Dreams in folklore. (Tr: Richards, A. M. O.) (Intro:JS) NY: IUP 1958, 19-65. SE 12:180-203.

It: Sogni nel folklore. Opere 6.

229

1913h   Träume von Toten. Erf Beisp Psa Prx [89] no. 20. Z 1913, 1:377-382.
10615   In *Die Traumdeutung*, 4th ed, 1914, or 5th ed, 1919. GS 1925, 3:135.
        GW 1942, 2-3:433.

Dreams of dead people. (Tr:AAB) In *The interpretation of dreams*,
3rd ed, 1932, 399-400.

Dreams about dead people. (Tr:JS) SE 5:431. SE 13:197.

FOR OTHER LANGUAGES, see under *Die Traumdeutung* [227].

230

1915c   Triebe und Triebschicksale. Z 1915, 3(2):84-100. SKSN 1918, 4:252-278.
10616   2nd ed, 1922. GS 1924, 5:443-465. Technik und Metapsychol 1924,
        165-187. Theoretische Schriften 1931, 58-82. GW 1946, 10:210-232.

Instincts and their vicissitudes. (Tr:CMB) CP 1925, 4:69-83. *Major
Works* 1952, 1955, 412-421. Extracts in Rickman, J. (ed) *A general
selection from the works of Sigmund Freud*, London: HPI 1937, 79-98.
(Revised tr:JS) SE 14:117-140.

Fr: Les pulsions et leurs destins. (Tr:MB & AB) In *Métapsychologie*, RFPsa
      1936, 9(1):29-47. Paris: Gallimard 1940, 1952, 25-36.

Pulsions et destins des pulsions. (Tr:JLa & Pontalis, J. B.) In *Métapsychologie*, Paris: Gallimard 1968, 11-44.

Heb: Yezarim vegoralot yezarim. Kitvei 4, chap. 3.

It: Pulsion e loro destini. (Tr:CLM) In *Freud con antologia freudiana*,
      Turin: Boringhieri 1959, 1970. Opere 8.

Jap: Oyobi honnō no unmei. (Tr: Hayashi, T.) In *Chōishiki shinrigaku*,
      CW-Ars 1932, 13:15-46. (Tr: Okonogi, K.) SelFr-JinSh 1970, 6:19 p.

Por: Os instintos e seus destinos. (Tr:CMdeF & IsIz) Obr Comp-P 8:139-164.

Rus: (Tr:MV) In *Osnovnye psikhologicheskie teorii v psikhoanalize. Psikholog
      i psikhoanal*, vyp. III, 206 p.

Sp: Los instintos y sus destinos. (Tr:LLBT) Obr Comp-Madrid 9. Obr
      Comp-BA 9:116-139. Obr Comp 1948, 1:1047-1056. Obr Comp 1967/
      1968, 1:1035-1044.

231

1917c   Über Triebumsetzungen, insbesondere der Analerotik. Z 1917, 4(3):
10617   125-130. SKSN 1918, 4:139-148. 2nd ed, 1922. GS 1924, 5:268-276.
        Psychoanalyse der Neurosen 1926, 40-49. Sexualtheorie und Traumlehre
        1931, 116-124. GW 1946, 10:402-410.

On the transformation of instincts with special reference to anal erotism.
(Tr:EG) CP 1924, 2:164-171.

On transformations of instinct as exemplified in anal erotism. (Tr:JS)
SE 17:127-133.

Fr: Sur les transformations des pulsions, particulièrement dans l'érotisme anal. (Tr: Pichon, E. & Hoesli, H.) RFPsa 1928, 2(4):609-616. (Tr: Berger, D.) In *La vie sexuelle*, Paris: PUF 1969, 106-112.

It: Trasformazioni pulsionali, particolarmente dell'erotismo anale. Opere 8.

Jap: Honnō tenkan toku ni komo seiyoku no tenkanni tsuite. (Tr: Konuma, M.) In *Ijō seiyoku no bunseki*, CW-Ars 1933, 15:192-204. (Tr: Tanaka, M.) SelFr-JinSh 1969, 5:6 p.

Por: Em tôrno das transformações dos instintos e particularmente do erotismo anal. (Tr:OG & MG) Obr Comp-P 5:245-252.

Rus: (Tr:MV) In *Osnovnye psikhologicheskie teorii v psikhoanalize. Psikholog i psikhoanal*, vyp. III, 206 p.

Sp: Sobre las transmutaciones de los instintos y especialmente del erotismo anal. (Tr:LLBT) Obr Comp-Madrid 13:154-162. Obr Comp-BA 13: 125-131. Obr Comp 1948, 1:1011-1014. Obr Comp 1967/1968, 1: 999-1002.

232

19101 Typisches Beispiel eines verkappten Ödipustraumes. C 1910, 1:44-45.
10618 In *Die Traumdeutung* (from 1925 on). GW 1942, 2-3:404, note.

A typical example of a disguised Oedipus dream. (Tr:AAB) In *The interpretation of dreams*, 3rd ed, 1932, 374, footnote. (Tr:JS) SE 5:398, footnote.

FOR OTHER LANGUAGES, see under *Die Traumdeutung* [227].

233

1930a Das Unbehagen in der Kultur. Vienna: Int Psa Verlag 1930, 1931,
10619 136 p. GS 1934, 12:29-114. GW 1948, 14:421-506. Chap 1, Psa B 1929, 1:289-298. Chap 5 [In part] Psa B 1930, 2:5-13. In *Über die Psychoanalyse*, Frankfurt/M: Fischer 1953, 90-222.

Civilization and its discontents. (Tr:JRiv) London: HPI; NY: Cape & Smith 1930, 144 p. *Major Works* 1952, 1955, 767-802. NY: Doubleday 1958, 105 p. Excerpts in Rickman, J. (ed) *Civilization, war and death: selections from three works by Sigmund Freud*, London: HPI 1939, 26-81. (Tr:JS) SE 21:64-145. NY: Norton 1962, 112 p; 1964, 109 p.

Dan: Kulturens byrde. (Tr: Raun, C.) Copenhagen: Hans Reitzel 1966, 99 p.

Fr: Malaise dans la civilisation. (Tr: Odier, C. & Mme. C.) RFPsa 1934, 7(4):692-769. (Les documents bleus, no. 54) Paris: Denoël & Steele 1934, 81 p. RFPsa 1970, 34(1):9-80. Paris: PUF 1971.

Gr: Politismos pighi dystihias. (Tr: Cohen, A.) Athens: Gavotsis 1932. (Tr: Meranaios, K. & Zographou, M.) Athens: Tsongas 1950.

Heb: Tarbut belo nachat. (Tr: Baer, A.) Kitvei 5:118-184. Excerpt in *Hatarbut vehadat*, Merchavia: Hakibut Haarzi 1943.

It: Il disagio nella civiltà. (Tr: Flescher, J.) Rome: Ed. Scienza Moderna 1949, 151 p. (Tr: Sagittario, E.) In *Il disagio della civiltà e altri saggi,* Turin: Boringhieri 1971. Opere 10. (Tr: Weiss, E.) Chap 1 in *Il saggiatore,* Rome, 455-463.

Jap: Bunmei to fuman. (Tr: Hasegawa, S. & KO) In *Shakai, shūkyō, bunmei,* Tokyo: Shunyōdō 1931. (Tr: KO) In *Furido seishinbunsekigaku zenshu,* FCW-S 1931, 3:226-361.

Bunka no funa. (Tr: Kikuchi, E.) In *Sensō to shi no seishinbunseki,* CW-Ars 1932, 14:3-146. (Tr: Doi, M.) In *Bunka ron,* SelFr-K 1953, 6:148 p. Rev ed (Tr: Yoshida, M.) SelFr-K 1970, 6:134 p. (Tr: Kimura, M.) SelFr-JinSh 1969, 3:66 p.

Jug: Nelagodnost u kulturi. (Tr: Matić, V.; Jeretić, V.; & Bogičević, D.) In *Iz kulture i umetnosti,* [Collected Works, Vol. 5] Novi Sad: Matica Srpska 1969.

Nor: Unbehaget i kulturen. (Tr: Larsen, P.) Oslo: Cappelen 1966, 94 p.

Sp: El malestar en la civilizacion. (Tr: Novoda, C., A.) Santiago: Ediciones Extras, Empressa Letras 1936, 138 p.

El malestar en la cultura. (Tr:LR) Obr Comp-BA 19:11-90. Obr Comp 1967/1968, 3:1-66. Madrid: Afrodisio Aguado 1966.

Sw: Vi vantrivs i kulturen. (Tr:S.J.S.) Stockholm: Bonniers 1932, 117 p. (Revised tr:Löfgren, I.) Stockholm: Bonniers 1969, 99 p.

234

46295 Ein unbekannter Freud-Brief. [A hitherto unknown letter to the editor of the *Berliner Illustrierte Zeitung,* 1926.] Aufbau 1956, 22(21):18.

235

1915e Das Unbewusste. Z 1915, 3(4):189-203; (5):257-269. SKSN 1918,
10620 4:294-338. GS 1924, 5:480-519. Technik und Metapsychol 1924, 202-241. Theoretische Schriften 1931, 98-140. GW 1946, 10:264-303.

The unconscious. (Tr:CMB) CP 1925, 4:98-136. *Major Works* 1952, 1955, 428-443. (Tr:JS) SE 14:166-215.

Dan: Det ubevidste. (Tr: Gelsted, O.) In *Det ubevidste. Om psykoanalyse. Om drømmen,* Copenhagen: Martin 1920, 1944.

Fr: L'inconscient. (Tr:MB & AB) In *Métapsychologie,* RFPsa 1936, 9(1): 58-90. Paris: Gallimard 1940, 91-161. 1952. (Tr:JLa & Pontalis, J. B.) Paris: Gallimard 1968, 65-123.

Heb: Halo muda. Kitvei 4, chap. 5.

It: L'inconscio. Opere 8.

Jap: Muishiki ni tsuite. (Tr: Imura, T.) In *Jiga ron,* SelFr-K 1929, 1937, 1954, 1970, 4:193-240. SelFr-JinSh 1970, 6:27 p.

Muishiki. (Tr: Hayashi, T.) In *Chōishiki shinrigaku,* CW-Ars 1932, 13:65-119.

Por: O inconsciente. (Tr:CMdeF & IsIz) Obr Comp-P 8:179-220.

Rus: (Tr:MV) In [Psychological theories], Moscow(?)

Sp: Lo inconsciente. (Tr:LLBT) Obr Comp-Madrid 9. Obr Comp-BA 9:154-190. Obr Comp 1948, 1:1063-1080. Obr Comp 1967/1968, 1:1051-1068.

236

1919h Das Unheimliche. Imago 1919, 5(5-6):297-324. SKSN 1922, 5:229-273.
10621 GS 1924, 10:369-408. Dichtung und Kunst 1924, 99-138. GW 1947, 12:229-268.

The "uncanny." (Tr:ASt) CP 1925, 4:368-407. (Revised tr:JS) SE 17: 219-256.

Fr: L'inquiétante étrangeté. (Tr: Marty, Mme. E. & MB) In *Essais de psychanalyse appliquée*, Paris: Gallimard 1933, 163-211.

Heb: Hameuyam. Kitvei 4, chap. 1.

It: Sulla precarietà. In Zolla, E. *La psicoanalisi*, Milan: Garzanti 1960, 92-96.

Il perturbante. Opere 9. In *Saggi sull'arte, la letteratura e il linguaggio*, Turin: Boringhieri 1969, vol. 1.

Jap: Kimi warusa. (Tr:KO) In *Bunseki geijutsu ron*, FCW-S 1931, 1937, 6:302-352.

Bukimi na mono. (Tr: Shinoda, H. & Hamano, O.) In *Geijutsu no bunseki*, Tokyo: Ars 1933.

(Tr:YT) In *Geijutsu ron*, SelFr-K 1953, 7:56 p. SelFr-JinSh 1969, 3:31 p. Rev ed (Tr:YT & Ikeda, K.) SelFr-K 1970, 7:58 p.

(Tr: Imura, T. & YT) In *Sei no seishin bunseki*, Tokyo: Kawade Shobō Shinsha 1957. (Tr: Kikumori, H.) Tokyo: Kawade Shobō Shinsha 1972, 38 p.

Sp: Lo siniestro. (Tr:LR) Obr Comp-BA 18:151-186.

237

1924d Der Untergang des Ödipuskomplexes. Z 1924, 10(3):245-252. GS 1924,
10622 5:423-430. Psychoanalyse der Neurosen 1926, 169-177. Neurosenlehre und Technik 1931, 191-199. GW 1940, 13:395-402.

The passing of the Oedipus complex. (Tr:JRiv) J 1924, 5(4):419-424. CP 1924, 2:269-276.

The dissolution of the Oedipus complex. (Revised tr:JS) SE 19:173-179.

Fr: Le déclin du complexe d'Oedipe. (Tr:AB) RFPsa 1934, 7(3):394-399.

La disparition du complexe d'Oedipe. (Tr: Berger, D.) In *La vie sexuelle*, Paris: PUF 1969, 117-122.

It: Il tramonto del complesso edipico. (Tr:CLM) In *Freud con antologia freudiana,* Turin: Boringhieri 1959, 1970. In *La vita sessuale,* Turin: Boringhieri 1970. Opere 10.

Jap: Edipusu fukugō no suimetsu. (Tr: Konuma, M.) In *Ijo seiyoku no bunseki,* CW-Ars 1933, 15:70-80.

Edepusu konpurekusu no shōmetsu. (Tr:YT) In Aijō no shinrigaku, SelFr-K 1960, 14:14 p. (Tr: Agō, Y.) SelFr-JinSh 1970, 6:6 p.

Por: O fim do complexo de Édipo. (Tr:OG & GP) Obr Comp-P 14:23-30.

Sp: El final del complejo de Edipo. (Tr:LLBT) Obr Comp-Madrid 14: 263-270. Obr Comp-BA 14:210-215. Obr Comp 1948, 2:409-411. Obr Comp 1967/1968, 2:501-503.

238

1915d Die Verdrängung. Z 1915, 3(3):129-138. SKSN 1918, 4:279-293.
10623 GS 1924, 5:466-479. Technik und Metapsychol 1924, 188-201. Theoretische Schriften 1931, 83-97. GW 1946, 10:248-261.

Repression. (Tr:CMB) CP 1925, 4:84-97. *Major Works* 1952, 1955, 422-427. Extracts in Rickman, J. (ed) *A general selection from the works of Sigmund Freud,* London: HPI 1937, 99-110. (Tr:JS) SE 14:146-158.

Fr: Le refoulement. (Tr:MB & AB) In *Métapsychologie,* RFPsa 1936, 9(1):48-58. Paris: Gallimard 1940, 67-90. 1952. (Tr:JLa & Pontalis, J. B.) Paris: Gallimard 1968, 45-63.

Heb: Hahadchaka. Kitvei 4, chap. 4.

It: La rimozione. (Tr:CLM) In *Freud con antologia freudiana,* Turin: Boringhieri 1959, 1970. Opere 8.

Jap: Appaku genshō. (Tr: Hayashi, T.) In *Chōishiki shinrigaku,* CW-Ars 1932, 13:47-64.

Yokuatsu. (Tr: Imura, T. & Katō, M.) In *Fuan no mondai,* SelFr-K 1955, 10. Rev ed (Tr: Katō, M.) SelFr-K 1969, 10:18 p. (Tr: Imura, T.) SelFr-JinSh 1970, 6:9 p.

Por: A repressão. (Tr:CMdeF & IsIz) Obr Comp-P 8:165-178.

Rus: (Tr:MV) In *Osnovnye psikhologicheskie teorii v psikhoanalize. Psikholog i psikhoanal,* vyp. III, 206 p.

Sp: La represión. (Tr:LLBT) Obr Comp-Madrid 9. Obr Comp-BA 9: 140-153. Obr Comp 1948, 1:1057-1062. Obr Comp 1967/1968, 1: 1045-1050.

239

1916a Vergänglichkeit. In *Das Land Goethes 1914-1916,* (ed Berliner Goethe-
(1915) bund) Stuttgart: Deutsche Verlagsanstalt 1916, 37-38. Almanach 1927,
10624 1926:39-42. GS 1928, 11:291-294. GW 1946, 10:358-361.

On transcience. (Tr:JS) J 1942, 23(2):84-85. CP 1950, 5:79-82. SE 14: 305-307.

Fr: Fugitivité. (Tr:MB) In Bonaparte, M. "Deux personnes devant l'abîme," RFPsa 1956, 20(3):307-315.

It: Caducità. Opere 8.

Jap: Mujō to yukoto. (Tr:YT) In *Aijō no shinrigaku*, SelFr-K 1960, 14:8 p. SelFr-JinSh 1969, 3:4 p. (Tr: Kikumori, H.) Tokyo: Kawade Shobō Shinsha Pr 1972, 4 p.

Sp: Lo perecedero. (Tr:LR) Obr Comp-Madrid 9. Obr Comp-BA 19: 253-256. Obr Comp 1948, 1(10). Obr Comp 1967/1968, 3:172-174.

240

1925h Die Verneinung. Imago 1925, 11(3):217-221. Psychoanalyse der
10625 Neurosen 1926, 199-204. GS 1928, 11:3-7. Theoretische Schriften 1931, 399-404. GW 1948, 14:11-15.

Negation. (Tr:JRiv) J 1925, 6(4):367-371. Extracts in Rickman, J. (ed) *A general selection from the works of Sigmund Freud*, London: HPI 1937, 63-67. (Revised tr:JRiv) CP 1950, 5:181-185. (Tr: Rapaport, D.) Extracts in Rapaport, D. *Organization and pathology of thought*, NY: Columbia Univ Pr 1951, 338-348. (Tr:JS) SE 19:235-239.

Fr: La négation. (Tr: Hoesli, H.) RFPsa 1934, 7(2):174-177.

Heb: Hashlila. Kitvei 4, chap. 9.

It: La negazione. In Zolla, E. *La psicanalisi*, Milan: Garzanti 1960, 116-121. Opere 10.

Jap: (Tr:YT) SelFr-JinSh 1969, 3:4 p.

Por: A negação. (Tr:ED) Obr Comp-P 11:293-298.

Sp: La negación. (Tr:LLBT) Rev Psicol gen apl, Madrid, 1948, 3:19-24. Obr Comp 1948, 2:1042-1043. Obr Comp 1967/1968, 2:1134-1135. (Tr:LR) Obr Comp-BA 21:195-202.

241

1913h Verschämte Füsse. Erf Beisp Psa Prx [89] no. 13. Z 1913, 1:377-382.
10626 GS 1928, 11:301-303. Neurosenlehre und Technik 1931, 306-308. GW 1946, 10:41.

Disgraced feet (shoes). (Tr:JS) SE 13:196.

242

1919f Victor Tausk. (obituary). [Signed "Die Redaktion"] Z 1919, 5:225-227.
10627 GS 1928, 11:277-279. GW 1947, 12:316-318.

Victor Tausk. (Tr:JS) SE 17:273-275.

It: Necrologio di Victor Tausk. Opere 9.

Sp: En memoria de Victor Tausk. (Tr:LR) Obr Comp-BA 20:201-203. Obr Comp 1967/1968, 3:324-325.

243

1920b   Zur Vorgeschichte der analytischen Technik. Z 1920, 6:79-81. SKSN
10628   1922, 5:141-145. Technik und Metapsychol 1924, 148-151. GS 1925,
        6:148-151. Neurosenlehre und Technik 1931, 423-426. GW 1947,
        12:309-312.

        A note on the prehistory of the technique of analysis. (Tr:JS) CP 1950,
        5:101-104. SE 18:263-265.

Heb: Lekedem toldoteha shel hatechnika haanlitit. Kitvei 3, chap. 5.

It: Preistoria della tecnica analitica. Opere 9.

Jap: (Tr:KO) FCW-S 1933, 8:7 p. Bunseki gihō zenshi ni tsuite. (Tr: Kosawa,
        H.) In *Seishinbunseki ryōhō*, SelFr-K 1959, 15:211-216. Rev ed (Tr:
        Okonogi, K.) SelFr-K 1969, 15.

Por: Para a pré-história da técnica psicanalítica. (Tr:JPP, OG & GP) Obr
        Comp 10:313.

Rus: (Tr:MV) In *Metodika i tekhnika psikhoanaliza. Psikholog i psikhoanal*,
        vyp. IV, 136 p.

Sp: Para la prehistoria de la técnica psicoanalítica. (Tr:LLBT) Obr Comp-
        Madrid 14. Obr Comp-BA 14:168-170. Obr Comp 1948, 2:361-363.
        Obr Comp 1967/1968, 2:453-456.

244

(1916-   Vorlesungen zur Einführung in die Psychoanalyse. [First published in
1917)   three separate parts.] Part I: Die Fehlleistungen (Lectures 1-4), Leipzig/
10629   Vienna: Heller 1916. Part II: Der Traum (Lectures 5-15), Leipzig/
         Vienna: Heller 1916; with title, Vorlesungen über den Traum, Leipzig/
         Vienna/Zurich: Int Psa Verlag 1922. Part III: Allgemeine Neurosen-
         lehre (Lectures 16-28), Leipzig/Vienna: Heller 1917; with title,
         Allgemeine Neurosenlehre, Leipzig/Vienna/Zurich: Int Psa Verlag
         1922. In one volume, Leipzig/Vienna: Heller 1917, viii+545 p. 2nd ed
         (revised, with index), 1918, viii+553 p. 3rd ed (revised), Leipzig/
         Vienna/Zurich: Int Psa Verlag 1920, viii+553 p. 4th ed (revised), 1922,
         viii+554 p. Pocket edition (without index) 1922, iv+495 p; (with index)
         1922, iv+502 p. GS 1924, 7:483 p. 5th ed, Leipzig/Vienna/Zurich:
         Int Psa Verlag 1926, 483 p; 1930, 501 p. Berlin: Kiepenheuer 1933,
         524 p. GW 1940, 11:495 p.

         A general introduction to psychoanalysis. (Foreword: Hall, G. S.) NY:
         Boni & Liveright 1920, x+406 p.

         Introductory lectures on psycho-analysis. (Tr:JRiv) (Pref:EJ) London:
         Allen & Unwin 1922, 1923, 395 p. 2nd ed (revised), 1929, 1933, 1936,
         395 p. *Major Works* 1952, 1955, 449-638.

         A general introduction to psychoanalysis. (Tr:JRiv) (Pref: Hall, G. S.;
         EJ) with introductory note by Freud, Nov 1934, NY:Liveright 1935,
         412 p. Garden City, NY: Garden City Publ 1943. NY: Perma Giants

1949, 412 p. NY: Doubleday 1953. NY: Washington Sq Pr 1960. Toronto: Smithers.

Introductory lectures on psycho-analysis. (Tr:JS) SE 15-16:15-239, 243-463. In *The complete introductory lectures on psychoanalysis*, NY: Norton 1966.

Arab: Derasat l'ousoud al-ta'lil. (Tr: Al-Nafseah, N. W. A.) Cairo: Dār El-Ma'aref 1950, 1953.

Chin: (Tr: Kao, Chio-Fu) Shanghai: Commercial Pr 1933.

Cz: Uvod do psychoanalysy. (Tr: Friedmann, O.) Prague: Julius Albert 1936, 389 p. 1945.

Dan: Forelaesninger til indføring i psykoanalysen. (Tr: Boisen, M.) Copenhagen: Hans Reitzel 1958, 1960, 1965, 1966, 376 p.

Dut: Inleiding tot de studie der psychoanalyse. (Tr, intro & foreword: Renterghem, A. W. van) Antwerp/Amsterdam: Maatsch. voor goede en goedkoope lectuur 1918, 1919, 2 vols: xxv+268 p, 270 p. 1933, xxxiii+660 p. Wereldbibliotheek 1936, 1950, 1951, 1952, 1955, 1958, 1963, 1967, 423 p.

Fin: Johdatus psykoanalyysiin. (Tr: Puranen, E.) Jyväskylä: K. J. Gummerus Osakeyhtiö 1964, 588 p. (Includes [166].)

Fr: Introduction à la psychanalyse. (Tr: Jankélévitch, S.) Paris: Payot 1922, 1951, 1962, 1969, 443 p.

Gr: Isaghoghi tis psychanalyssis. (Tr: Ferentinos, S.) Athens: Gavotsis 1932. (Tr: Lillis, M.) Athens: Prometheus 1950.

Issagōgē is tēn psuhanalussē. (Tr: Pangalos, A.) Athens: Gobostēs 1960.

Issaghoghistin psychanalyssi. (Tr: Syrros, P.) Athens: Panekdotiki 1962.

Heb: Mavo lapsichoanalysa. (Tr: Dvossis, I.) Tel-Aviv: A. J. Steibel 1930, 1935. Kitvei 1.

Shiurim bemavo lepsichoanalisa. Tel-Aviv: Stiebl 1938. [Lectures 5-15, 19] in *Al hachalom. Revisia al torat hachalom*. Jerusalem: Ever 1954.

Hin: Phrāyaḍ manovišleṣan. (Tr: Vedalankar, D.) Delhi: Rajpal 1958.

Hun: Bevezetés a pszichoanalizisbe. Huszonnyolc előadás. (Tr: Hermann, I.) In Ferenczi, S. & Storfer, A. (eds) *Collected papers of Sigmund Freud*, Vol. 1, Vienna: Int Psa Verlag & Budapest: Somló 1932, 407 p. Chapters VII, XI, XXIII in Buda, B. *A pszichoanalizis és modern irányzatai*, Budapest: Gondolat 1971, 94-133.

It: Introduzione allo studio della psicoanalisi. (Tr: Weiss, E.) (Pref:MLB) Zurich/Naples/Vienna: Libreria Psicoanalitica Internazionale 1922, vii+441 p. Rome: Astrolabio 1947, 494 p; 1965, 526 p.

Introduzione alla psicoanalisi. (Tr: Dogana, F. & Sagittario, E.) In *Introduzione all psicoanalisis, Prima e seconda serie di lezioni*. Turin: Boringhieri 1969, 1970, 1972. Opere 8.

Jap: Seishinbunseki nyūmon. (Tr: Yasuda, T.) Tokyo: Ars. Vol. 1, 1926, 349 p; Vol. 2, 1928, 328 p. CW-Ars 1931, 7:3-349 p; 8:353-680 p.
(Tr: Marui, K.) Part 1, SelFr-K 1952, 1:331 p. Part 2, SelFr-K 1953, 2:323 p. (Tr: Imura, T. & Baba K.) Part 1, SelFr-K 1970, 1:353 p. Part 2, SelFr-K 1970, 2:356 p.
(Tr: Yasuda, T. & Yasuda, I.) Tokyo: Kadokawa Shoten Pr 1953, 515 p. (Tr: Toyokawa, N.) Tokyo: Shinchōsha Pr 1956, Vol. 1, 297 p; Vol. 2, 283 p. (Tr: Kakeda, K.) Tokyo: Chuō Kōronsha 1966, 478 p; 1967, 346 p. (Tr: Kakeda, K. & YT) SelFr-JinSh 1971, 1:377 p.

Jug: Uvod us psihoanalizu. (Tr: Lorenc, B.) (Intro: Klajn, H. & Kirin, V.) Belgrad: Kosmos 1933, xv+448 p; 1937, xxv+448 p; 1958, 1961, xli+381 p; 1964, xliii+424 p. [Collected Works, Vol. 2] Novi Sad: Matica Srpska 1969, 434 p.

Nor: Forelaesninger til indførelse i psykoanalyse. (Tr: Schjelderup, K.) Oslo: Gyldendal 1929, 510 p. Rev ed 1930, 500 p. 2nd ed, 1957, 380 p. 3rd ed, 1961, 384 p. Rev ed, 1962, 384 p. Rev ed, 1964, 384 p. 4th ed, 1967, 384 p.

Pol: Wstep do psychoanalizy. (Tr: Klempnerówna, S. & Zaniewicki, W.; revised: Bychowski, G.) Warsaw: Wydawnictwo, J. Przoworskiego 1935, 583 p; Ksiazka i Wiedza 1958.

Por: Introdução à psicanálise. (Tr:ED) Obr Comp-P 12:9-274; 13:5-258.

Rus: Letsii po vvedeniiu v psikhoanaliz. (Tr:MV) Psikholog i psikhoanal, vyp. I, II, 250, 249 p. 2nd ed (vol. I), 1922.

Sp: Introducción a la psicoanálisis. (Tr:LLBT) Obr Comp-Madrid 4:9-305; 5:9-278. Obr Comp-BA 4:303 p; 5:289 p. Obr Comp 1948, 2:59-300. Obr Comp 1967/1968, 2:151-392.

Sw: Orientering i psykoanalysen. (Tr: Asker, A.) Stockholm: Natur och Kultur 1955, 549 p.

Yid: Areinfier in psichoanalise. (Tr: Weinrich, W.) Wilna: Yiddischer Visenschaftlicher Institute. Vol. 1 (Lectures 1-4) 1936, 61+3 p. Vol. 2 (Lectures 5-10) 1937, 65-144. Vol. 3 (Lectures 11-15) 1938, 145-207. Vol. 4, set in type but never published.

245

1893h Vortrag "Über den psychischen Mechanismus hysterischer Phänomene."
10634 [Lecture delivered by Dr. Sigm. Freud at a meeting of the 'Wiener medizinischer Club', 11 Jan 1893. Special shorthand report by the Wiener medizinische Presse, revised by the lecturer.]*
Abs Wien med Presse 1893, 34(4:22 Jan):121-126; (5:29 Jan): 165-167.
* SE 3:27, footnote.

On the psychical mechanism of hysterical phenomena. [A lecture.] (Tr:JS) J 1956, 37(1):8-13. (Revised tr:JS) SE 3:27-39.

246

1907a Der Wahn und die Träume in W. Jensens *Gradiva*. Leipzig/Vienna:
10641 Heller 1907, 81 p (*Schriften zur angewandten Seelenkunde* I). Leipzig/
Vienna: Deuticke 1908, 81 p. 2nd ed (with Postscript) 1912, 87 p.
3rd ed, 1924. GS 1925, 9:273-367. GW 1941, 7:31-125.

Delusion and dream. (Tr: Downey, H. M.) (Intro: Hall, G. S.) (Omits
"Postscript") NY: Moffat, Yard 1917, 243 p. London: Allen & Unwin
1921, 213 p. In Rieff, P. *Delusion and dream and other essays*, (Tr:
Zohn, H.) (Intro: Rieff, P.) (Includes "Postscript") Boston: Beacon Pr
1956, 25-121.

Delusions and dreams in Jensen's *Gradiva*. (Tr:JS) (Includes "Postscript")
SE 9:7-95.

Fr: Délires et rêves dans la *Gradiva* de Jensen. (Tr:MB) Paris: Gallimard
1931, 1933, 1949, 1971, 221 p.

Heb: Hashigyonot vehachalomot basipur *Gradiva* shel Yansen. Kitvei 2,
chap. 4.

It: Delirio e sogni nella *Gradiva* di W. Jensen. (Tr: Benedicty, G. de)
(Pref:MLB) Zurich/Naples/Vienna: Libreria Psicoanalitica Internazionale 1923, 96 p.

Gradiva. Un racconto di Wilhelm Jensen e uno etudio analitico di
Sigmund Freud. (Tr:CLM) Turin: Boringhieri 1961, 283 p. With title:
Il diliro e i sogni nella *Gradiva* di Wilhelm Jensen. Opere 5:263-338.

Jap: Yume to bōsō. (Tr: Yasuda, T.) In *Geijutsu to seishin bunseki*, Tokyo:
Logos Pr 1929, 115-250.

(Tr: Chino, S.) CW-Ars n.d., 10. (Tr: Ikeda, K.) SelFr-JinSh 1969,
3:76 p. (Tr: Kikumori, H.) Tokyo: Kawade Shobō Shinsha Pr 1972,
77 p.

Jug: Sumanutost i snovi u *Gradivi* V. Jensena. (Tr: Matić, V.; Jeretić, V.;
& Bogičević, D.) In *Iz kulture i umetnosti*, [Collected Works, Vol. 5]
Novi Sad: Matica Srpska 1969.

Por: O delírio e os sonhos na *Gradiva* de W. Jensen. (Tr:OG & MG) Obr
Comp-P 5:5-100.

Rus: Bred i sny v "Gradive" Iensena. Moskva 1912.

Sp: El delirio y los sueños en la *Gradiva* de W. Jensen. (Tr:LLBT) Obr
Comp-Madrid 3:301-332. Obr Comp-BA 3:209-377. Obr Comp 1948,
1:589-634. Obr Comp 1967/1968, 1:585-628.

247

1933b Warum Krieg? Paris: Internationales Institut für geistige Zusammen-
(1932) arbeit (Völkerbund) 1933, 25-62. GS 1934, 12:349-363. GW 1950,
10642 16:13-27. Part in Psa B 1933, 5:207-216.

Why war? (Tr: Gilbert, S.) Paris: International Institute of Intellectual

Cooperation (League of Nations) 1933, 57. London: Peace Pledge Union 1939, 24 p. Excerpts in Rickman, J. (ed) *Civilization, war and death: selections from three works by Sigmund Freud*, London:HPI 1939, 82-97. (Tr:JS) CP 1950, 5:273-287. SE 22:203-215. In Ebenstein, W. *Great political thinkers*, NY: Rinehart 1960, 860-868. In Bramson, L. & Goethals, G. W. *War: studies from psychology, sociology, anthropology*, NY: Basic Books 1964, 71-80.

Dut: Waarom oorlog? (Tr: Straat, E.) Amsterdam: Seijffardt's Boek-en Muziekh 1933, 61 p.

Fr: Lettre à Einstein. (Tr: Briod, B.) In *Pourquoi la guerre?* Institut International de Coopération Intellectuelle, Paris: Stock 1933, 25-63. RFPsa 1957, 21(6):757-768.

Heb: Milchama lama? (Tr: Baer, A.) Kitvei 5:7-18.

Hun: Kell-e haboru? Emberismeret 1936, 2.

It: Perché la guerra? (Tr: Candreva, S. & Sagittario, E.) In *Il disagio della civiltà e altri saggi*, Turin: Boringhieri 1971. Opere 11.

Jap: (Tr: Itō, T.) FCW-S 1930, 4:27 p.

Naniyue no sensō ka. (Tr:KO) Tokyo: Shunyodo 1940.

(Tr: Doi, M. & Yoshida, M.) In *Gensō no mirai*, SelFr-K 1955, 8:26 p.

Sp: El porqué de la guerra? (Tr:LR) Obr Comp-BA 18:245-258.

248

1919a   Wege der psychoanalytischen Therapie. [Address delivered at 5th Int
(1918)   Psa Cong, Budapest, 29 Sept 1918] Z 1919, 5(2):61-68. SKSN 1922,
10643   5:146-158. Technik und Metapsychol 1924, 136-147. GS 1925, 6:
           136-147. Neurosenlehre und Technik 1931, 411-422. GW 1947, 12:
           183-194.

Turnings in the ways of psycho-analytic therapy. (Tr:JRiv) CP 1924, 2:392-402.

Lines of advance in psycho-analytic therapy. (Tr:JS) SE 17:159-168.

Fr: Les voies nouvelles de la thérapeutique psychanalytique. (Tr:AB) In *La technique psychanalytique*, Paris: PUF 1953, 1967, 1970, 131-141.

It: Vie della terapia psicoanalitica. Opere 9.

Jap: (Tr:KO) FCW-S 1933, 8:23 p.

Seishinbunseki ryōhō no michi. (Tr: Kosawa, H.) In *Seishinbunseki ryōhō*, SelFr-K 1959, 15:194-210. Rev ed (Tr: Okonogi, K.) SelFr-K 1969, 15.

Nor: (Tr: Schjelderup, K.) In *Psykoanalysen i praksis. Et utvalg mindre arbeider*, Oslo: Gyldendal 1930, 174 p.

Por: Caminhos da terapêutica psicanalítica. (Tr:JPP, OG & GP) Obr Comp-P 10:303-312.

Rus: (Tr:MV) In *Metodika i tekhnika psikhoanaliza. Psikholog i psikhoanal,* vyp. IV, 136 p.

Sp: Los caminos de la terapia psicoanalítica. (Tr:LLBT) Obr Comp-BA 14: 159-167. Obr Comp 1948, 2:357-360. Obr Comp 1967/1968, 2:449-452.

249

1931b Über die weibliche Sexualität. Z 1931, 17(3):317-322. GS 1934, 12:
10644 120-140. GW 1948, 14:517-537.

Concerning the sexuality of woman. (Tr: Jackson, E. B.) Q 1932, 1(1):191-199.

Female sexuality. (Tr:JRiv) J 1932, 13(3):281-297. CP 1950, 5:252-272. (Revised tr:JS) SE 21:225-243.

Fr: Sur la sexualité féminine. (Tr: Berger, D.) In *La vie sexuelle,* Paris: PUF 1969, 139-155.

It: Sessualità femminile. (Tr: Campione, A.; Candreva, S.; Montinari, M.; CLM; & Sagittario, E.) In *La vita sessuale,* Turin: Boringhieri 1970. Opere 11.

Jap: (Tr: Kakeda, K.) SelFr-K 1953, 5:36 p. (Tr: Kakeda, K. & Shimura, H.) SelFr-JinSh 1969, 5:18 p.

Sp: Sobre la sexualidad femenina. (Tr:LR) Obr Comp-BA 21:279-300. Obr Comp 1967/1968, 3:518-532.

250

1896b Weitere Bemerkungen über die Abwehr-Neuropsychosen. Neurol Zbl
10645 1896, 15(10, 15 May):434-448. SKSN 1906, 1:112-134. 2nd ed, 1911. 3rd ed, 1920. 4th ed, 1922. GS 1925, 1:363-387. GW 1952, 1:379-403. Abs Inhalts wiss Arb 35.

Further observations on the defense neuropsychoses. (Tr:AAB) SPH 1909, 155-174. *Major Works* 1952, 1955, 97-106.

Further remarks on the defence neuro-psychoses. (Tr:JR) CP 1924, 1:155-182.

Further remarks on the neuro-psychoses of defence. (Revised tr:JS) SE 3:162-185.
Abs (Tr:JS) SE 3:253.

Fr: Nouvelles remarques sur les psychonévroses de défense. (Tr:JLa) In *Névrose, psychose et perversion.* Paris: PUF 1973, 61-81.

It: Nuove osservazioni sulle neuropsicosi da difesa. (Tr: Campione, A.) Opere 2:307-330.

Por: Novas observações sôbre as neuropsicoses de defesa. (Tr:CMdeF) Obr Comp-P 2:251-272.

Sp: Nuevas observaciones sobre las neuropsicosis de defensa. (Tr:LLBT)

Obr Comp-Madrid 11:236-264. Obr Comp-BA 11:175-194. Obr Comp 1948, 1:220-232. Obr Comp 1967/1968, 1:219-230.

251

1913c   Weitere Ratschläge zur Technik der Psychoanalyse (I) [This general title
10646   dropped after 1918]: Zur Einleitung der Behandlung. Die Frage der
           ersten Mitteilungen—Die Dynamik der Heilung. Z 1913, 1(1):1-10;
           (2):139-146. SKSN 1918, 4:412-440. 2nd ed, 1922. Technik und
           Metapsychol 1924, 84-108. GS 1925, 6:84-108. Neurosenlehre und
           Technik 1931, 359-385. GW 1943, 8:454-478.

Further recommendations in the technique of psycho-analysis: on beginning the treatment. The question of the first communications. The dynamics of the cure. (Tr:JRiv) CP 1924, 2:342-365.

On beginning the treatment (further recommendations on the technique of psycho-analysis I). (Modified tr:JS) SE 12:123-144.

Fr: Le début du traitement. (Tr:AB) In La technique psychanalytique, Paris: PUF 1953, 1970, 80-104.

Hun: A pzaichoanalitikus kezelés elöfeltételei (tanacsik a gyakorlo analitikus szamara). (Tr:SFe) Gyogyaszat 1913, 53:129-133.

It: Nuovi consigli sulla tecnica della psicoanalisi: 1. Inizio del trattamento. Opere 7.

Jap: (Tr:KO) FCW-S 1933, 8:34 p.

Bunsekichiryō no kaishi ni tsuite. (Tr: Kosawa, H.) In Seishinbunseki ryōhō, SelFr-K 1959, 15:118-156. Rev ed (Tr: Okonogi, K.) SelFr-K 1969, 15.

Por: A iniciação do tratamento. (Tr:JPP, OG & GP) Obr Comp-P 10: 247-270.

Rus: In Psikhoterapiia 1913, no. 2. (Tr:MV) In Metodika i tekhnika psikhoanaliza. Psikholog i psikhoanal, vyp. IV, 136 p.

Sp: La iniciación del tratamiento. (Tr:LLBT) Obr Comp-BA 14:119-138. Obr Comp 1948, 2:334-344. Obr Comp 1967/1968, 2:426-436.

252

1914g   Weitere Ratschläge zur Technik der Psychoanalyse (II) [This general title
10647   dropped after 1918]: Erinnern, Wiederholen und Durcharbeiten.
           Z 1914, 2(6):485-491. SKSN 1918, 4:441-452, 2nd ed, 1922. Technik
           und Metapsychol 1924, 109-119. GS 1925, 6:109-119. Neurosenlehre
           und Technik 1931, 385-396. GW 1946, 10:126-136.

Further recommendations in the technique of psychoanalysis: recollection, repetition and working through. (Tr:JRiv) CP 1924, 2:366-376.

Remembering, repeating and working-through. (Further recommendations on the technique of psycho-analysis II). (Modified tr:JS) SE 12: 147-156.

Fr: Remémoration, répétition, et élaboration. (Tr:AB) In *La technique psychanalytique*, Paris: PUF 1953, 1970, 105-115.

It: Rievocazione, ripetizione ed elaborazione nelle tecnica del tratamento psicoanalitico. (Tr:CLM) Riv Psa 1955, 1(1):11-17.

Nuovi consigli sulla tecnica della psicoanalisis: 2. Ricordare, ripetere ed elaborare. (Tr:CLM) In *Freud con antologia freudiana*, Turin: Boringhieri 1959, 1970. Opere 7.

Jap: (Tr:KO) FCW-S 1933, 8:15 p.

Sōki, hampuku, tettei sōsa. (Tr: Kosawa, H.) In *Seishinbunseki ryōhō*, SelFr-K 1959, 15:157-171. Rev ed (Tr: Okonogi, K.) SelFr-K 1969, 15.

(Tr: Okonogi, K.) SelFr-JinSh 1970, 6:10 p.

Por: Recordar-se, repetir e elaborar. (Tr:JPP, OG & GP) Obr Comp-P 10:279-288.

Rus: (Tr:MW) In [Methods], Moscow: Staatsverlag 1913.

Sp: Recuerdo, repetición y elaboración. (Tr:LLBT) Obr Comp-BA 14: 139-146. Obr Comp 1948, 2:345-349. Obr Comp 1967/1968, 2:437-441.

253

1915a Weitere Ratschläge zur Technik der Psychoanalyse (III) [This general
10648 title dropped after 1918]: Bemerkungen über die Übertragungsliebe. Z 1915, 3(1):1-11. SKSN 1918, 4:453-469. 2nd ed, 1922. Technik und Metapsychol 1924, 120-135. GS 1925, 6:120-135. Neurosenlehre und Technik 1931, 385-396. GW 1946, 10:306-321.

Further recommendations in the technique of psycho-analysis: observations on transference-love. (Tr:JRiv) CP 1924, 2:377-391.

Observations on transference-love. (Further recommendations on the technique of psycho-analysis III). (Modified tr:JS) SE 12:159-171.

Fr: Observations sur l'amour de transfert. (Tr:AB) In *La technique psychanalytique*, Paris: PUF 1953, 1970, 116-130.

It: Osservazione sull'amore di traslazione. (Tr:CLM) Riv Psa 1955, 1(2): 3-13.

Nuovi consigli sulla tecnica della psicoanalisi: 3. Osservationi sull'amore di traslazione. (Tr:CLM) In *Freud con antologia freudiana*, Turin: Boringhieri 1959, 1970. Opere 7.

Jap: (Tr:KO) FCW-S 1933, 8:22 p.

Kanjō teni seirenai ni tsuite. (Tr: Kosawa, H.) In *Seishinbunseki ryōhō*, SelFr-K 1959, 15:172-193. Rev ed (Tr: Okonogi, K.) SelFr-K 1969, 15.

Por: Observações sôbre o "amor de transferência." (Tr:JPP, OG & GP) Obr Comp-P 10:289-302.

Rus: (Tr:MV) In *Metodika i tekhnika psikhoanaliza. Psikholog i psikhoanal*, vyp. IV, 136 p.

Sp: Observaciones sobre el "amor de transferencia." (Tr:LLBT) Obr Comp-BA 14:147-158. Obr Comp 1948, 2:350-356. Obr Comp 1967/1968, 2:442-448.

254

1937e   Wenn Moses ein Ägypter war ... Imago 1937, 23(4):387-419. GW 1950,
10649   16:114-155. First three sections: Almanach 1938, 1937:9-43. In *Der Mann Moses und die monotheistische Religion*, 29-94.

If Moses was an Egyptian.... (Tr: Jones, K.) J 1939, 20(1):1-32. Part II of *Moses and Monotheism*, 29-85. (Tr:JS) SE 23:17-53.

Sp: Si Moisés era egipcio. (Tr:LR) Obr Comp-BA 20:23-56. Obr Comp 1967/1968, 3:188-218.

255

1910k   Über "wilde" Psychoanalyse. C 1910, 1(3):91-95. SKSN 1913, 3:299-305.
10651   Technik und Metapsychol 1924, 37-44. GS 1925, 6:37-44. GW 1943, 8:118-125.

Concerning "wild" psychoanalysis. (Tr:AAB) SPH 2nd ed, 1912, 3rd ed, 1920, 201-206.

Observations on "wild" psycho-analysis. (Tr:JRiv) CP 1924, 2:297-304. *Major Works* 1952, 1955, 128-130.

"Wild" psycho-analysis. (Revised tr:JS) SE 11:221-227.

Fr: À propos de la psychanalyse dite "sauvage." (Tr:AB) In *La technique psychanalytique*, Paris: PUF 1953, 1967, 1970, 35-42.

Heb: Al psichoanalisa "perua." Kitvei 3, chap. 6.

It: Psicoanalisis "selvaggia." (Tr:CLM) In *Freud con antologia freudiana*, Turin: Boringhieri 1959, 1970. Opere 6.

Jap: Rambō na bunseki ni tsuite. (Tr: Kosawa, H.) In *Seishinbunseki ryōhō*, SelFr-K 1959, 15:52-63. Rev ed (Tr: Okonogi, K.) SelFr-K 1969, 15.

Nor: (Tr: Schjelderup, K.) In *Psykoanalysen i praksis*, Oslo: Gyldendal Norsk Forlag 1930.

Por: A psicanálise inculta. (Tr:JPP, OG & GP) Obr Comp-P 10:207-214.

Rus: (Tr:MV) In *Metodika i tekhnika psikhoanaliza. Psikholog i psikhoanal*, vyp. IV, 136 p.

Sp: La psicoanalisis "silvestre." (Tr:LLBT) Obr Comp-BA 14:83-88. Obr Comp 1948, 2:315-317. Obr Comp 1967/1968, 2:407-409.

256

1905c   Der Witz und seine Beziehung zum Unbewussten. Leipzig/Vienna:
10652   Deuticke 1905, ii+206 p. 2nd ed (with additions) 1912, iv+207 p. 3rd ed, 1921. 4th ed, 1925. GS 1925, 9:1-269. GW 1940, 6:1-285.

Wit and its relation to the unconscious. (Tr, pref: AAB) NY: Moffat, Yard 1916, 1917; London: T. Fisher Unwin 1917, ix+388 p. London: Kegan Paul 1922, ix+388 p. BWSF 1938, 633-803.

Jokes and their relation to the unconscious. (Tr:JS) SE 8:9-236.

Fr: Le mot d'esprit et ses rapports avec l'inconscient. (Tr:MB & Nathan, M.) Paris: Gallimard 1930, 285 p; 1953, 1969, 377 p.

It: Il motto di spirito e la sua relazione con l'inconscio. (Tr: Daniele, S. & Sagittario, E.) Opere 5:7-214.

Jap: Share no seishinbunseki. (Tr: Masaki, F.) CW-Ars 1930, 9:5-320.

Kichi to sono muishiki ni taisuru kankei to. (Tr:KO) In *Bunseki geijutsu ron*, FCW-S 1931, 6:2-131, 1937.

(Tr: Ikumatsu, K.) SelFr-JinSh 1970, 4:185 p.

Jug: Dosetka i njen odnos prema nesvesnom. (Tr: Bekić, T.) [Collected Works, Vol. 3] Novi Sad: Matica Srpska 1969.

Por: O chiste e sua relação com o inconsciente. (Tr:CMdeF) Obr Comp-P 7:7-246.

Rus: Ostroumie i ego otnoshenie k bessoznatel'nomu. (Tr: Kogan, IA. M.) In *Nauchnaia biblioteka "Sovremennyky problem,"* Moskva: Kn-vo "Sovremennye problemy" 1925, 318 p.

Sp: El chiste y su relacion con lo inconsciente. (Tr:LLBT) Obr Comp-Madrid 3:5-300. Obr Comp-BA 3:9-208. Obr Comp 1948, 1:833-948. Obr Comp 1967/1968, 1:825-938.

Sw: Vitsen och dess förhällande till det omedvetna. (Tr: Palmen, R.) Helsingfors: Söderström & Co Forlagsaktiebolag 1954, 269 p.

257

1938a   Ein Wort zum Antisemitismus. Die Zukunft: ein neues Deutschland ein
10653   neues Europa 1938, (No. 7, 25 Nov), 2.

On antisemitism. Die Zukunft: ein neues Deutschland ein neues Europa 1939, (N. 7, 25 Nov), 2.

A comment on anti-semitism. (Tr:JS) SE 23:291-293.

It: Una parola sull'antisemitismo. Opere 11.

Sp: Un comentario sobre el antisemitismo. Obr Comp 1967/1968, 3: 1007-1008.

258

1954b   28 Dec 1919. *News of the Yivo* 1954, Dec (55):9.
(1919)
10522B

259

1915b Zeitgemässes über Krieg und Tod. Imago 1915, 4(1):1-21. SKSN 1918,
10654 4:486-520. GS 1924, 10:315-346. Leipzig/Vienna/Zurich: Int Psa
        Verlag 1924, 35 p. GW 1946, 10:324-355.

        Reflections on war and death. (Tr:AAB & Kuttner, A. B.) NY: Moffat,
        Yard 1918, iii+72 p.

        Thoughts for the times on war and death. (Tr:ECM) CP 1925, 4:
        288-317. *Major Works* 1952, 1955, 755-766. Extracts in Rickman, J.
        (ed) *Civilization, war and death: selections from three works by Sigmund
        Freud*, London: HPI 1939, 1-25. [In part] Ment Health Bull, Danville,
        1945, 23:13-23. (Revised tr:JS) SE 14:275-300.

  Dut: Beschouwingen over oorlog en dood. (Tr: Emden, J. E. G. van) Leiden:
        S. C. van Doesburgh 1917, 40 p.

   Fr: Considérations actuelles sur la guerre et la mort. (Tr: Jankélévitch, S.)
        In *Essais de psychanalyse*, Paris: Payot 1927, 1948, 1951, 219-250.
        (Revised tr: Hesnard, A.) Paris: Payot 1970, 235-267.

   Gr: O polemos kai o thanatos. (Tr: Ferentinos, S.) Athens: Gavotsis 1941.

   It: Considerazioni attuali sulla guerra e la morte. (Tr:CLM) In *Freud con
        antologia freudiana*, Turin: Boringhieri 1959, 1970. In *Il disagio della
        civiltà e altri saggi*, Turin: Boringhieri 1971. Opere 8.

  Jap: Sensō to shi no seishinbunseki. (Tr: Ishinaka, S.) CW-Ars 1932, 14:
        237-287.

        (Tr: Moriyama, K.) SelFr-JinSh 1969, 5:24 p.

  Por: Considerações de atulaidade sôbre a guerra ea morte. (Tr:ED) Obr
        Comp-P 11:205-234.

   Sp: Sobre la guerra y la muerte. (Tr:LR) Obr Comp-BA 18:219-244.

        Consideraciones de actualidad sobre la guerra y la muerte. (Tr:LLBT)
        Obr Comp 1948, 2:1002-1015. Obr Comp 1967/1968, 2:1094-1107.

260

1927c Die Zukunft einer Illusion. Leipzig/Vienna/Zurich: Int Psa Verlag 1927,
10655 1928, 91 p. GS 1928, 11:411-466. GW 1948, 14:325-380.

        The future of an illusion. (Tr: Robson-Scott, W. D.) London: HPI 1928,
        98 p. NY: Liveright 1928, 1949, 98 p. Garden City, NY: Doubleday
        1957. (Tr:JS) SE 21:5-56. Excerpts in Kaufman, W. A. *Religion from
        Tolstoy to Camus*, NY: Harper 1961, 273-278.

   Cz: Budoucnost jedné iluse. (Tr: Schütz, H. & Navrátil, F.) Prague:
        Nakladazelstci Volné Myšlensky 1929, 82 p.

  Dut: De toekomst eener illusie. (Tr: Veen, J. van) Amsterdam: Vrijdenkers-
        vereen De Dageraad 1929, 101 p.

        En illusions fremtid. (Tr: Boisen, M.) In *Totem og tabu*, Amsterdam:
        Hans Reitzel 1961.

Fr: L'avenir d'une illusion. (Tr:MB) Paris: Denoël & Steele 1932, 197 p.

Gr: To mellon mias aftarpias. (Tr: Meranaios, C.) Athens: Gavotsis 1930.

To mellon mias outopias. (Tr: Dimakou, E.) Athens: Panekdotiki 1969.

Heb: Atida shel ashlaya. (Tr: Baer, A.) Kitvei 5:78-117. Excerpt in *Hatarbut vehadat*, Merchavia: Hakibut Haarzi 1943.

Hun: Egy illuzió jövője. (Tr: Schönberger, I.) Budapest: Bibliotheca 1945, 72 p.

It: L'avvenire di un'illusione. (Tr: Candreva, S. & Panaitescu, E. A.) In *Il disagio della civiltà e altri saggi*, Turin: Boringhieri 1971. Opere 10.

Jap: Shūkyō no mirai. (Tr: Hasegawa, M.) FCW-S 1931, 3:137-224.

Gensō no mirai. (Tr: Kimura, K.) CW-Ars 1932, 12:3-67. (Tr: Doi, M. & Yoshida, M.) SelFr-K 1955, 8:86 p.

(Tr: Hamakawa, S.) SelFr-JinSh 1969, 3:44 p.

Pers: Āyandehe yek pendār. (Tr: Razi, H.) Tehran: Kaveh 1962, x+506 p.

Por: O futuro de uma ilusão. (Tr:JPP, OG & GP) Rio de Janeiro: Waissman, Koogan 1934, 152 p. Obr Comp-P 10:5-64.

Rus: Budushchnost' odnoĭ illiuzii. Ateist 1928, (32):58-96. (Tr: Ermakov, I. D.) Moskva/Leningrad: Gosizdat 1930, 59 p.

Sp: El porvenir de una ilusión. (Tr:LLBT) Obr Comp-BA 14:7-54. Obr Comp 1948, 1:1277-1303. Obr Comp 1967/1968, 2:73-100. Madrid: Alianza Editorial 1969.

Sw: En illusion och dess framtid. (Tr: Bratt, S.) Stockholm: Bonniers 1928, 95 p.

Yid: Die zukunft fun an ilusie. (Tr: Dudnick, I.) Cleveland, Ohio: Progressing Printing Co 1932, 63 p.

261

1910d Die zukünftigen Chancen der psychoanalytischen Therapie. (Read at
10656 2nd Psa Cong, Nuremberg, 30-31 Mar, 1910) C 1910, 1(1-2):1-9. SKSN 1913, 3:288-298. 2nd ed, 1922. Technik und Metapsychol 1924, 25-36. GS 1925, 6:25-36. GW 1943, 8:104-115.

The future chances of psychoanalytic therapy. (Tr:AAB) SPH 1912, 207-215.

The future prospects of psycho-analytic therapy. (Tr:JRiv) CP 1924, 2:285-296. In *Major Works* 1952, 1955, 123-127. (Revised tr:JS) SE 11: 141-151.

Fr: Perspectives d'avenir de la thérapeutique analytique. (Tr:AB) In *La technique psychanalytique*, Paris: PUF 1953, 1967, 1970, 23-34.

It: Le prospettive future della terapia psicoanalitica. Opere 6.

Jap: (Tr:KO) FCW-S 1933, 8:18 p.

Seishinbunseki ryōhō no kongo no kanōsei. (Tr: Kosawa, H.) In *Seishin-bunseki ryōhō*, SelFr-K 1959, 15:33-51. Rev ed (Tr: Okonogi, K.) SelFr-K 1969, 15.

Por: O futuro da terapêutica psicanalítica. (Tr:JPP, OG & GP) Obr Comp-P 10:195-206.

Rus: (Tr:MV) In *Metodika i tekhnika psikhoanaliza. Psikholog i psikhoanal*, vyp. IV, 136 p.

Sp: El porvenir de la terapia psicoanalítica. (Tr:LLBT) Obr Comp-BA 14: 73-82. Obr Comp 1948, 2:310-314. Obr Comp 1967/1968, 2:402-406.

262

1907b   Zwangshandlungen und Religionsübungen. (Read at Vienna Psa Soc,
10658   2 Mar 1907) Z Religionspsychol 1907, 1(1 Apr):4-12. SKSN 1909,
2:122-131. GS 1924, 10:210-220. GW 1941, 7:129-139.

Obsessive acts and religious practices. (Tr:RCM) CP 1924, 2:25-35.

Obsessive actions and religious practices. (Revised tr:JS) SE 9:117-127.

Dut: Dwanghandelingen en godsdienstoefening. (Tr: Stärcke, A.) Baarn: Hollandia Drukkerij 1914, 33-43.

Fr: Actes obsédants et exercises religieux. (Tr:MB) In *L'avenir d'une illusion*, Paris: Denoël & Steele 1932, 157-183.

Actions compulsionelles et exercises religieux. (Tr: Guérineau, D.) In *Névrose, psychose et perversion*. Paris: PUF 1973, 133-142.

It: Azioni ossessive e pratiche religiose. (Tr:CLM) In *Freud con antologia freudiana*, Turin: Boringhieri 1959, 1970. Opere 5:341-352.

Jap: (Tr: Yamamoto, I.) SelFr-JinSh 1969, 5:8 p.

Por: Os atos obsessivos e as práticas religiosas. (Tr:ED) Obr Comp-P 11: 97-108.

Rus: Naviazchivyia dieistviia i religionznye obriady. In *Psikhologicheskie ètiudy. Biblioteka "Psikhoterapiia"* no. 1. Izd. 2-e. Moskva: Red. zhurnala "Psikhoterapiia" 1912, 55 p.

Sp: Los actos obsesivos y los ritos religiosos. (Tr:LR) Obr Comp-BA 18: 35-46. (Tr:LLBT) Obr Comp 1948, 2:956-960. Obr Comp 1967/1968, 2:1048-1052.

263

1913g   Zwei Kinderlügen. Z 1913, 1(4):359-362. SKSN 1918, 4:189-194.
10659   2nd ed, 1922. GS 1924, 5:238-243. Psychoanalyse der Neurosen 1926,
16-22. Neurosenlehre und Technik 1931, 17-21. GW 1943, 8:422-427.

Infantile mental life: two lies told by children. (Tr:ECM) CP 1924, 2:144-149.

Two lies told by children. (Modified tr:JS) SE 12:305-309.

Fr: Deux mensonges d'enfants. (Tr: Jury, P. & Engel, F.) RFPsa 1934, 7(4):606-610. (Tr: Berger, D. & JLa) In *Névrose, psychose et perversion*, Paris: PUF 1973, 183-187.

Heb: Shnei shikrei yeladim. Kitvei 3, chap. 12.

It: Due bugie di bambini. Opere 7.

Jap: Kodomo no kyo futatsu. (Tr:KO) In *Bunseki renai ron*, FCW-S 1932, 9:124-130.

(Tr: Iida, M.) SelFr-JinSh 1969, 5:4 p.

Por: Duas mentiras infantis. (Tr:OG, IsIz & MG) Obr Comp-P 9:137-142.

Sp: Dos mentiras infantiles. (Tr:LLBT) Obr Comp-Madrid 13:125-130. Obr Comp-BA 13:102-106. Obr Comp 1948, 1:1193-1194. Obr Comp 1967/1968, 1:1179-1180.

264

1913h   Zwei Zimmer und eines. Erf Beisp Psa Prx [89] no. 9. Z 1913, 1:377-382.
10660   In *Die Traumdeutung* 4th ed, 1914, and later. GS 1925, 3:71-72. GW 1942, 2-3:359-360.

Two rooms and one. (Tr:AAB) In *The interpretation of dreams*, 3rd ed, 1932, 336-337.

Two rooms and one room. (Tr:JS) SE 5:354. SE 13:195.

FOR OTHER LANGUAGES, see under *Die Traumdeutung* [227].

SECTION III
INTRODUCTIONS AND PREFACES

Part A lists alphabetically Freud's introductions and prefaces to his own works. Only those prefaces and introductions that were published separately are included. Omitted are those published with the work, e.g., the prefaces of 1908, 1911, 1914, 1918, 1921, 1928, 1931 to *The interpretation of dreams*. Part B includes Freud's prefaces to works of others and his letters published as prefaces. Entries are listed alphabetically under the author's name, and in the instance of letter-prefaces, the recipient's name.

A. TO FREUD'S OWN WORKS

265

1920e Vorwort zu *Drei Abhandlungen zur Sexualtheorie.*
10432

   2nd edition 1910. [Omitted after 1920] SEE [79].

   3rd edition. SEE [79].

Sp: Prólogo de la tercera edición. Obr Comp 1967/1968, 3:316-317.

1920e Vorwort zur vierten Auflage der *Drei Abhandlungen zur Sexualtheorie.*
10637 Z 1920, 6:247-248. GW 1942, 5:31-32. SEE [79].

   Preface to the fourth edition of *Three essays on the theory of sexuality.* (Tr:JS) SE 7:133-134.

Fr: Préface à la quatrième édition de *Trois essais sur la théorie de la sexualité.* (Tr: Reverchon, B.) Paris: Gallimard 1923. (Revised tr:JLa & Pontalis, J. B.) Paris: Gallimard 1962, 1968, 11-13.

Sp: Prólogo de la cuarta edición de *Tres ensayos para la teoría sexual.* (Tr: LR) Obr Comp-BA 20:189-190. Obr Comp 1967/1968, 3:318.

   5th edition 1922. SEE [79].

   6th edition 1925. SEE [79].

266

1906b Vorwort zu *Sammlung kleiner Schriften zur Neurosenlehre I.* Leipzig/
10636 Vienna: Deuticke 1906, iii. GS 1925, 1:241-242. GW 1952, 1:557-558.

Preface to Freud's collection of shorter writings on the theory of the neuroses from the years 1893-1906. (Tr:JS) SE 3:3-6.

It: Prefazione alla prima edizione della "Raccolta di brevi scritti sulla teoria delle nevrosi 1893-1906." (Tr: Cinato, A.) Opere 5:255-258.

Sp: Prólogo para la primera edición de la "Recopilación de ensayos sobre la teoría de las neurosis, de los años 1893 a 1906." (Tr:LR) Obr Comp-BA 20:185-186. Obr Comp 1967/1968, 3:315.

267

1907e   Werbeschrift zu *Schriften zur angewandten Seelenkunde*. In *Der Wahn*
10571   *und die Träume in W. Jensen's "Gradiva,"* 1907, 82:1908.

Introduction to *Schriften zur angewandten Seelenkunde* [Papers on Applied Mental Science]. (Tr: Bunker, H. A.) In Bry, I. et al: "Ex Libris I. Early Monographic Series." Bull Am Psa Ass 1952, 8:214-215. J Am Psa Ass 1953, 1:519-520.

Prospectus for *Schriften zur angewandten Seelenkunde*. (Tr:JS) SE 9: 248-249.

It: Prospetto per la colana *Scritti di psicologia applicata*. (Tr: Cinato, A.) Opere 5:369-372.

268

1966b   Introduction to Freud, S. and Bullitt, W. C. *Thomas Woodrow Wilson,*
73593   *twenty-eighth president of the United States: a psychological study.*
(Tr: Bullitt, W. C.) Encounter 1966, 28(1):3. Book published Boston: Houghton Mifflin 1967, xi-xvii; London: Weidenfeld & Nicolson 1967. SEE [220].

Ger: In *Neurose und Genialität*, Frankfurt 1971.

Dut: In *Thomas Woodrow Wilson, President van 1913-1921. Een psychologische studie*. (Tr: Kraak-de Looze, E. M. A.) Meppel: J. A. Boom & Zoon 1967.

Fr: In *Le président Thomas Woodrow Wilson, portrait psychologique*. (Tr: Tadié, M.) Paris: Albin Michel 1968.

It: Introduzione allo studio psicologico su Thomas Woodrow Wilson. Opere 11. In *Il caso Thomas Woodrow Wilson, ventottesimo presidente degli Stati Uniti. Uno studio psicologico*. (Tr: Sorani, R. & Petrillo, R.) Milan: Feltrinelli 1967.

269

1934b   Vorrede zur hebräischen Ausgabe von *Totem und Tabu*. GS 1934,
(1930)   12:385. GW 1948, 14:569.
10631

Preface to the Hebrew translation of *Totem and taboo*. (Tr:JS) In *Totem and taboo*, London: Routledge & Kegan Paul 1950, xi. SE 13:xv.

Heb: (Tr: Dvossis, I.) Jerusalem Kirjeith Zefer 1939.

Sp: Prólogo para la edición hebrea de "Totem y tabú." (Tr:LR) Obr Comp-
BA 20:191-192. Obr Comp 1967/1968, 3:319.

270

1934a   Vorrede zur hebräischen Ausgabe der *Vorlesungen zur Einführung in*
(1930) *die Psychoanalyse.* GS 1934, 12:383-384. GW 1950, 16:274-275.
10632
Preface to the Hebrew translation of *Introductory lectures in psycho-
analysis.* (Tr:JS) SE 15:11-12.

Heb: (Tr: Dvossis, I.) In *Mavo lapsichoanalysa,* Tel-Aviv: A. J. Steibel 1935.
Kitvei 1.

Sp: Prólogo para la edición hebrea de la "Introducción al psicoanálisis."
(Tr:LR) Obr Comp-BA 20:193-194. Obr Comp 1967/1968, 3:320.

B. TO THE WORKS OF OTHERS

271

AICHHORN, AUGUST

1925f   Geleitwort zu *Verwahrloste Jugend.* Leipzig/Vienna/Zurich: Int Psa
10465 Verlag 1925, 1931, 5-6. GS 1928, 11:267-269. Neurosenlehre und
Technik 1931, 319-320. GW 1948, 14:565-567.

Foreword to *Wayward youth.* NY: Viking Pr 1935; London: Putnam
1936, v-vii.

Psycho-analysis and delinquency. (Tr:JS) CP 1950, 5:98-100. In
Aichhorn, A. *Wayward youth,* London: IPC 1951, vii-ix.

Preface to Aichhorn's *Wayward youth.* (Tr:JS) SE 19:273-275.

Dut: (Tr: Zuring, J.) In Aichhorn, A. *Verwaarloosde jeugd. De psychoanalyse
en de heropvoeding.* Utrecht: J. Bijleveld 1957, 1968.

It: Prefazione a "Infanzia abbandonata" di August Aichhorn. Opere 10.
(Tr: Giordano, A.) In *Gioventù traviata,* Milan: V. Bompiani 1950.

Sp: Prefacio para un libro de August Aichhorn. (Tr:LR) Obr Comp-BA
20:171-173. Obr Comp 1967/1968, 3:309-310.

272

BERG, CHARLES

1941h   Preface to *War in the mind.* [In English] London: Macauley Pr 1941.
(1939)
10567

Sp: Carta a Charles Berg sobre su libro "War in the mind." (Tr:LR) Rev Psicoanál 1955, 12:126. Obr Comp-BA 21:409. Obr Comp 1967/1968, 3:1004.

273

BERNHEIM, HIPPOLYTE-MARIE

1888- Vorrede zur Übersetzung von *De la suggestion et de ses applications à*
1889 *la thérapeutique* [Suggestion and its therapeutic effects]. In Bernheim, H.
10630 *Die Suggestion und ihre Heilwirkung*, Leipzig/Vienna: Deuticke 1888. 2nd ed, 1896 [With new preface], iii-xii. With title: Hypnotismus und Suggestion. Wien med Bl 1888, 11(38: 20 Sept):1189-1193; (39: 27 Sept):1226-1228. Extract with title: Hypnose durch Suggestion, Wien med Wschr 1888, 38(26: 30 Jun):898-900.

Hypnotism and suggestion. (Tr:JS) J 1946, 27(1-2):59-64. (Revised) CP 1950, 5:11-24.

Preface to the translation of Bernheim's *Suggestion*. (Revised tr:JS) SE 1:75-87.

It: Prefazione alla traduzione di "Della suggestione" di Hippolyte Bernheim. (Tr: Schwarz, L.) Opere 1:69-80.

Sp: Prólogo y notas al libro de Bernheim, "La sugestión y sus aplicaciones terapéuticas." (Tr:LR) Obr Comp-BA 21:374-387. Obr Comp 1967/1968, 3:977-987.

274

BONAPARTE, MARIE

1933d Préface à *Edgar Poe, étude psychanalytique*. [First published in French]
10561 Paris: Denoël & Steele 1933, xi. PUF 1958.

Vorwort zu *Edgar Poe, eine psychoanalytische Studie*. Vienna: Int Psa Verlag 1934, v. GS 1934, 12:391. GW 1950, 16:276.

Preface to *The life and works of Edgar Allan Poe: a psychoanalytic interpretation*. (Tr: Rodker, J.) London: IPC 1949, xi. (Tr:JS) SE 22: 254.

It: Prefazione a *Edgar Poe, studio psicoanalitico*. Opere 11.

Sp: Prólogo para un libro de Marie Bonaparte. (Tr:LR) Obr Comp-BA 20:181-182. Obr Comp 1967/1968, 3:314.

275

BOURKE, JOHN GREGORY

1913k Geleitwort zu *Der Unrat in Sitte, Brauch, Glauben und Gewohnheits-*
10466 *recht der Völker*. Leipzig: Ethnologischer Verlag 1913. GS 1928, 11:249-251. Sexualtheorie und Traumlehre 1931, 242-245. GW 1946, 10:453-455. Written by Freud for the German translation of Bourke's *Scatalogic rites of all nations*.

Foreword to *Scatalogic rites of all nations. A dissertation upon the employment of excrementitious remedial agents in religion, therapeutics, divination, witchcraft, love-philters, etc., in all parts of the globe.* NY: American Anthropological Society 1934, vii-ix.

The excretory functions in psycho-analysis and folklore. (Tr:JS) CP 1950, 5:88-91.

Preface to *Scatalogic rites of all nations.* (Revised tr:JS) SE 12:335-337.

It: Prefazione alla traduzione di "Ritti scatologici di tutti popoli" di J. G. Bourke. Opere 7.

Sp: Prólogo para un libro de John Gregory Bourke. (Tr:LR) Obr Comp-BA 20:148-151. Obr Comp 1967/1968, 3:294-296.

276

CHARCOT, JEAN-MARTIN

1886f   Vorwort zu *Neue Vorlesungen über die Krankheiten des Nervensystems,*
10561A   *insbesondere über Hysterie,* Leipzig/Vienna: Toeplitz & Deuticke 1886, iii-iv. Written by Freud for his translation of Charcot's *Leçons sur les maladies du système nerveux: tôme troisième.*

Preface to the translation of Charcot's *Lectures on the diseases of the nervous system.* (Tr:JS) SE 1:21-22.

It: Prefazione alla traduzione delle *Lezioni sull malattie del sistema nervoso* di J.-M. Charcot. (Tr: Schwarz, L.) Opere 1:19-22.

277

CHARCOT, JEAN-MARTIN

1892-   Vorwort zu Poliklinische Vorträge, Vol. 1, Akademisches Jahr 1887-
1893a   1888. Leipzig/Vienna: Deuticke 1892-4, iii-vi. Written by Freud for
10562   his translation of Charcot's *Leçons du Mardi de la Salpêtrière (1887-1888).* Includes Freud's added footnotes.

Preface and footnotes to the translation of Charcot's *Tuesday Lectures.* (Tr:JS) SE 1:133-143.

It: Prefazione e note alla traduzione delle "Lezioni del martedí della Salpêtrière" di J.-M. Charcot. (Tr: Schwarz, L.) Opere 1:151-162.

278

DISQUE VERT

1924a   Lettre préface à *Disque Vert,* 26 Feb 1924. [In French] In *Disque Vert II,*
10657   Special number: *Freud et la psychanalyse.* Paris/Brussels: Le Disque Vert 1924, 2(3rd series: June):3. Z 1924, 10:206-208. GS 1928, 11:266. GW 1940, 13:446.

No German text extant.

Letter to *Le Disque Vert.* (Tr:JS) SE 19:290.

It: Lettera alla rivista "Le Disque vert." Opere 10.

Sp: Carta a la revista "Le Disque Vert." (Tr:LR) Obr Comp-BA 20:232. Obr Comp 1967/1968, 3:346.

279
DORYON, ISRAEL

1940g Nov. 1938. [German with Hebrew translation] In Doryon, I. *Lynkeus'*
(1938) *new state.* Jerusalem 1939, 1940. In Doryon, I. *The man Moses.*
Jerusalem 1945, 1946.

280
EITINGON, MAX

1923g Vorwort zu *Bericht über die Berliner psychoanalytische Poliklinik (März*
10635 *1920 bis Juni 1922).* Leipzig/Vienna/Zurich: Int Psa Verlag 1923, 3.
GS 1928, 11:265. GW 1940, 13:441.

Preface to *Report on the Berlin Psycho-Analytical Policlinic (March 1920
to June 1922).* (Tr:JS) SE 19:285.

It: Prefazione a "Rapporto sul Policlinico psicoanalitico di Berlino" di
Max Eitingon. Opere 9.

Sp: Prólogo para un libro de Max Eitingon. (Tr:LR) Obr Comp-BA 20:
169-170., Obr Comp 1967/1968, 3:308.

281
FARROW, E. PICKWORTH

1926c Vorbemerkung zu *Eine Kindheitserinnerung aus dem 6. Lebensmonat*
10404 [A childhood memory from the sixth month of life]. Z 1926, 12(1):79.
GW 1948, 14:568.

Preface to *A practical method of self-analysis.* London: Allen & Unwin
1942; NY: IUP 1945.

Prefatory note to a paper by E. Pickworth Farrow. (Tr:JS) SE 20:280.

It: Premessa a un articolo di E. Pickworth Farrow. Opere 10.

Sp: Nota para un trabajo de E. Pickworth Farrow. (Tr:LR) Obr Comp-BA
20:174. Obr Comp 1967/1968, 3:311.

282
FERENCZI, SÁNDOR

1910b Dec 1909. Vorwort zu (Eloszo) *Lélekelemzés: értekezések a pszicho-*
(1909) *analizis köréből.* [German with Hungarian translation] (Tr:SFe)
10564 Budapest: Szilagyi 1910, 3-4; Manó Dick 1914, 1918, 3-4.

GS 1928, 11:241. GW 1941, 7:469.

Preface to *Psycho-analysis: essays in the field of psycho-analysis.* (Tr:JS) SE 9:252.

It: Prefazione a "Psicoanalisi: saggi nel campo della psicoanalisi" di Sándor Ferenczi. Opere 6.

Sp: Prólogo para un libro de Sándor Ferenczi. (Tr:LR) Obr Comp-BA 20:137-138. Obr Comp 1967/1968, 3:288.

283

FERENCZI, SÁNDOR; ABRAHAM, KARL; SIMMEL, ERNST; JONES, ERNEST

1919d Einleitung zu *Psychoanalyse der Kriegsneurosen.* (Diskussion auf dem V.
10439 Internationalen Psychoanalytischen Kongress in Budapest, 28 and 29 September 1918.) Leipzig/Vienna: Int Psa Verlag 1919, 3-7. GS 1928, 11:252-255. Neurosenlehre und Technik 1931, 310-315. GW 1947, 12:321-324.

Introduction to *Psycho-analysis and the war neuroses.* (Tr:EJ) In *Psychoanalysis and the war neuroses,* London/Vienna/NY: Int Psa Pr 1921, 1-4.

Psycho-analysis and the war neuroses. (Tr:JS) CP 1950, 5:83-87.

Introduction to *Psycho-analysis and the war neuroses.* SE 17:207-210.

It: Introduzione al libro "Psicoanalisi delle nevrosi di guerra." Opere 9.

Sp: Introduccion al simposio sobre las neurosis de guerra. (Tr:LR) Obr Comp-BA 20:154-158. Obr Comp 1967/1968, 3:297-300.

284

HUG-HELLMUTH, HERMINE VON

1919i 27 Apr 1915. In *Tagebuch eines halbwüchsigen Mädchens,* Leipzig/
(1915) Vienna/Zurich: Int Psa Verlag 1919, 1921, 1922, iii. GS 1928, 11:261.
10416 GW 1946, 10:456.

(Tr: Paul, E. & Paul, C.) In *A young girl's diary,* London: Allen & Unwin; NY: Seltzer 1921, 1936, p. 5.

Letter to Dr. Hermine von Hug-Hellmuth. (Tr:JS) SE 14:341.

It: Lettera alla dottoressa Hermine von Hug-Hellmuth. Opere 8.

Sp: Carta a la doctora Von Hug-Hellmuth. (Tr:LR) Obr Comp-BA 20: 152-153. Obr Comp 1967/1968, 3:297.

285

NUNBERG, HERMANN

1923b Geleitwort zu *Allgemeine Neurosenlehre auf psychoanalytischer Grund-*

(1931) *lage.* Berne/Berlin: Huber 1932, iii. GS 1934, 12:390. GW 1950,
10467 16:273.

Foreword to *Principles of psychoanalysis.* (Tr: Kahr, M. & Kahr, S.)
NY: IUP 1955, xi.

Preface to *General theory of the neuroses on a psycho-analytic basis.*
(Tr:JS) SE 21:258.

Fr: Préface à Nunberg, N. *Principes de psychanalyse. Leur application aux
névroses.* (Tr: Rocheblave, A. M.) Paris: PUF 1957.

It: Prefazione a "Teoria generale delle nevrosi secondo i principi psicoanalitici" di Hermann Nunberg. Opere 11.

Sp: Prefacio para un libro de Hermann Nunberg. (Tr:LR) Obr Comp-BA
20:180. Obr Comp 1967/1968, 3:314.

286

MEDICAL REVIEW OF REVIEWS
SPECIAL PSYCHOPATHOLOGY NUMBER

1930c Preface. [First published in English] Medical Review of Reviews 1930,
10563 36(3:Mar):103-104.

Introduction to the special psychopathology number of *The Medical
Review of Reviews.* (Tr:JS) SE 21:254-255.

Geleitwort zu *Medical Review of Reviews.* [Incorrectly given as "Geleitwort zu *Psychoanalytic Review.*"] GS 1934, 12:386-387. GW 1948,
14:570-571.

It: Prefazione a un numero speciale di "The Medical Review of Reviews."
Opere 11.

Sp: Mensaje para la "Medical Review of Reviews." (Tr:LR) Obr Comp-BA
20:177-178. Obr Comp 1967/1968, 3:312.

287

PFISTER, OSKAR

1913b Geleitwort zu *Die psychoanalytische Methode. Eine erfahrungswissen-*
10468 *schaftlichsystematische Darstellung.* In Pfister, O. *Die psychoanalytische
Methode, Pädagogium.* Leipzig/Berlin: Klinkhardt 1913, 1:iv-vi.
2nd ed, 1921. 3rd ed, 1924. GS 1928, 11:244-246. Neurosenlehre und
Technik 1931, 315-318. GW 1946, 10:448-450.

Introduction to *The psychoanalytic method.* (Tr: Payne, C. R.) NY:
Moffat, Yard; London: Kegan Paul 1917, v-viii.

Introduction to *The psycho-analytic method.* (Tr:JS) SE 12:329-331.

It: Prefazione a "Il metodo psicoanalitico" di Oskar Pfister. Opere 7.

Sp: Prefacio para un libro de Oskar Pfister. (Tr:LR) Obr Comp-BA 20:
142-145. Obr Comp 1967/1968, 3:290-292.

288

DAS PSYCHOANALYTISCHES VOLKSBUCH

1939c [Facsimile] In Federn, P. & Meng, H. (eds) *Das psychoanalytisches*
10519 *Volksbuch* (3rd ed), Berne: Huber 1939. In Holstätter, P. R. *Einführung*
in die Tiefenpsychologie ("Erkenntnis und Besinnung" No. 1) Vienna:
Braumüller 1948, between pages 224-225.

289

PUTNAM, JAMES J.

1921a Preface to *Addresses on psycho-analysis*. [Published in English] (Tr:EJ)
10565 London/Vienna/NY: Int Psa Pr 1921. London: HPI 1951, iii-v.
GS 1928, 11:262-263. GW 1940, 13:437-438. SE 18:269-270.

No German text extant.

It: Prefazione a "Discorsi di psicoanalisi" di J. J. Putnam. Opere 9.

Sp: Prólogo para un libro de J. J. Putnam. (Tr:LR) Obr Comp-BA 20:
164-166. Obr Comp 1967/1968, 3:305-306.

290

REIK, THEODOR

1919g Vorrede zu *Probleme der Religionspsychologie*, I Teil. Leipzig/Vienna:
10633 Int Psa Verlag 1919, vii-xii. 2nd ed, with title *Das Ritual: psychoan-*
alytische Studien, Leipzig/Vienna: Int Psa Verlag 1928, GS 1928,
11:256-260. GW 1947, 12:325-329.

Preface to *Ritual: psycho-analytic studies*. (Tr:DB) London: HPI;
NY: Norton 1931, 5-10.

Psycho-analysis and religious origins. (Tr:JS) CP 1950, 5:92-97.

Preface to *Ritual: psycho-analytic studies*. (Tr:JS) SE 17:259-263.

Fr: Préface à Reik, T. *Le rituel, psychanalyse des rites religieux*. (Tr: Demet,
M. F.) Paris: Denoël 1974, 21-25.

It: [Prefazione.] (Tr: Ferrarotti, F.) (Intro:CLM) In *Il rito religioso: studi*
psicanalitici, Turin: G. Einaudi 1949, 359 p.

Prefazione a "Il rito religioso: studi psicanalitici" di Theodor Reik.
Opere 9.

Sp: Prólogo para un libro de Theodor Reik. (Tr:LR) Obr Comp-BA 20:
159-163. Obr Comp 1967/1968, 3:301-304.

291

SAUSSURE, RAYMOND DE

1922e Préface à *La méthode psychanalytique*. [First published in French]
10566 Lausanne/Geneva: Payot 1922, vii-viii.

German text unpublished.

Preface to Raymond de Saussure's *The psycho-analytic method*. (Tr from original German text: Richards, A.) SE 19:283-284.

It: Prefazione a "Il metodo psicoanalitico" di Raymond de Saussure. Opere 9.

292

STEINER, MAXIM

1913e Vorwort zu *Die psychischen Störungen der männlichen Potenz*. Leipzig/
10638 Vienna: Deuticke 1913. 2nd ed, 1917. 3rd ed, 1926. 4th ed, 1931, iii-iv. GS 1928, 11:247-248. Sexualtheorie und Traumlehre 1931, 239-240. GW 1946, 10:451-452.

Preface to *The psychical disorders of male potency*. (Tr:JS) SE 12: 345-346.

It: Prefazione a "Il disturbi psichici della potenza virile" di Maxim Steiner. Opere 7.

Sp: Prólogo para un libro de Maxim Steiner. (Tr:LR) Obr Comp-BA 20: 146-147. Obr Comp 1967/1968, 3:293.

293

STEKEL, WILHELM

1908f Vorwort zu *Nervose Angstzustände und ihre Behandlung*. Berlin/
10639 Vienna: Urban & Schwarzenburg 1908, iii. 2nd ed, 1912, v. GS 1928, 11:239-240. GW 1941, 7:467-468.

Preface to *Nervous anxiety states and their treatment*. (Tr:JS) SE 9: 250-251.

It: Prefazione a "Stati nervosi d'angoscia e loro trattamento" di Wilhelm Stekel. (Tr: Dogana, M. T.) Opere 5:435-438.

Sp: Prólogo para un libro de Wilhelm Stekel. (Tr:LR) Obr Comp-BA 20: 135-136. Obr Comp 1967/1968, 3:287.

294

STERBA, RICHARD

1936b 3 July 1932. [Facsimile] In *Handwörterbuch der Psychoanalyse*. Vienna:
(1932) Int Psa Verlag 1936.
10419A

Preface to Richard Sterba's *Dictionary of psycho-analysis*. (Tr:JS) SE 22:253.

It: Prefazione al *Piccolo dizionario di psicoanalisi* di R. Sterba. Opere 11.

295

TORRES, LUIS LOPEZ-BALLESTEROS Y DE

1923h 7 May 1923. [First published in Spanish; probably written in Spanish.]

10418 Unas palabras del doctor Freud sobre la edicion castellana de sus *Obras Completas*. Obr Comp-Madrid 4:7. GS 1928, 11:266. GW 1940, 13:442.

Letter to Senor Luis Lopez-Ballesteros y de Torres. (Tr:JS) SE 19:289.

No German text extant.

It: Lettera a Luis Lopez-Ballesteros y de Torres. Opere 9.

296

VARENDONK, JULIAN

1921b   Introduction to *The psychology of day-dreams*. [In English] London:
10488 Allen & Unwin 1921, 9-10. SE 18:271-272.

Geleitwort zu *Über das vorbewusste phantasierende Denken*. [First paragraph only] (Tr: Furrer, A.) Vienna/Leipzig/Zurich: Int Psa Verlag 1922, iii. GS 1928, 11:264. GW 1940, 13:439-440 (Includes English version of last part of text). No complete German text extant.

It: Prefazione a "La psicologia dei sogni ad occhi aperti" di J. Varendonck. Opere 9.

Sp: Prólogo para un libro de J. Varendonck. (Tr:LR) Obr Comp-BA 20: 167-168. Obr Comp 1967/1968, 3:307.

297

WEISS, EDOARDO

1931c   Prefazione a *Elementi di psicoanalisi*. [German facsimile with Italian
(1930)   translation.] (Tr: Weiss, E.) Milan: Hoepli 1931, vi-viii; 1933, 1937,
10469 viii-x. Opere 11.

Geleitwort zu *Elementi di psicoanalisi*. GS 1934, 12:389. GW 1948, 14:573.

Introduction to *Elements of psycho-analysis*. (Tr: Richards, A.) SE 21: 256.

Sp: Palabras preliminares para un libro de Edoardo Weiss. (Tr:LR) Obr Comp-BA 20:179. Obr Comp 1967/1968, 3:313.

298

1930b   Vorwort zu *Zehn Jahre Berliner psychoanalytisches Institut*. In *Zehn*
10640 *Jahre Berliner psychoanalytisches Institut*, Leipzig/Vienna/Zurich: Int Psa Verlag 1930, 5. GS 1934, 12:388. GW 1948, 14:572.

Preface to *Ten years of the Berlin Psycho-analytic Institute*. In *Max Eittingon in memoriam*, Jerusalem: Israel Psa Soc 1951, 47. (Tr:JS) SE 21:257.

It: Prefazione a "Dieci anni dell'Instituto psicoanalitico di Berlino." Opere 11.

Sp: Prólogo de folleto "Décimo aniversario del Instituto Psicoanalítico de Berlin." (Tr:LR) Obr Comp-BA 20:175-176. Obr Comp 1967/1968, 3:311.

SECTION IV
ABSTRACTS AND REVIEWS

This section includes Freud's abstracts and reviews of the writings of others. Entries are listed alphabetically according to the last name of the author of the work.

299

1887c Adamkiewicz, Albert, "Monoplegia anaesthetica." Neurol Zbl 1887,
10672 37(6):131-133.

300

1887a Averbeck, Heinrich, *Die akute Neurasthenie, ein ärztliches Kulturbild.*
10673 Wien med Wschr 1887, 37(5:29 Jan):138.

Review of Averbeck's *Die akute Neurasthenie* [Acute neurasthenia]. (Tr:JS) SE 1:35.

It: Recensione a "La nevrastenia acuta" di H. Averbeck. (Tr: Schwarz, L.) Opere 1:37.

301

1904c Baumgarten, Alfred, *Neurasthenie, Wesen, Heilung, Vorbeugung.* Neue
10674 Freie Presse 1904, 4 Feb (Morgenblatt) p 22.

It: Recensione a "Nevrastenia, natura, guargione e prevenzione" di Alfred Baumgarten. Opere 4:420.

302

1903a Biedenkapp, Georg, *Im Kampfe gegen Hirnbacillen.* Neue Freie Presse
10675 1903, 8 Feb (Morgenblatt):41.

Review of Georg Biedenkapp's *Im Kampfe gegen Hirnbacillen* [The fight against brain bacilli]. (Tr: Richards, A.) SE 9:253-254.

It: Recensione a "Nevrastenia, natura, guarigione e prevenzione" di Alfred (Tr: Dogana, M. T.) Opere 4:417-418.

303

1904b Bigelow, John, *The mystery of sleep.* Neue Freie Presse 1904, 4 Feb
10676 (Morgenblatt):22.

Review of John Bigelow's *The mystery of sleep.* (Tr: Richards, A.) SE 9:254-255.

It: Recensione a "Il mistero del sonno" di John Bigelow. (Tr: Dogana, M. T.) Opere 4:419.

304

1887h Borgherini, Alessandro, "Beiträge zur Kenntnis der Leitungsbahnen im
10676A Rückenmarke." Neurol Zbl 1887, 6(4):79.

305

1895a Edinger, Ludwig, "Eine neue Theorie über die Ursachen einiger Nerven-
10677 krankheiten, insbesondere der Neuritis und Tabes." Wien klin Rdsch
1895, 9(2):cols 27-28.

306

1889a Forel, August, *Der Hypnotismus, seine Bedeutung und seine Hand-*
10678 *habung.* Wien med Wschr 1889, 39(28:13 July):cols 1097-1100;
(47:23 Nov):cols 1892-1896.

Review of August Forel's *Hypnotism.* (Tr:JS) SE 1:91-102.

It: Recensione a "L'ipnotismo" di August Forel. (Tr: Schwarz, L.) Opere
1:81.

307

1911g Greve, G., "Sobre psicologia y psicoterapie de ciertos estados angusti-
10671 osos." C 1911, 1:594-595.

308

1904f Löwenfeld, Leopold, *Die psychischen Zwangerscheinungen.* J Psychol
73594 Neurol 1904, 3:190-191.

An unknown review by Freud. (Tr:JS) J 1967, 48:319-320.

It: Recensione a "I fenomeni psichici de coazione" di Leopold Löwenfeld.
Opere 4:422-423.

309

1887b Mitchell, S. Weir, *Die Behandlung gewisser Formen von Neurasthenie*
10679 *und Hysterie.* Wien med Wschr 1887, 37(5:29 Jan):col 138.

Review of Weir Mitchell's *Die Behandlung gewisser Formen von
Neurasthenie und Hysterie.* (Tr:JS) SE 1:36.

It: Recensione alla traduzione di "Grasso e sangue" di S. W. Mitchell.
(Tr: Schwarz, L.) Opere 1:38.

310

1910m Neutra, Wilhelm, *Briefe an nervöse Frauen.* C 1910, 1:49-50.
10680

Review of Wilhelm Neutra's *Letters to neurotic women.* (Tr:JS) SE 11:238.

It: Recensione a "Lettere a donne nevrose" di Wilhelm Neutra. Opere 6.

311

1887i   Nussbaum, J., "Über die wechselseitigen Beziehungen zwischen den
10680A centralen Ursprungsgebieten der Augenmuskelnerven." Neurol Zbl
        1887, 6(23):543.

312

1887e   Obersteiner, Heinrich, *Anleitung beim Studium des Baues der nervösen*
10681   *Centralorgane im gesunden und kranken Zustande.* Wien med Wschr
        1887, 37(50):cols 1642-1644.

313

1887g   Pal, Jakob, "Ein Beitrag zur Nervenfärbetechnik." Neurol Zbl 1887,
10681A 6(3):53.

314

        (Unsigned) [In English] Spina, Arnold, *Studies on the bacillus of tuber-*
73572   *culosis.* Medical News, Philadelphia 1883, 42(7 Apr):401-402. In
        Grinstein, A. "Freud's first publications in America." J Am Psa Ass 1971,
        19:243-246.

315

1905f   Wickmann, R., *Lebensregeln für Neurastheniker.* Neue Freie Presse
10682   1905, 31 Aug (Morgenblatt):21.

SECTION V
TRANSLATIONS

This section includes Freud's translations of the writings of others. Entries are listed alphabetically under the last name of the author of the work.

316

1892a Bernheim, Hippolyte-Marie, *Hypnotisme, suggestion et psychothérapie:*
10664 *études nouvelles,* under the title, *Neue Studien über Hypnotismus, Suggestion und Psychotherapie.* Leipzig/Vienna: Deuticke 1892, xii+380 p.

317

1888- Bernheim, Hippolyte-Marie, *De la suggestion et de ses applications à*
1889 *la thérapeutique,* under the title, *Die Suggestion und ihre Heilwirkung.*
10665 Leipzig/Vienna: Deuticke 1888, 1889, xxvi+415 p. [with introduction, notes and postscript]. 2nd ed (Revised: Kahane, M.; new preface by Freud) 1896, xi+218 p. (Note: case histories in Part II, translated by O. Springer. Portion of translation appeared in Wien med Wschr 1888, 38:898-900. For preface, see [273].)

318

1939b (& Freud, Anna) Bonaparte, Marie, *Topsy, Chow-Chow au poil d'or,*
(1938) under the title *Topsy, der Goldhaarige Chow.* Amsterdam 1939.
10666

319

1892- Charcot, Jean-Martin, *Leçons du mardi à la Salpêtrière (1887-1888),*
1894 under the title *Poliklinische Vorträge, I.* Vienna: Deuticke 1892, 1893,
10668 xii+480 p. Includes preface [277] and footnotes.

320

1886f Charcot, Jean-Martin, *Leçons sur les maladies du système nerveux,*
10667A *Vol. III,* under the title *Neue Vorlesungen über die Krankheiten des Nervensystems, insbesondere über Hysterie.* Leipzig/Vienna: Toeplitz & Deuticke 1886, xi+357 p. [With preface and footnotes]. Includes [321]. For preface and footnotes, see [276].

321

1886e Charcot, Jean-Martin, "Sur un cas de coxalgie hystérique de cause
10667 traumatique chez l'homme," under the title "Über einen Fall von

hysterischer Coxalgie aus traumatischer Ursache bei einem Manne."
Wien med Wschr 1886, 36(20:15 May):711-715; (21:22 May):756-759.
Incorporated in [320].

(Tr:JS) SE 1:19.

322

1926g   Levine, Israel, *The unconscious* (Part I, Section 13: "Samuel Butler"),
10669   under the title *Das Unbewusste*, Vienna 1926. [Remainder translated
        by Freud, A.] Includes footnote on Hering [102].

323

1880a   Mill, John Stuart, "Enfranchisement of women" (1851); Grote's *Plato*
10670   *and other companions of Sokrates* (1866); "Thornton on labour and its
        claims" (1869); "Chapters on Socialism" (1879), under the titles "Über
        Frauenemancipation"; "Plato"; "Die Arbeiterfrage"; "Der Sozialismus."
        In Mill, J. S. *Gesammelte Werke*, Vol. 12, Leipzig: Fuez 1880.

324

1911j   Putnam, James J., "On the etiology and treatment of the psychoneuro-
10670A   ses," (1910) under the title "Über Ätiologie und Behandlung der Psycho-
         neurosen." C 1911, 1:137. [with footnote]

(Tr:JS) In editor's footnote to "James J. Putnam" [127], SE 17:271 n.

SECTION VI
FREUD'S LETTERS

Entries in this section are arranged alphabetically under the name of the recipient. The names of the recipients of special interest and "open" letters, as well as the names of the recipients of letters used as prefaces are listed but are unnumbered here. The reader is referred to the entry number in the appropriate section where complete bibliographical information is given.

The full bibliographic citation for *Briefe; Letters* showing all known translations is given only once, at the beginning of this section below. Use of the abbreviated reference thereafter implies the existence of French, Italian, Norwegian and Spanish translations.

325

Briefe 1873-1939. (Ed: Freud, E. L.) Frankfurt: S. Fischer 1960, 511 p. 2nd ed (Ed: Freud, E. L. & Freud, L.) S. Fischer 1968, 538 p.

The letters of Sigmund Freud. (Ed: Freud, E. L.) (Tr: Stern, T. & Stern, J.) NY: Basic Books 1960, viii+470 p.

Fr: Correspondance 1873-1939. (Ed: Freud, E. L.) (Tr:AB & Grossein, J. P.) Paris: Gallimard 1966, 517 p.

It: Lettere 1873-1939: lettere alla fidanzata e ad altri corrispondenti. (Ed: Freud, E. L.) (Tr: Montinari, M.) Turin: Boringhieri 1960, 475 p.

Nor: Brev 1873-1939. (Eds: Freud, E. L. & Freud, L.) (Tr: Hagerup, I. & Hagerup, A.) Oslo: Aschehoug 1971.

Sp: Epistolario 1873-1939. (Tr: Merino Pérez, J.) Madrid: Biblioteca Nueva 1963.

326

ABRAHAM, KARL

1907-1926. *Sigmund Freud/Karl Abraham. Briefe 1907 bis 1926.* (Eds: 46270A Abraham, H. C. & Freud, E. L.) Frankfurt am Main: Fleischer 1965.

A psychoanalytic dialogue: the letters of Sigmund Freud and Karl Abraham, 1907-1926. (Eds: Abraham, H. C. & Freud, E. L.) (Tr: Marsh, B. & Abraham, H. C.) NY: Basic Books 1965.

Fr: *Freud, S. & Abraham, K.: Correspondance 1907-1926.* (Eds: Abraham, H. C. & Freud, E. L.) (Tr: Cambon, F. & Grossein, J. P.) Paris: Gallimard 1969, 410 p.

46270A 5 July 1907-21 July 1925. [In part] Jones 2, 3.

8 Oct 1907-21 July 1925. *Briefe; Letters.*

327

ABRAHAMSEN, DAVID

1946a   14 Mar 1938, 11 June 1939. [German facsimiles with English translation]
(1938- In Abrahamsen, D. *The mind and death of a genius* [i.e. Otto Wein-
1939)   inger]. NY: Columbia Univ Pr 1946, [41-42], 202, 207-209.
10506A

  Sp: Dos cartas a David Abrahamsen sobre Weininger. (Tr:LR) Obr Comp-
      BA 21:410. Obr Comp 1967/1968, 3:1004-1006.

328

ACHELIS, WERNER

    30 Jan 1927. *Briefe; Letters.*

329

ALDINGTON, HILDA (H. D.)

1956c   18 Dec 1932 - 28 Nov 1938. In H. D. *Tribute to Freud.* NY: Pantheon
(1932- Books 1956, 173-180.
1938)
10506B

330

ALEXANDER, FRANZ

46270B   17 May, 23 July 1926, 13 May 1928, Jones 3.

331

ANDREAS-SALOMÉ, LOU

        1 Oct 1912 - May 1936. *Sigmund Freud/Lou Andreas-Salomé, Brief-*
73591 *wechsel.* (Ed: Pfeiffer, E.) Frankfurt: S. Fischer 1966.

        Sigmund Freud and Lou Andreas-Salomé: Letters. (Ed: Pfeiffer, E.)
        (Tr: Robson-Scott, E. & Robson-Scott, W.) NY: Harcourt Brace
        Jovanovich 1972.

  Fr: *Andreas-Salomé, L.: Correspondance avec Sigmund Freud 1912-1936.*
      (Tr: Jumel, L.) Paris: Gallimard 1970.

      30 July 1915 - 16 May 1935. *Briefe; Letters.*
46270C   10 Oct 1921 - 16 May 1935. Jones 3.

      23 Mar 1930. *Briefe* (2nd ed).

332

ANONYMOUS

        27 Sept 1910. [To a gentleman about taking on the analysis of his
10523A daughter.] In J. A. Stargardt Katalog #537, Marburg 13 May 1958,
        item #321.

333
ANONYMOUS

29 July 1917. *Briefe*, 2nd ed.

334
ANONYMOUS

28 Apr 1918. *Briefe; Letters.*

335
ANONYMOUS

8 Feb 1930. *Briefe; Letters.*

336
ANONYMOUS

27 June 1934. *Briefe; Letters.*

337
ANONYMOUS

14 Dec 1937. *Briefe; Letters.*

338
ANONYMOUS

18 June 1938. *Briefe; Letters.*

339
ANONYMOUS

21 Dec 1938. [In part, English translation] In "The Freud collection of the Menninger Foundation Museum." Bulletin of the Menninger Clinic 1965, 29(5) Sept:281.

340
EINEN ARZT ÜBER DIE PSYCHOANALYTISCHE BEHANDLUNG EINER PATIENTIN

25 Jan 1922. [In part] In J. A. Stargardt Katalog #580, Marburg

23 May 1967, item #384.

341
BAUER, VICTOR

1952b   1931. [French translation] In *Journal de la maison* (Ed: Veillon, C.)
(1931) Lausanne 1952, 9(7:Dec):101.
10507

342
BAUMGARDT, DAVID

3 Nov 1938. *Briefe; Letters.*

343
BEER-HOFMANN, RICHARD

10 July 1936. *Briefe* (2nd ed).

344
BENNET, E. A.

73579 9 M. 1930. [German facsimile with English translation.] In "The Freud-Janet controversy: an unpublished letter." Brit med J 1965, 5426(2 Jan): 53.

345
BERDACH (BARDI), RACHEL

27 Dec 1938. *Briefe; Letters.*

BERG, CHARLES

See [272].

BERLINER ILLUSTRIERTE ZEITUNG, EDITOR OF

See [234].

346
BERNAYS, ANNA FREUD

1940f   14 May 1939. [Published in English] In Bernays, A. F. "My brother
(1939)   Sigmund Freud." American Mercury 1940, Nov:335-342.
10508

Ger: Original text unpublished.

347
BERNAYS, EDWARD L.

27 Sept 1919-10 Aug 1929. In Bernays, E. L. *Biography of an idea: memoirs of public relations counsel Edward L. Bernays.* NY: Simon & Schuster 1965, 254-275.

10 Aug 1929. *Briefe; Letters.*

348
BERNAYS, EMMELINE

16, 21 Oct 1887. *Briefe; Letters.*

349

BERNAYS, MARTHA

19 June 1882 - 13 May 1886. *Brautbriefe*. Frankfurt am Main: Fischer
1968. Jones 1. *Briefe; Letters*.

It: *Lettere alla fidanzata (1882-1887)*. (Tr: Montinari, M.) Turin: Boringhieri 1963, 1969, 202 p.

Sp: *Cartas a la novia*. (Tr: Merino Pérez, J.) Barcelona: Tusquets 1969.

46271 19 June 1882. Aufbau 1960, 26:19-20.

10 May 1883. [In part, with English translation] In Grinstein, A.
"Freud's first publications in America." J. Am Psa Ass 1971, 19:241-242.

28 Oct 1882. [In part, with English translation] (Intro: Freud, E. L.)
(Tr: Schrier, I.) In "Some early unpublished letters of Freud." J. 1969,
50:419.

25 Apr 1885. [With English translation] (Tr: Schur, M.) In Schur, M.
Freud: living and dying. NY: IUP 1972, 33, 530.

350

BERNAYS, MINNA

21 Feb 1883 - 13 July 1891. *Briefe; Letters*.

6 Apr 1892. *Briefe* (2nd ed).

351

BINSWANGER, LUDWIG

1955   17 May 1909 - 19 July 1938 [Includes extracts]. In Binswanger, L.
(1909-   *Sigmund Freud: Erinnerungen an Sigmund Freud*, Berne: A. Francke
1938)   AG 1955.
10508A
          In Binswanger, L. *Sigmund Freud: reminiscences of a friendship*,
          (Tr: Guterman, N.) NY/London: Grune & Stratton 1957.

Fr: Discours, parcours et Freud. (Tr: Lewinter, R.) In *Souvenirs sur
Sigmund Freud*, Paris: Gallimard 1970, 278-366.

14 Apr 1912, 12 Apr 1929, 8 Oct 1936. *Briefe; Letters*.

11 Jan 1929. [In part] Jones 2.

352

BLANTON, SMILEY

8 July 1929. [English facsimile] Blanton, S. *Diary of my analysis with
Sigmund Freud*. NY: Hawthorn Books 1971, dust jacket.

353

BLEULER, EUGEN

73582
28 Sept 1910-25 Apr 1912. [Excerpts in English translation] In Alexander, F. & Selesnick, S. T. "Freud-Bleuler correspondence." Arch gen Psychiat 1965, 12:1-19.

354

BLUMGART, DR. LEONARD

73583
12 May 1921. [English facsimile] In Wangh, M. *Fruition of an idea: fifty years of psychoanalysis in New York.* NY: IUP 1962, 89, 91.

B'NAI B'RITH LODGE

See [47].

355

BONAPARTE, MARIE

46217A 1926-16 June 1939. [In part] Jones 2, 3.

27 Apr 1926-16 June 1939. [German with English translation] (Tr: Schur, M.) In Schur, M. *Freud: living and dying.* NY: IUP 1972, 391-524; 555-567.

10 May 1926-28 Apr 1939. *Briefe; Letters.*

22 Oct 1932-27 Jan 1937. [German with English translation] (Tr: Schur, M.) In Schur, M. *Drives, affects, behavior.* NY: IUP 1965, 2:10-20.

27 Jan 1938. *Briefe* (2nd ed).

356

BOSE, GIRINDRASEKHAR

46272 1921-1937. Samiksa 1956, 10:104-110, 155-166.

357

BOUTONIER, JULIETTE

1955e 11 Apr 1930. [German with French translation] In Favez-Boutonier, J.
(1930) "Psychanalyse et philosophie." Bull Soc fr Philos 1955, 49(1):3-4.
10508B

358

BÓVEDA, XAVIER

1956f 6 Dec 1933. [German facsimile with English translation] Q 1956,
(1933) 25:153-154. Jones 3.
10508C

359

BRAMSON, JAMES S. H.

46272A 25 Mar 1934. Jones 3.

360

BRAUN-VOGELSTEIN, JULIE

1956g 30 Oct 1927. [German with English translation] In Grotjahn, M.
10508D "A letter by Sigmund Freud with recollections of his adolescence."
J Am Psa Ass 1956, 4:645-649. *Briefe; Letters.*

361

BRETON, ANDRÉ

1933e 13, 14, 26 Dec 1932. [Original publication in French; one German
(1932) facsimile] In *Le surréalisme au service de la révolution*, Paris 1933,
10509A May (5-6):10-11. In Breton, A. *Les vases communicants*, Paris:
Gallimard 1970, 173.

In Davis, F. "Three letters from Sigmund Freud to André Breton."
J Am Psa Ass 1973, 21(1):127-134.

1938b 8 Dec 1937. [In German] In *Trajectoire du rêve. Documents recueillis*
(1937) *par André Breton*, Paris: G.L.M. 1938. [German with English trans-
10509 lation] In Calas, N. "Surrealist intentions." Transformation: Arts,
Communications, Environment 1950, 1:49.

362

BREUER, JOSEF

23 June 1884 - 7 Jan 1898. *Briefe; Letters.*

1 Sept 1886. Jones 1.

See also [65].

363

BREUER, MATILDE

13 May 1926. Jones 3. *Briefe; Letters.*

364

BROD, MAX

11 Mar 1913. [In part] In J. A. Stargardt Katalog #591, 13-14 Nov 1969,
item #422.

365

CAROSSA, HANS

4 May 1939. *Briefe.*

Fr: *Correspond.*

366

CARRINGTON, HEREWARD

1957b   24 July 1921. [German with English translation] In "An unpublished
(1921)   letter on parapsychology." Psychoanalysis, J Nat Psychol Ass Psycho-
10509B   analysis 1957, "Psychoanalysis and the future" special issue, 4(4),
           5(1):12-13. *Briefe; Letters.*

367

CHARCOT, JEAN-MARTIN

1886(?). Jones 1.

368

CLAPARÈDE, ÉDOUARD

1921e   1921. [Extract, in French] In Freud, S. *La psychanalyse* (Tr: LeLay, Y.)
10510   Geneva: Des Editions Sonor 1921, 69-70.

           (Tr:JS) SE 11:214 footnote.

369

COHEN, ISRAEL
["Hamazkir" (The Secretary)]

1924i   1938/1939. [English translation] (Tr: Cohen, I.) In Jewish Observer &
10522C   Middle East Review, 1954,* 3(23:4 June):10.

           * 1954 was the actual publication date, not 1924 as has been previously
           believed.

370

AU-DELÀ DE L'AMOUR

1926h   1926. [In French] [Response to a questionnaire regarding the nature of
10523   love beyond the domain of sex.] In *Au delà de l'amour*, Paris: Les Cahiers
           Contemporains 1926, 77-78.

           (Tr: Winston, R.) In Reik, T. *From thirty years with Freud.* NY/
           Toronto: Farrar & Rinehart 1940; London: HPI 1942, 157; NY: IUP
           1949, 175-176.

LE DISQUE VERT

See [278].

371

A DOCTOR

19 Aug 1929. [In part, with English translation] In Paul C. Richards
Catalogue #47, item #101.

DORYON, ISRAEL

See [279].

372

DYER-BENNET, RICHARD S.

9 Dec 1928. *Briefe; Letters.*

373

EDER, MONTAGUE DAVID

1945b 11 May 1926. [In English] In Hobman, J. (ed) *David Eder. Memoirs of*
(1926) *a modern pioneer.* London: Gollancz 1945, 20-21.
10511

    Sp: Carta a David Eder. (Tr:LR) Obr Comp-BA 21:400. Obr Comp 1967/
    1968, 3:997.

EEDEN, FREDERIK VAN

See [140].

374

EINSTEIN, ALBERT

3 May 1936. *Briefe; Letters.*

See [247].

375

EITINGON, MAX

7 Jan 1913 - 6 June 1938. Jones 2, 3. *Briefe; Letters.*

21 Jan 1920 - 5 Mar 1939. [German with English translation] (Tr: Schur,
M.) In Schur, M. *Freud: living and dying,* NY: IUP 1972, 317-566.

June 1931. In *Max Eitingon. In memoriam.* Jerusalem: Israel Psycho-
Analytical Society 1950, between pages 46 and 47.

376

ELLIS, HAVELOCK

1954c 12 Sept 1926, 12 May 1928. *Briefe; Letters.*
(1934)
10512A
    Sept 1934. [English translation] In Wortis, J. *Fragment of an analysis*
    with Freud, NY: Simon & Schuster 1954, 13-14.

    Fr: (Tr: Rousseau, P.) In Wortis, J. *Psychanalyse à Vienne, 1934. "Notes*
    sur mon analyse avec Freud." Paris: Denoël 1974, 24-25.

377

FAGG, CHARLES

25 Oct 1923 - 3 Dec 1933. [In part, in English, with précis] In Dawsons of Pall Mall Catalogue, item #36.

378

FEDERN, PAUL

4 Feb 1927. [Facsimile of part] In Bruce Gimelson, Autographs, item #1117.

Sp: 1931. Carta a Paul Federn. (Tr: LR) Obr Comp-BA 21:401-402. Obr Comp 1967/1968, 3:998.

379

FERENCZI, SÁNDOR

46273A 4 Aug 1908 - 16 Sept 1930. Jones 2, 3. *Briefe; Letters.*

6 Oct 1910, 26 Nov, 9 Dec 1912. [German with English translation] (Tr: Schur, M.) In Schur, M. *Freud: living and dying.* NY: IUP 1972, 256-257, 266-268, 552-553.

20, 26 Mar 1924. [In part] In Taft, J. *Otto Rank.* NY: Julian Pr 1958, 90-93.

380

FISCHER-COLBRIE, ARTUR

28 June 1917 - 3 Jan 1921. [In part, facsimile of part of one] In Karl Faber Katalog, 25-26 Jan 1966, items 2106-2112.

28 Oct 1917. [In part] In J. A. Stargardt Katalog #585, Marburg, 11-12 June 1968, item #393.

23 May 1927. [In part] In Carnegie Book Shop Catalogue #302, item #156.

381

FLATTER, RICHARD

30 Mar 1930. [English translation, presumably by Flatter] In Flatter, R.
10513 "Queries and notes: Sigmund Freud on Shakespeare." Shakespeare Quarterly 1951, 2(4):368-369. Jones 3. *Briefe; Letters.*

20 Sept 1932. [English translation, presumably by Flatter] In Flatter, R.
10513 "Queries and notes: Sigmund Freud on Shakespeare." Shakespeare Quarterly 1951, 2(4):368-369.

382

FLIESS, WILHELM

See Aus den Anfängen der Psychoanalyse [46].

1 Aug 1890 - 11 Mar 1902. *Briefe; Letters.*

18 Oct 1893 - 19 Sept 1901. [German with English translation] (Tr: Schur, M.) In Schur, M. *Freud: living and dying,* NY: IUP 1972, 41-219, 530-550.

4 Mar 1895 - 9 June 1901. [German with English translation] (Tr: Schur, M.) In Schur, M. "Some additional 'day residues' of 'The Specimen Dream of Psychoanalysis.'" In *Psychoanalysis—a general psychology.* (eds) Loewenstein, R.; Newman, L. M.; Schur, M.; & Solnit, A. J. NY: IUP 1966, 55-84.

1906e   23, 27 July 1904. In Pfenning, R. *Wilhelm Fliess und seine Nach-*
(1904) *entdecker: O. Weininger und H. Swoboda,* Berlin: E. Goldschmidt
10513A 1906.

383

FLUSS, EMIL

18 Sept 1872 - 19 Apr 1874. "Jugendbriefe Sigmund Freuds." (Intro:
73581 Freud, E. L.) Neue Rundschau 1969, 80(4):678-693.

Some early unpublished letters of Freud. (Intro: Freud, E. L.) (Tr: Schrier, I.) J 1969, 50:419-427.

Fr: Lettres de Freud adolescent. (Tr: Pontalis, J. B.) Nouvelle Revue de psychanalyse 1970(1):167-184.

1941i   16 June 1873. Z Imago 1941, 26:5-8. *Briefe; Letters.*
(1873)
10493

Sp: Carta sobre el bachillerato. (Tr:LR) Rev Psicoanál 1955, 12:122-126. Obr Comp-BA 21:369-373. Obr Comp 1967/1968, 973-976.

384

FODOR, NANDOR

1955-   22 Nov 1938. [German with English translation] (Tr: Fodor, N.) Psycho-
1956   analysis, J Nat Psychol Ass Psychoanalysis 1955-56, 4(2):25-26.
(1938) Tomorrow 1956, 5(2):124-125.
10513B

385

FREUD, ADOLFINE

22 July 1930. *Briefe; Letters.*

386

FREUD, ALEXANDER

17 Sept 1905 - 22 June 1938. *Briefe; Letters.*

387

FREUD, AMALIE

26 Jan 1920. [In part] In J. A. Stargardt Katalog #540, Marburg 14 Nov *10513C* 1958, item #372. *Briefe; Letters.*

17 Oct 1923. *Briefe; Letters.*

388

FREUD, ANNA

7 July 1908, 28 Nov, 13 Dec 1912. *Briefe; Letters.*

1 Aug 1915. *Correspond.*

16 Apr 1927. Jones 2.

389

FREUD, ERNST

3 Apr 1922 - 12 May 1938. *Briefe; Letters.*

12 May 1938. Jones 3.

390

FREUD FAMILY

20 Apr 1905 - 25 Sept 1908. *Briefe; Letters.*

391

FREUD, LUCIE

29 Dec 1921. *Briefe; Letters.*

392

FREUD, MARGIT

4 Mar 1927. *Briefe; Letters.*

393

FREUD, MARTHA

7 June 1894 - 25 Sept 1912. Jones 2, 3. *Briefe; Letters.*

See also Bernays, Martha [349].

394

FREUD, MARTIN

3 Aug 1929, 8 July 1935. [In part, English translation] In Rendell Catalogue #56, item 71.

16 Aug 1937. *Briefe; Letters.*

26 Aug, undated, 20 Dec 1914. [English translation] (Tr: Freud, M.)
In Freud, M. *Sigmund Freud: man and father.* NY: Vanguard Pr 1958,
180-181.

395
FREUD, MATHILDE

19 Mar 1908. *Briefe; Letters.*

396
FREUD, ROSA

8 Mar 1886. *Briefe* (2nd ed).

397
FREUD, SOPHIE

20 July 1912. *Briefe; Letters.*

398
VON FREUND, ANTON

9 Aug, 17 Sept 1918. *Briefe; Letters.*

399
VON FREUND, ROZSI

9 Aug 1918, 14 May 1920, 17 Dec 1926. *Briefe; Letters.*

400
FRIENDS
["Rundbriefe"]

15 Dec 1922. [English translation] In Grotjahn, M. "Notes on reading
the 'Rundbriefe.'" Journal of Otto Rank Assoc. Winter '73-'74, 8(2):
69-72.

15 Feb 1924. In Abraham, H. C. & Freud, E. L. (eds) *Sigmund Freud/
Karl Abraham. Briefe 1907 bis 1926.* Frankfurt am Main: Fleischer 1965.

[English translation] Jones 3. In Taft, J. *Otto Rank*, NY: Julian Pr 1958,
84-88. In Abraham, H. C. & Freud, E. L. (eds) *A psychoanalytic
dialogue: the letters of Sigmund Freud and Karl Abraham, 1907-1926.*
(Tr: Marsh, B. & Abraham, H. C.) NY: Basic Books 1965, 344-348.
In Robinson, V. P. "Introduction—the committee." Journal of Otto Rank
Assoc. Winter '73-'74, 8(2):25-29.

Fr: In Abraham, H. C. & Freud, E. L. (eds) *Freud, S. & Abraham, K.:
Correspondance 1907-1926.* (Tr: Cambon, F. & Grossein, J. P.) Paris:
Gallimard 1969.

25 Feb 1924. In Abraham, H. C. & Freud, E. L. (eds) *Sigmund Freud/
Karl Abraham. Briefe 1907 bis 1926.* Frankfurt am Main: Fleischer 1965.

[English translation] In Abraham, H. C. & Freud, E. L. (eds) *A psycho-analytic dialogue: the letters of Sigmund Freud and Karl Abraham, 1907-1926.* (Tr: Marsh, B. & Abraham, H. C.) NY: Basic Books 1965, 349-350.

401
FUCHS, GEORG

1931f 1931. In Fuchs, G. *Wir Zuchthäusler. Erinnerungen des Zellen-*
46274, *gefangenen,* Nr. 2911. Munich: Albert Langen 1931, x. J 1961, 42:
46275 199-200. Excerpt in Meng, H. "Sigmund Freud in Brief, Gespräch, Begegnung und Werk." Psyche, Heidel 1956, 10:523.

(Tr: Eissler, K. R.) In Eissler, K. R. "A hitherto unnoticed letter by Sigmund Freud." J 1961, 42:199-200. (Tr:JS) SE 22:251.

FÜRST, M.

See [212].

402
GOMPERZ, ELISE

25 Nov, 8 Dec 1901; 12 Nov 1913. *Briefe; Letters.*

403
GOMPERZ, HEINRICH

15 Nov 1899. *Briefe; Letters.*

404
GREEN, J. G.

16 Nov 1934. [In part] Jones 3.

405
GRODDECK, GEORG

5 June 1917 - 4 Mar 1934. In Honegger, M. (ed) *G. Groddeck, Der Mensch und sein Es. Briefe, Aufsätze, Biografisches.* Wiesbaden: Limes Verlag 1970, 14-90.

5 June 1917 - 21 Dec 1924. *Briefe; Letters.*

406
A GROUP OF JEWS FROM BRAILA, RUMANIA

29 Apr 1929. [In memory of Eduard Silberstein]. In Stanescu, H. "Young Freud's letters to his Rumanian friend, Silberstein." (Tr: Meron, J.) Israel Annals of Psychiatry and Related Disciplines 1971, 9(3:Dec): 197-198.

407
GUILBERT, YVETTE

8 Mar 1931, 24 Oct 1938. *Briefe; Letters.*

408
HALBERSTADT, MAX

7 July 1912 - 18 Sept 1916. *Briefe; Letters.*
25 Jan 1920. *Briefe* (2nd ed).

409
HALBERSTADT, SOPHIE

18 Sept 1916. *Briefe; Letters.*

410
HALL, G. STANLEY

28 Aug 1923. [German with English translation] (Tr: Erikson, E. H. &
46276 Rapaport, D.) Q 1960, 29:310-312.

23 Nov 1913. *Briefe; Letters.*

"HAMAZKIR"

See [369].

411
HELLER, HUGO
(THE ANTIQUARY HINTERBERGER)

1907d 1 Nov 1906 (1907). Antwort auf eine Rundfrage *Vom Lesen und von*
10396 *guten Büchern, eine Rundfrage veranstaltet von der Redaktion der*
"Neuen Blätter für Literatur und Kunst." Vienna: Heller 1907, ix.
In Feigl, H. *Jahrbuch deutscher Bibliophilen und Literaturfreunde,*
Zurich/Leipzig: Amalthea Verlag 1931, 16-17:117-119. *Briefe.*

(Tr: Eissler, K. R.) In Eissler, K. R. "An unknown autobiographical
letter by Freud and a short comment," J 1951, 32:319-320. Jones 3.
Letters.

Contribution to a questionaire on reading. (Revised tr:JS) SE 9:245-247.

It: Risposta a un questionario sulla lettura e sui buoni libri. (Tr: Montinari,
M.) Opere 5:367-368.

412
HÉRENGER, ALEXANDER

10 May 1929. *Briefe* (2nd ed).

413

EINEN HERRN IN FRANKREICH

29 Aug 1926. [In part] In J. A. Stargardt Katalog #549, Marburg, 11 Nov 1960, item #338.

414

HESSE, HERMANN

23 Aug 1918. [Postcard] In Zeller, B. "Ansprache bei der Eröffnung des
73585 Hermann-Hesse-Archivs im Schiller-Nationalmuseum, Marbach A.N. am 23. Februar 1965." *Jahrbuch der Deutschen Schillergesellschaft*, Stuttgart: Alfred Kröner Verlag 1965, 9:637-642.

415

HESSING, SIEGFRIED

46277 In Hessing, S. *Spinoza-Festschrift*, Heidelberg 1933, 222.

416

HILLER, KURT

1950b 9 Nov 1936. In Hiller, K. *Köpfe und Tröpfe, Profile aus einem Viertel-*
(1936) *jahrhundert.* Hamburg/Stuttgart: Rowohlt 1950, 308. [In part] Jones 3.
10514

417

HIRSCHFELD, MAGNUS

1906d [Two letters] In Monatsbericht des wissenschaftlichhumanitären Komitee,
10515 Leipzig 1906, 5:30. [First letter incomplete].

418

HITSCHMANN, EDUARD

Aug 1914. [In part] Jones 2.

7 May 1916. *Briefe; Letters.*

1956b 5 July 1916. [German with English translation] Q 1956, 25:361-362.
(1916)
10515A

419

HOLLÓS, ISTVÁN

4 Oct 1928. [German with English translation] (Tr: Schur, M.) In Schur, M. *The id and the regulatory principles of mental functioning.* NY: IUP 1966, 21-22.

420

ON HOMOSEXUALITY

1951a   9 Apr 1935. [In English] P 1951, 107:786-787. J 1951, 32:331. *Letters.*
(1935)   *Briefe* [In English with German translation].
10524

421

HOOPER, FRANKLIN

4 Sept 1924. *Briefe; Letters.*

HUG-HELLMUTH, HERMINE VON

See [284].

422

INDRA, ALFRED

20 July 1938. *Briefe; Letters.*

423

JELLIFFE, SMITH ELY

2 Oct 1933 - Feb 1939. [3 in English, 1 English translation] In Lewis, N. D. C. "Psychosomatic Medicine in America." In Alexander, F.; Eisenstein, S.; & Grotjahn, M. (eds) *Psychoanalytic pioneers,* London/ NY: Basic Books 1966, 227-228.

424

JONES, ERNEST

46277A   22 Feb 1909 - 3 Mar 1939. [Some originally written in English] Jones 2, 3.

30 Dec 1925 - 7 Mar 1938. *Briefe; Letters.*

1 July 1928 - 1 Nov 1938. [German with English translation] (Tr: Schur, M.) In Schur, M. *Freud: living and dying.* NY: IUP 1972, 405-512, 557-565.

425

JONES, HERBERT

1914. *Briefe; Letters.*

426

JONES, LOE

1914. *Briefe; Letters.*

JÜDISCHE PRESSZENTRALE, EDITOR

See [63].

427

JUNG, CARL GUSTAV

11 Apr 1906 - 27 Jan 1913. *The Freud/Jung letters.* (Ed: McGuire, W.) (Tr: Manheim, R. & Hill, R. F. C.) Princeton, N.J.: Princeton Univ Pr 1974, xlii+650 p.

46277A 7 Oct 1906 - 7 Dec 1911. Jones 2.

26 May 1907 - 22 Dec 1912. *Briefe; Letters.*

16 Apr 1909. [German with English translation] (Tr: Schur, M.) In Schur, M. *Freud: living and dying.* NY: IUP 1972, 228-233, 550-551.

16 Apr 1909, 12 May, 15 June 1911. (Tr: Winston, R. & Winston, C.) *73586* In Jung, C. G. *Memories, dreams, reflections.* (Ed: Jaffé, A.) NY: Pantheon 1963, 361-364.

Fr: (Tr: Cohen, R. & LeLay, Y.) In Jung, C. G. *Ma vie.* Paris: Gallimard 1973, 419-422.

19 Dec 1909. [German with English translation] (Tr: Schur, M.) In Schur, M. *The id and the regulatory principles of mental functioning.* NY: IUP 1966, 17-18.

428

KEYSERLING, COUNT HERMANN

10 Aug 1932. *Briefe; Letters.*

429

KNÖPFMACHER, WILHELM

6 Aug 1878. *Briefe; Letters.*

430

KOLLER, CARL

23 July 1880 - 1 Jan 1887. *Briefe* (2nd ed).

23 July 1880 - 13 Sept 1887. (Tr: Freud, E. L. & Becker, H. K.) In Becker, H. K. "Carl Koller and cocaine." Q 1963, 32:316-361.

431

KRAUS ,KARL

12 Jan 1906. *Briefe; Letters.*

KRAUSS, DR. FRIEDRICH S.

See [64].

432

LAFORGUE, RENE

1 Nov 1923 - 5 Nov 1929. [Extracts, in French] In Bourguignon, A. "Les relations epistolaires de Freud et Laforgue." Ann med-psychol 1968, 1(2):169-176.

433

LAMPL-DE GROOT, HANS

11 Feb 1926. *Briefe; Letters.*

434

LAMPL-DE GROOT, JEANNE

11 Feb 1926. *Briefe; Letters.*

435

LAY, WILFRED

1956e
(1920)
10515B
13 Dec 1920. [In English] Q 1956, 25:152.

436

LEHRMAN, PHILIP

73583
5 June 1928. [English facsimile] In Wangh, M. *Fruition of an idea: fifty years of psychoanalysis in New York.* NY: IUP 1962, 90.

LEROY, MAXIME

See [141].

437

LEVY, KATÁ

11 June 1923. *Briefe; Letters.*

438

LEVY, LAJOS

11 June 1923. *Briefe; Letters.*

439

LEYENS, ERICH

1956d
(1923)
(1936)
10515C
4 July 1923, 25 July 1936. [German with English translation. In English] Q 1956, 25:148-150. Jones 3.

440

LIPSCHÜTZ, ALEXANDER

12 Aug 1931. *Briefe; Letters.*

441

LOW, BARBARA

1945c   19 Apr 1936. [In English] In Hobman, J. *David Eder. Memoirs of a*
(1936)   *modern pioneer.* London: Gollancz 1945, 21. *Briefe; Letters.*
10516

Sp: (Tr:LR) Obr Comp-BA 21:403. Obr Comp 1967/1968, 3:999.

442

LÖWY, HEINRICH

30 Mar 1930. *Briefe; Letters.*

443

MAGGIE

14 Aug 1911. [A patient. In part] J. A. Stargardt Katalog #540, Marburg
14 Nov 1958, item #392, insert after p. 85.

444

MAGNES, JUDAH LEON

1954a   17 Nov 1933. [English translation] (Tr: Glaser, K. & Glaser, Mrs.) In
(1933)   Rosenbaum, M. "Freud-Eitingon-Magnes correspondence, psychoan-
10516A alysis at the Hebrew University." J Am Psa Ass 1954, 2(2):314-315.

1954a   5 Dec 1933. [English translation] (Tr: Glaser, K. & Glaser, Mrs.) In
(1933)   Rosenbaum, M. "Freud-Eitingon-Magnes correspondence, psychoan-
10516A alysis at the Hebrew University." J Am Psa Ass 1954, 2(2):315-316.
          Briefe; Letters.

445

MANN, THOMAS

1935c   June 1935. [For Thomas Mann's 60th Birthday] Almanach 1936, June
10607   1935:18. GW 1950, 16:249. *Briefe.*

         Letters. (Tr:JS) SE 22:255.

It: A Thomas Mann per il suo sessantesimo compleanno. Opere 11.

Sp: A Thomas Mann, en su sesenta aniversario. (Tr:LR) Obr Comp-BA 20:
     221. Obr Comp 1967/1968, 3:337.

1941g   29 Nov 1936. [Under title: "Entwurf zu einem Brief an Thomas Mann."]
(1936)   [On Napoleon] Z 1941, 26:217-219. *Briefe.*
10441

         Jones 3. *Letters.*

Sp: Borrador de una carta a Thomas Mann. (Tr:LR) Obr Comp-BA 21: 404-406. Obr Comp 1967/1968, 3:1000-1001.

446
MARCONDES, DURVAL

27 June 1928. [German facsimile with Portuguese translation] Revista Brasileira de Psicanálise 1967, 1(1):cover.

447
MEITLIS, JACOB

1951b 8 June 1938-19 Aug 1939. In Meitlis, J. "The last days of Sigmund
(1938- Freud." Jewish Frontier 1951, Sept:20-22.
1939)
10517

19 Aug 1939. [In part] Jones 3.

448
MENDELSOHN, B.

6 Dec 1934, 22 Jan 1937. [German facsimiles with English translation] In Winnik, H. Z. "Two unpublished letters of S. Freud." Israel Annals of Psychiatry and Related Disciplines 1974, 12(1:March):4-9.

449
MONOD-HERZEN, ÉDOUARD

9 Feb 1923. *Briefe; Letters.*

450
MONTESSORI, MARIE

20 Dec 1917. *Briefe; Letters.*

451
MORDELL, ALBERT

46278A 21 May 1920. Jones 3.

452
MORSELLI, ENRICO

18 Feb 1926. *Briefe; Letters.*

453
MÜLLER-BRAUNSCHWEIG, CARL

21 July 1935. [Published in English] (Tr: Stierlin, H.) In Burnham, D. L.

"Freud and female sexuality: a previously unpublished letter." Psychiatry 1971, 34(Aug):329.

Original German text unpublished.

NEUE FREIE PRESSE

See [77].

454

PÁLOS, GISELA

30 Apr 1917. [In part] Jones 2.

455

PAQUET, ALFONS

26 July 1930. *Briefe; Letters.*

See also [48].

456

PFISTER, OSKAR

1963a 18 Jan 1909 - 27 Mar 1937. *Sigmund Freud/Oskar Pfister. Briefe 1909*
73592 *bis 1939.* (Eds: Freud, E. L. & Meng, H.) Frankfurt: S. Fischer 1963,
46280 168 p. Schweiz Z Psychol 1956, 15:108-113. Excerpts in Meng, H.
46279 "Sigmund Freud in Brief, Gespräch, Begegnung und Werk." Psyche,
Heidel 1956, 10:520-521.

Psychoanalysis and faith. Dialogues with the Reverend Oskar Pfister.
(Eds: Freud, E. L. & Meng, H.) (Tr: Mosbacher, E.) London: Hogarth
Pr; NY: Basic Books 1963, 152 p.

Fr: *Correspondance avec le pasteur Pfister, 1909-1939.* (Tr: Jumel, L.)
Paris: Gallimard 1966, 216 p.

It: *Psicologia e fede. Carteggio con il pastore Pfister (1909-1939).* (Tr:
Daniele, S.) *Epistolari di Sigmund Freud,* Vol. 3. Turin: Boringhieri
1970, 151 p.

Sp: *Correspondencia 1909-1939.* (Tr: Cabo, M. R.) Mexico, Fondo de
cultura economica 1966.

18 Jan 1909 - 13 June 1934. *Briefe; Letters.*

9 Feb 1909 - 9 May 1920. [Excerpts] Jones 2, 3.

457

PILZ, ROBERT VON

30 July 1927. [In part] In J. A. Stargardt Katalog #548, Marburg 17 May
1960.

PŘÍBOR, BÜRGERMEISTER OF

See [62].

458

POPPER-LYNKEUS, JOSEF

4 Aug 1916. *Briefe; Letters.*

DAS PSYCHOANALYTISCHE VOLKSBUCH

See [288].

459

PUTNAM, JAMES JACKSON

5 Dec 1909 - 1 Oct 1916. [German with English translation] (Tr: Heller, J. B.) In Hale, Nathan G. (ed) *James Jackson Putnam and psychoanalysis.* Cambridge: Harvard Univ Pr 1971, 86-202; 351-379.

1 Jan 1913, 8 July 1915. *Briefe; Letters.*

9 Mar, 7 June, 8 July 1915. Jones 2.

460

RANK, OTTO

8 July 1922 - 27 Aug 1924. (Tr: Taft, J.) In Taft, J. *Otto Rank.* NY: Julian Pr 1958, 74-109.

25 Aug 1924. *Briefe; Letters.*

461

REIK, THEODOR

1956 1911 - 3 July 1938. [English facsimile of one] (Tr: Reik, T.) In Reik, T.
(1911- *The search within.* NY: Straus & Cudahy 1956, 75, 172-173, 195-196,
1938) 630-657.
10521A

13 Nov 1913, 1926, 14 Apr 1929. In Reik, T. *From thirty years with Freud.* (Tr: Winston, R.) NY/Toronto: Farrar & Rinehart 1940; London: HPI 1942, 64, 155-157, 176. NY: IUP 1949, 173-175.

1930f 14 Apr 1929. In Reik, T. *Freud als Kulturkritiker.* Vienna/Leipzig:
(1929) Präger Verlag 1930, 63-65. In Reik, T. *The search within,* 75. (Revised
10520 tr: JS) As "Appendix to 'Dostoevsky and parricide.'" SE 21:195-196.

1952a 3 July - 3 Oct 1938. In "Three letters to America." Psychoanalysis, J Nat
(1938) Psychol Ass Psychoanalysis 1952, 1:5-6.
10521

Fr: Trois lettres inedites de Sigmund Freud a Theodor Reik. (Tr: Choisy, M.) Psyche, Paris 1953, 8:369-371.

462

RIE, OSKAR

4 Aug 1921. *Briefe; Letters.*

463

ROBACK, ABRAHAM AARON

1957   25 Jan 1930 - 10 July 1939. In Roback, A. A. *Freudiana.* Cambridge,
(1930- Mass: Sci-Art Publ 1957. Jones 3.
1931)
10512B
20 Feb 1930. *Briefe; Letters.*

464

ROLLAND, ROMAIN

4 Mar 1923 - May 1931. *Briefe; Letters.*

1923-1936. [In French] In Cornubert, C. *Freud et Romain Rolland.
Essai sur la découverte de la pensée psychanalytique par quelques
ecrivains français.* Paris: Thèse de Medecine 1966, 74 p.

See also [66, 206].

465

RUBENS, VICTOR

12 Feb 1929. [On smoking] In NY Public Library, George Arents
10521C Collection, catalogue #3270, accession #5062.

466

SCHAEFFER, ALBRECHT

19 Sept 1939. *Briefe; Letters.*

467

SCHILLER, MAX

26 Mar 1931. *Briefe; Letters.*

468

SCHNIER, JACQUES

5 July 1938. [In part] Jones 3.

469

SCHNITZLER, ARTHUR

1955b 8 May 1906 - May 1931. Die neue Rundschau 1955, 66(1):1-12.
(1906-
1931)
10420A

[Extracts and summaries] (Tr: Sulzberger, C. F.) In Sulzberger, C. F. "Two new documents on Freud." Psychoanalysis, J Nat Psychol Ass Psychoanalysis 1955, 4(2):9-21.

8 May 1906, 14 May 1922. *Briefe; Letters.*

14 May 1922. Jones 3.

14 May 1912, 24 Mar, 24 May 1926. [In part] In J. A. Stargardt Katalog #576, Marburg, 24-25 May 1966, items #373-375.

470

SCHUR, MAX

10 Jan, 9 Sept 1930. [German with English translation] (Tr: Schur, M.) In Schur, M. *Freud: living and dying,* NY: IUP 1972, 409, 411, 557-558.

28 June 1930, 26 July 1938. *Briefe; Letters.*

471

SEROTA, HERMAN, M.

14 Apr 1938. [German facsimile with English translation] (Tr: Eissler, 73587 R. S.) Bull Phila Ass Psa 1968, 18:12-13.

472

SILBERER, HERBERT

17 Apr 1922. In Meng, H. "Sigmund Freud in Brief, Gespräch, Begeg- 46282 nung und Werk." Psyche, Heidel 1956, 10:521.

473

SILBERSTEIN, EDUARD

8 Nov 1874-7 Feb 1882. [Facsimiles of two in Spanish. Letters signed 73587A "Cipion."] In Stanescu, H. "Unbekannte Briefe des jungen Sigmund Freuds an einen rumänischen Freund." Neue Literatur 1965, 16(3): 123-129. In Stanescu, H. "Ein Gelegenheitsgedicht des jungen Sigmund Freud." Deutsch für Ausländer 1967, Jan:13-18. In Gedo, J. & Wolf, E. "Die Ichthyosaurusbriefe." Psyche 1970, 24:785-797.

In Stanescu, H. "Young Freud's letters to his Rumanian friend, Silberstein." (Tr: Meron, J.) Israel Annals of Psychiatry and Related Disciplines 1971, 9(3:Dec):195-207.

22 Aug 1874. *Briefe* (2nd ed).

474

SIMMEL, ERNST

20 Feb 1918-9 Jan 1939. [One written in English] (Tr: Brunswick, D. 73588 & Deri, F.) In "Freud's letters to Ernst Simmel." (Intro: Brunswick, D. & Lachenbuech, R.) J Am Psa Ass 1964, 12:93-109.

11 Nov 1928. *Briefe; Letters.*

475
SINGER, CHARLES
31 Oct 1938. *Briefe; Letters.*

476
STÄRCKE, AUGUST
25 Feb, 25 Aug 1912. [In part] Jones 2.

477
STEINIG, LEON
June 1932. *Briefe; Letters.*

478
STEKEL, WILHELM
13 Jan 1924. *Briefe; Letters.*

STERBA, RICHARD
See [294].

479
STRACHEY, LYTTON
25 Dec 1928. *Briefe* (2nd ed).

480
STRUCK, HERMANN
7 Nov 1914. *Briefe; Letters.*

27 July 1914. [In part] In J. A. Stargardt Katalog #563, 28-29 May 1963, item #314.

481
SZONDI, LIPOT
46283 [In part] In Meng, H. "Sigmund Freud in Brief, Gespräch, Begegnung und Werk." Psyche, Heidel 1956, 10:521.

482
TANDLER, JULIUS
8 Mar 1925. *Briefe; Letters.*

TIME AND TIDE
See [49].

483

TINTY, BARON KARL FERDINAND

46283A 10 July 1934. Jones 3.

484

VELIKOVSKY, IMMANUEL

1957c 24 June 1931. [German with English translation] In *Psychoanalysis and*
(1931) *the future.* Psychoanalysis, J Nat Psychol Ass Psychoanalysis 1957, 15-16.
10522AA

485

VIERECK, GEORGE SYLVESTER

20 July 1928, 16 Apr 1933. *Briefe; Letters.*

486

VOIGTLÄNDER, ELSE

1 Oct 1911. *Briefe; Letters.*

487

WECHSLER, ISRAEL SPANIER

8 May 1929. *Briefe; Letters.*

488

WEISS, EDOARDO

29 June 1919 - 1936. [English translation] (Tr: Grotjahn, E. & Grotjahn,
M.) In Weiss, E. *Sigmund Freud as a consultant.* NY: Intercontinental
Med Book Corp 1970, 23-82.

3 Oct 1920 - 12 Apr 1933. [German with English translation] In Grotjahn, M. "Sigmund Freud as a consultant and therapist; from Sigmund
Freud's letters to Edoardo Weiss." Psa Forum 1966, 1(2):223-231.

28 May 1922 - 9 Feb 1934. [German facsimiles with English translation]
In Grotjahn, M. "Freud as a psychoanalytic consultant: from some
unknown letters to Edoardo Weiss." Psa Forum 1966, 1(1):132-137.

46283B 24 Apr 1932 - 22 Sept 1932. Jones 3.

12 Apr 1933. [In part] Jones 2. *Briefe; Letters.*

489

WEISSMAN, KARL

46283C 21 Mar 1938. Jones 3.

490

WELLS, HERBERT GEORGE

16 July 1939. *Briefe; Letters.*

491

WITTELS, FRITZ

1924g   18 Dec 1923. [First published in English] (Tr: Paul, E. & Paul, C.) In
1923   Wittels, F. *Sigmund Freud, his personality, his teaching and his school,*
10415 London: Allen & Unwin; NY: Dodd, Mead 2nd ed, 1924, 11-13. Jones 3.
        Letters. SE 19:286-288.

Ger: *Briefe.*

 Fr: Extrait d'une lettre à F. Wittels. (Tr: Herbert) In Wittels, F. *Freud,*
     l'homme, la doctrine, l'école, Paris: Alcan 1929.

 It: Lettera a Fritz Wittels. Opere 9.

     15 Aug 1924. *Briefe; Letters.*

492

WORRALL, R. L.

10 Sept 1937. [In part] Jones 3.

493

WORTIS, JOSEPH

1954d   21 May, 14 July, 20 Oct 1935. [German facsimile with English trans-
(1934- lation] (Tr: Wortis, J.) In Wortis, J. *Fragment of an analysis with Freud.*
1935)   NY: Simon & Schuster 1954, 7, 168-171.
10522A
        29 Sept 1934. [In English] In Wortis, J. *Fragment of an analysis with*
        Freud. NY: Simon & Schuster 1954, 15.

 Fr: Quatre lettres à Joseph Wortis. (Tr: Rousseau, P.) In *Psychanalyse à*
     Vienne, 1934, "Notes sur mon analyse avec Freud." Paris: Denoël 1974,
     26, 186.

494

YABE, YAEKICHI

25 Nov 1930. [Published in Japanese] (Tr: Yabe, Y.) In *Furoido seishin*
bunsekigaku zenshu, Tokyo: Shunyodo Publ Co 1931, 5:appendix-19.

Original English text not extant.

YIVO

See [258].

495

ZWEIG, ARNOLD

20 Mar 1927 - 31 May 1936. *Briefe; Letters.*

1968a 20 Mar 1927 - 5 Mar 1939. *Briefwechsel von Sigmund Freud und Arnold*
(1927- *Zweig, 1927-1939.* (Ed: Freud, E. L.) Frankfurt am Main: S. Fischer
1939) 1968, 202 p.
73576

The letters of Sigmund Freud and Arnold Zweig, 1927-1939. (Ed: Freud, E. L.) (Tr: Robson-Scott, E. & Robson-Scott, W.) London: HPI 1970; NY: Harcourt, Brace & World 1970, 190 p.

Fr: *Freud, S. et Zweig, A.: Correspondance 1927-1939.* (Tr: Weibel, L.) Paris: Gallimard 1973.

21 Mar, 18 Aug 1933, 14 Oct 1935. [German with English translation] (Tr: Schur, M.) In Schur, M. *Freud: living and dying,* NY: IUP 1972, 444, 448, 459, 561-563.

29 July 1933. [Extracts, in German] In J. A. Stargardt Katalog #560, Marburg, 28 Nov 1962, item #1031.

46283D 28 Jan 1934 - 13 Dec 1938. Jones 3.

496

ZWEIG, STEFAN

3 May 1908 - 20 July 1938. *Briefe; Letters.*

17 Nov 1937, 20 July 1938. [In part] Jones 3.

SECTION VII
CHRONOLOGICAL LISTING OF
THE WORKS OF SIGMUND FREUD

This section lists Freud's writings according to the year of publication and/or writing when known. Under each year heading the publications are arranged sequentially using the Tyson-Strachey number which refers to the year of publication. Another number in parentheses may follow this number in those instances where the year of writing of a particular work was known to be different from the year of publication.

Each title is given in the language of the original publication of the article, book or monograph. The entry number used in this work, *Sigmund Freud: A Comprehensive Bibliography*, immediately follows the title.

This chronological listing omits Freud's abstracts, reviews, translations, letters, prefaces and introductions to his own works and to the works of others. These may be found in the appropriate sections (III through VI) of this work.

1871

1871 —Zerstreute Gedanken, 40

1877

1877a—Über den Ursprung der hinteren Nervenwurzeln im Rückenmarke von Amnocoetes, 37

1877b—Beobachtungen über Gestaltung und feineren Bau der als Hoden beschriebenen Lappenorgane des Aals, 9

1878

1878a—Über Spinalganglien und Rückenmark des Petromyzon, 34

1879

1879a—Notiz Über eine Methode zur anatomischen Präparation des Nervensystems, 31

1882

1882a—Über den Bau der Nervenfasern und Nervenzellen beim Flusskrebs, 5

1884

1884a—Ein Fall von Hirnblutung mit indirekten basalen Herdsymptomen bei Skorbut, 17

1884b,1884d—Eine neue Methode zum Studium des Faserverlaufes im Centralnervensystem, 30

1884c —A new histological method for the study of nerve-tracts in the brain and
spinal cord, 30
1884e —Ueber Coca, 14
1884f —Die Struktur der Elemente des Nervensystems, 35
The bacillus of syphilis, 4
Cocaine, 15

1885

1885a—Beitrag zur Kenntnis der Cocawirkung, 7
1885b—Über die Allgemeinwirkung des Cocaïns, 1
1885c —Ein Fall von Muskelatrophie mit ausgebreiteten Sensibilitätsstörungen
(Syringomyelie), 18
1885d—Zur Kenntnis der Olivenzwischenschicht, 26
1885e —[Gutachten über das Parke Cocaïn], 20
1885f —Nachträge über Coca, 28

1886

1886a—Akute multiple Neuritis der spinalen und Hirnnerven, 3
1886b—(& Darkschewitsch, L.) Über die Beziehung des Stickkörpers zum
Hinterstrang und Hinterstrangskern nebst Bemerkungen über zwei
Felder der Oblongata, 11
1886c —Über den Ursprung des Nervus acusticus, 38
1886d—Beobachtung einer hochgradigen Hemianästhesie bei einem hysterischen
Manne, 8
1956a(1886)—Report on my studies in Paris and Berlin carried out with the
assistance of a travelling bursary granted from the University Jubilee
Fund, 204

1887

1887d—Beiträge über die Anwendung des Cocaïn, 6
1887f —Das Nervensystem, 29

1887-1902

1950a—Aus den Anfängen der Psychoanalyse; Briefe an Wilhelm Fliess,
Abhandlungen und Notizen aus den Jahren 1887-1902, 46

1888

1888a—Über Hemianopsie in frühesten Kindesalter, 21
1888b—[Contribution to] Villaret, A. *Handwörterbuch der gesamten Medizin*,
39

1890

1890a—Psychische Behandlung (Seelenbehandlung), 183

1891

1891a—(& Rie, O.) Klinische Studie über die halbseitige Cerebrallähmung der
Kinder, 27

1891a (excerpt)—Cerebrale Kinderlähmung und Poliomyelitis infantilis, 13
1891b—Zur Auffassung der Aphasien. Eine kritische Studie, 2
1891c—Kinderlähmung, spinale, 39
1891c—Lähmung, 39
1891d—Hypnose, 22

1892

1893a(1892)—(& Breuer, J.) Über den psychischen Mechanismus hysterischer
Phänomene: Vorläufige Mitteilung, 185
1940d(1892)—(& Breuer, J.) Zur Theorie des hysterischen Anfalls, 219
1941a(1892)—Brief an Josef Breuer, 65
1941b(1892)—Notiz "III," 172
[Contribution to] Rosenthal, E. *Contribution a l'étude des diplégies cérébrales de l'enfance*, 33

1892-1893

1892-93—Ein Fall von hypnotischer Heilung: nebst Bemerkungen über die
Entstehung hysterischer Symptome durch den "Gegenwillen," 97

1893

1893b—Zur Kenntnis der cerebralen Diplegien des Kindesalters (im Anschluss
an die Little'sche Krankheit), 25
1893c—Quelques considérations pour une étude comparative des paralysies
motrices organiques et hystériques, 200
1893d—Über familiäre Formen von cerebralen Diplegien, 19
1893e—Les diplégies cérébrales infantiles, 16
1893f—Charcot. (obituary), 69
1893g—Über ein Symptom das häufig die Enuresis nocturna der Kinder begleitet, 36
1893h—Vortrag über den psychischen Mechanismus hysterischer Phänomene,
245
[Contribution to] Rosenberg, L. *Casuistische Beiträge zur Kenntnis der cerebralen Kinderlähmungen und der Epilepsie*, 32

1894

1894a—Die Abwehr-Neuropsychosen, 42
1895b(1894)—Über die Berechtigung von der Neurasthenie einen bestimmten
Symptomenkomplex als "Angstneurose" abzutrennen, 59
1895c(1894)—Obsessions et phobies. Leur mécanisme psychique et leur étiologie,
173

1895

1895d—(& Breuer, J.) Studien über Hysterie, 214
1895e—Über die Bernhardt'sche Sensibilitätsstörung am Oberschenkel, 10
1895f—Zur Kritik der "Angstneurose," 138
1950a(1895)—[Entwurf einer Psychologie], 88

1896

1896a—L'hérédité et l'étiologie des névroses, 118
1896b—Weitere Bemerkungen über die Abwehr-Neuropsychosen, 250
1896c—Zur Ätiologie der Hysterie, 50

1897

1897a—Die infantile Cerebrallähmung, 23
1897b—Inhaltsangaben der wissenschaftlichen Arbeiten des Privatdocenten
Dr. Sigm. Freud (1877-1897), 24

1898

1898a—Die Sexualität in der Ätiologie der Neurosen, 211
1898b—Zum psychischen Mechanismus der Vergesslichkeit, 184
1898c,1899b,1900b—Cerebrale Kinderlähmung, 12

1899

1899a—Über Deckerinnerungen, 72
1900a(1899)—Die Traumdeutung, 227
1901c(1899)—Autobiographical note, 52
1941c(1899)—Eine erfüllte Traumahnung, 90

1901

1901a—Über den Traum, 223
1901b—Zur Psychopathologie des Alltagslebens, 197
1905e(1901)—Bruchstück einer Hysterie-Analyse, 67

1904

1904a—Die Freud'sche psychoanalytische Methode, 109
1904d—[Note on] "Magnetische Menschen," 169
1904e—Professor S. Hammerschlag: obituary, 182
1905a(1904)—Über Psychotherapie, 198

1905

1905c—Der Witz und seine Beziehung zum Unbewussten, 256
1905d—Drei Abhandlungen zur Sexualtheorie, 79
1906a(1905)—Meine Ansichten über die Rolle der Sexualität in der Ätiologie der
Neurosen, 149

1905-1906

1905-06—Psychopathic characters on the stage, 196

1906

1906c—Tatbestandsdiagnostik und Psychoanalyse, 217

1907

1907a—Der Wahn und die Träume in W. Jensens *Gradiva,* 246
1907b—Zwangshandlungen und Religionsübungen, 262
1907c—Zur sexuellen Aufklärung der Kinder, 212

1907-1908

1955a(1907-08)—Original record of the case of obsessional neurosis (The Rat Man), 177

1908

1908a—Hysterische Phantasien und ihre Beziehung zur Bisexualität, 120
1908b—Charakter und Analerotik, 68
1908c—Über infantile Sexualtheorien, 124
1908d—Die "kulturelle" Sexualmoral und die moderne Nervosität, 139
1908e—Der Dichter und das Phantasieren, 73

1909

1909a—Allgemeines über den hysterischen Anfall, 43
1909b—Analyse der Phobie eines fünfjährigen Knaben, 45
1909c—Der Familienroman der Neurotiker, 98
1909d—Bemerkungen über einen Fall von Zwangsneurose, 57
1910a(1909)—Über Psychoanalyse, 186

1910

1910c—Eine Kindheitserinnerung des Leonardo da Vinci, 135
1910d—Die zukünftigen Chancen der psychoanalytischen Therapie, 261
1910e—"Über den Gegensinn der Urworte." Referat über die gleichnamige Brochüre von Karl Abel, 111
1910f—Brief an Dr. Friedrich S. Krauss über die *Anthropophyteia,* 64
1910g—Zur Einleitung der Selbstmord-Diskussion, 86
1910h—Über einen besonderen Typus der Objektwahl beim Manne, 60
1910i—Die psychogene Sehstörung in psychoanalytischer Auffassung, 193
1910j—Beispiele des Verrats pathogener Phantasien bei Neurotikern, 54
1910k—Über "wilde" Psychoanalyse, 255
1910l—Typisches Beispiel eines verkappten Ödipustraumes, 232

1911

1911a—Nachträge zur Traumdeutung, 164
1911b—Formulierungen über zwei Prinzipien des psychischen Geschehens, 106
1911c—Psychoanalytische Bemerkungen über einen autobiographisch beschriebenen Fall von Paranoia (Dementia paranoides), 192
1911d—Die Bedeutung der Vokalfolge, 53
1911e—Die Handhabung der Traumdeutung in der Psychoanalyse, 116
1911f—"Gross ist die Diana der Epheser," 115
1911h—[Footnote to] Stekel, W. "Zur Psychologie des Exhibitionismus," 105
1911i—Ein Beitrag zum Vergessen von Eigennamen, 55
1911j—[Footnote to] Putnam, J. J. "Über Ätiologie und Behandlung der Psychoneurosen," 104

1912a(1911)—Nachtrag zu dem autobiographisch beschriebenen Fall von
    Paranoia (Dementia paranoides), 163
1913m(1911)—On psycho-analysis, 189
1957a(1911)—(& Oppenheim, D. E.) Träume im Folklore, 228

1912

1912b—Zur Dynamik der Übertragung, 80
1912c —Über neurotische Erkrankungstypen, 168
1912d—Über die allgemeinste Erniedrigung des Liebeslebens, 44
1912e —Ratschläge für den Arzt bei der psychoanalytischen Behandlung, 201
1912f —Zur Onanie-Diskussion. Einleitung; Schlusswort, 175
1912g —A note on the unconscious in psycho-analysis, 170
1912h—Nachfrage des Herausgebers über Kindheitsträume, 159
    [Paragraph on observations of coitus], 178

1912-1913

1912-13—Totem und Tabu, 221

1913

1913a—Ein Traum als Beweismittel, 224
1913c —Weitere Ratschläge zur Technik der Psychoanalyse: Zur Einleitung der
    Behandlung, 251
1913d—Märchenstoffe in Träumen, 146
1913f —Das Motiv der Kästchenwahl, 157
1913g—Zwei Kinderlügen, 263
1913h—Erfahrungen und Beispiele aus der analytischen Praxis, 89
in 1913h—Auftreten der Krankheitssymptome im Traume, 51
in 1913h—Der Mantel als Symbol, 145
in 1913h—Darstellung von Lebenszeiten im Traume, 71
in 1913h—Position beim Erwachen aus einem Traum, 179
in 1913h—Rücksicht auf Darstellbarkeit, 207
in 1913h—Selbstkritik der Neurotiker, 210
in 1913h—Tageszeiten im Trauminhalt, 216
in 1913h—Traum ohne kenntlichen Anlass, 225
in 1913h—Träume von Toten, 229
in 1913h—Verschämte Füsse, 241
in 1913h—Zwei Zimmer und eines, 264
in 1913h—Fragmentarische Träume, 108
1913i —Die Disposition zur Zwangsneurose. Ein Beitrag zum Problem der
    Neurosenwahl, 74
1913j —Das Interesse an der Psychoanalyse, 125
1913l —Kindheitsträume mit spezieller Bedeutung, 136

1914

1914a—Über fausse Reconnaissance ("déjà raconté") während der psychoan-
    alytischen Arbeit, 99
1914b—Der Moses des Michelangelo, 156
1914c —Zur Einführung des Narzissmus, 81

1919h—Das Unheimliche, 236
1919k—E. T. A. Hoffmann über die Bewusstseinsfunktion, 94
1954b(1919)—*Yivo*, 258

1920

1920a—Über die Psychogenese eines Falles von weiblicher Homosexualität, 194
1920b—Zur Vorgeschichte der analytischen Technik, 243
1920c—Dr. Anton v. Freund. (obituary), 75
1920d—Gedankenassoziation eines vierjährigen Kindes, 110
1920f —Ergänzungen zur Traumlehre, 91
1920g—Jenseits des Lustprinzips, 128
1955c(1920)—Memorandum on the electrical treatment of war neurotics, 151

1921

1921c—Massenpsychologie und Ich-Analyse, 147
1921d—Preiszuteilungen, 181
1941d(1921)—Psychoanalyse und Telepathie, 188

1922

1922a—Traum und Telepathie, 226
1922b—Über einige neurotische Mechanismen bei Eifersucht, Paranoia und
    Homosexualität, 84
1922c—Nachschrift zur Analyse des kleinen Hans, 161
1922d—Preisausschreibung, 180
1922f —Etwas vom Unbewussten, 95
1933b(1922)—Warum Krieg?, 247
1940c(1922)—Das Medusenhaupt, 148

1923

1923a—"Psychoanalyse" und "Libidotheorie," 187
1923b—Das Ich und das Es, 121
1923c—Bemerkungen zur Theorie und Praxis der Traumdeutung, 58
1923d—Eine Teufelsneurose im siebzehnten Jahrhundert, 218
1923e—Die infantile Genitalorganisation, 123
1923f —Josef Popper-Lynkeus und die Theorie des Traumes, 130
1923i —Dr. Ferenczi Sándor (zum 50. Geburtstag), 76
1924b(1923)—Neurose und Psychose, 167

1924

1924c—Das ökonomische Problem des Masochismus, 174
1924d—Der Untergang des Ödipuskomplexes, 237
1924e—Die Realitätsverlust bei Neurose und Psychose, 202
1924f —Psychoanalysis: exploring the hidden recesses of the mind, 190
1924h—Mitteilung des Herausgebers, 153
1925a(1924)—Notiz über den "Wunderblock," 171
1925d(1924)—"Selbstdarstellung," 209
    Beiträge zur Psychologie des Liebeslebens (published in book form;
    separate parts written earlier), 56

1925

1925b—Brief an den Herausgeber der *Jüdischen Presszentrale Zürich*, 63
1925c—To the opening of the Hebrew University, 176
1925e—Résistances à la psychanalyse, 205
1925g—Josef Breuer. (obituary), 129
1925h—Die Verneinung, 240
1925i —Einige Nachträge zum Ganzen der Traumdeutung, 83
1925j —Einige psychische Folgen des anatomischen Geschlechtsunterschieds, 85

1926

1926a—An Romain Rolland (zum 60. Geburtstag), 206
1926b—Karl Abraham. (obituary), 131
1926d—Hemmung, Symptom und Angst, 117
1926e—Die Frage der Laienanalyse. Unterredungen mit einem Unparteiischen,
       107
1926f —Psycho-analysis: Freudian School, 191
1926g—[Footnote on] Hering in Levine, I. *Das Unbewusste*, 102
1941e(1926)—Ansprache an die Mitglieder des Vereins B'nai B'rith, 47
       Dr. Reik und Kurpfuschereifrage. A letter to the *Neue Freie Presse*, 77
       Ein unbekannter Freud-Brief, 234

1927

1927a—Nachwort zur *Frage der Laienanalyse*, 165
1927b—Nachtrag zur Arbeit über den Moses des Michelangelo, 162
1927c—Die Zukunft einer Illusion, 260
1927d—Der Humor, 119
1927e—Fetischismus, 101

1928

1928a—Ein religiöses Erlebnis, 203
1928b—Dostojewski und die Vatertötung, 78

1929

1929a—Ernest Jones zum 50. Geburtstag, 93
1929b—Lettre à Maxime Leroy sur "Quelques rêves de Descartes," 141

1930

1930a—Das Unbehagen in der Kultur, 233
1930e—Ansprache im Frankfurter Goethe-Haus, 48

1931

1931a—Über libidinöse Typen, 142
1931b—Über die weibliche Sexualität, 249
1931d—Das Fakultätsgutachten im Prozess Halsmann, 96
1931e—Brief an den Bürgermeister der Stadt Příbor, 62

1932

1932a—Zur Gewinnung des Feuers, 114
1932c—Meine Berührung mit Josef Popper-Lynkeus, 150
1933a(1932)—Neue Folge der Vorlesungen zur Einführung in die Psychoanalyse, 166
1933b(1932)—Warum Krieg?, 247

1933

1933c—Sándor Ferenczi. (obituary), 208

1935

1935a—Nachschrift 1935 zur *Selbstdarstellung*, 160
1935b—Die Feinheit einer Fehlhandlung, 100
1935c—Thomas Mann zum 60. Geburtstag, 445

1936

1936a—Brief an Romain Rolland: Eine Erinnerungsstörung auf der Akropolis, 66

1937

1937a—Lou Andreas-Salomé. (obituary), 143
1937b—Moses ein Ägypter, 155
1937c—Die endliche und die unendliche Analyse, 87
1937d—Konstruktionen in der Analyse, 137
1937e—Wenn Moses ein Ägypter war...., 254

1937-1939

1939a(1937-39)—Der Mann Moses und die monotheistische Religion, 144

1938

1938a—Ein Wort zum Antisemitismus, 257
1938c—Anti-semitism in England, 49
1940a(1938)—Abriss der Psychoanalyse, 41
1940b(1938)—Some elementary lessons in psycho-analysis, 213
1940e(1938)—Die Ichspaltung im Abwehrvorgang, 122
1941f(1938)—Ergebnisse, Ideen, Probleme, 92
1966b(1938)—(& Bullitt, W. C.) *Thomas Woodrow Wilson, twenty-eighth president of the United States: a psychological study*, 220

SECTION VIII
ALPHABETICAL LISTING OF THE ENGLISH TITLES
OF THE WORKS OF SIGMUND FREUD

This section is intended to provide a quick and ready reference to titles by employing their common usage. It is in no way a Subject Index of Freud's writings. For example, a reference will be found here to the "Schreber case," 192, and, under "Case histories," to "Schreber," 192, as well as to "Psycho-analytic notes on an autobiographical account of a case of paranoia (dementia paranoides)," 192.

Articles, books and monographs are listed alphabetically according to the principal words of their English titles. The entry number used in this work, *Sigmund Freud: A Comprehensive Bibliography*, immediately follows the title.

This alphabetical listing omits Freud's abstracts, reviews, translations, letters, prefaces and introductions to his own works and to the works of others. These may be found in the appropriate sections (III through VI) of this work.

EARLY, PRIMARILY NONPSYCHOLOGICAL WRITINGS

Abstracts of the scientific writings of Dr. Sigmund Freud (1877-1897), 24
Acoustical nerve, origin of, 38
Acute multiple neuritis of the spinal and cranial nerves, 3
Anatomical preparation of the nervous system, 31
Aphasia [in A. Villaret], 39
On aphasia, a critical study, 2

Bacillus of syphilis, 4
On Bernhardt's disease (meralgia paraesthetica), 10
Brain [in A. Villaret], 39

A case of cerebral hemorrhage with indirect basal focal symptoms in scurvy, 17
A case of muscular atrophy with extensive disturbances of sensitivity (syringomyelia), 18
Cerebral diplegias in childhood, 16, 19, 33
    in connection with Little's disease, 25
Cerebral hemorrhage with indirect focal symptoms in scurvy, case of, 17
Clinical contributions to the understanding of infantile cerebral paralysis and of epilepsy (Rosenberg), 32
A clinical study on unilateral cerebral paralysis in children, 27
Coca, 7, 14
Cocaine, 1, 6, 7, 15, 20

PSYCHOLOGICAL WRITINGS

"Rat Man," 57, 177
Recollection, repetition and working through, 252
Recommendations to physicians practising psycho-analysis, 201
Reflections on war and death, 259
The relation of the poet to day-dreaming, 73
A religious experience, 203
Remarks on the theory and practice of dream-interpretation, 58
Remembering, repeating and working through, 252
A reply to criticisms of paper on anxiety neurosis, 138
Report on studies in Paris and Berlin carried out with the assistance of a travelling
  bursary granted from the University Jubilee Fund (October 1885 - end of
  March 1886), 204
Representation of ages in dreams, 71
Representation of a "great achievement" in a dream, 70
Repression, 238
Request for examples of childhood dreams, 159
The resistances to psycho-analysis, 205
REVIEWS: SEE SECTION IV
Right to separate from neurasthenia a definite symptom-complex as "anxiety
  neurosis," 59
To Romain Rolland (on his 60th birthday), 206
To Romain Rolland on his 70th birthday (disturbance of memory on the
  Acropolis), 66

Sándor Ferenczi (obituary), 208
Schoolboy psychology, some reflections on, 195
Schreber case, 192
Scientific interest in psycho-analysis, 125
Screen memories, 72
Self-criticism by neurotics, 210
A seventeenth-century demonological neurosis, 218
The sexual enlightenment of children (an open letter to Dr. M. Fürst), 212
Sexual morality and modern nervousness, 139
Sexual perversions: "A child is being beaten," 133
On the sexual theories of children, 124
Sexuality in the aetiology of the neuroses, 149, 211
A short account of psycho-analysis, 190
The significance of sequences of vowels, 53
Sketches for the "Preliminary communication" of 1893, 65, 172, 219
Some additional notes on dream-interpretation as a whole, 83
Some character-types met with in psycho-analytic work, 82
Some dreams of Descartes: a letter to Maxime Leroy, 141
Some elementary lessons in psycho-analysis, 213
Some general remarks on hysterical states, 43
Some neurotic mechanisms in jealousy, paranoia and homosexuality, 84
Some points for a comparative study of organic and hysterical motor paralyses,
  200
Some psychical consequences of the anatomical distinction between the sexes, 85
Some reflections on schoolboy psychology, 195
Some remarks on the unconscious, 95
A special type of choice of object made by men, 60